# THE LEGAL AND MORAL ASPECTS OF INTERNATIONAL TRADE

Free trade has always been a moral and political, as well as an economic programme. Although free traders call for the liberalization of the economy from governmental interference, it is understood that international exchange can only operate within a framework of law. Defenders of free trade believe that it not only will promote economic prosperity but that it will enhance worldwide peace and understanding by substituting commercial competition for the pursuit of national goals by military means. Protection, on the other hand, has been defended as safeguarding those vulnerable to the fluctuations of world markets.

This collection of essays by international lawyers and moral philosophers arises from a prestigious multi-disciplinary conference to commemorate the 150th anniversary of the repeal of the Corn Laws in 1846. It examines the legal, moral and political dimensions of free trade. Contributors explore issues such as:

- the ethics and rules of competition
- the idea of global justice
- the problem of international exploitation
- the protection of the environment
- the regulation of services
- international taxation and the justification for barriers to trade.

*The Legal and Moral Aspects of International Trade* provides an important insight into the continuing debates surrounding free trade. It will appeal to experts across the fields of economics, politics and law as well as to those with an interest in international trade.

**Asif H. Qureshi** is reader in International Law and International Economic Law at the University of Manchester. He is the author of *The World Trade Organization* and *The Public International Law of Taxation.* **Hillel Steiner** is Professor of Political Philosophy in the Department of Government and the School of Philosophical Studies at the University of Manchester. His book *An Essay on Rights* was recently awarded the W.J.M. Mackenzie Prize by the Political Studies Association. **Geraint Parry** is W.J.M. Mackenzie Professor of Government at the University of Manchester. His publications include *Political Elites, John Locke* and *Political Participation and Democracy in Britain.*

# ROUTLEDGE STUDIES IN THE MODERN WORLD ECONOMY

1 INTEREST RATES AND BUDGET DEFICITS
A study of the advanced economies
*Kanhaya L. Gupta and Bakhtiar Moazzami*

2 WORLD TRADE AFTER THE URUGUAY ROUND
Prospects and policy options for the twenty-first century
*edited by Harald Sander and András Inotai*

3 THE FLOW ANALYSIS OF LABOUR MARKETS
*edited by Ronald Schettkat*

4 INFLATION AND UNEMPLOYMENT
Contributions to a new macroeconomic approach
*edited by Alvaro Cencini and Mauro Baranzini*

5 MACROECONOMIC DIMENSIONS OF PUBLIC FINANCE
Essays in honour of Vito Tanzi
*edited by Mario I. Blejer and Teresa M. Ter-Minassian*

6 FISCAL POLICY AND ECONOMIC REFORMS
Essays in honour of Vito Tanzi
*edited by Mario I. Blejer and Teresa M. Ter-Minassian*

7 COMPETITION POLICY IN THE GLOBAL ECONOMY
Modalities for cooperation
*edited by Leonard Waverman, William S. Comanor and Akira Goto*

8 WORKING IN THE MACROECONOMY
A study of the US labor market
*Martin F.J. Prachowny*

9 HOW DOES PRIVATIZATION WORK?
*edited by Anthony Bennett*

10 THE ECONOMICS AND POLITICS OF INTERNATIONAL TRADE
Freedom and trade, volume II
*edited by Gary Cook*

11 THE LEGAL AND MORAL ASPECTS OF INTERNATIONAL TRADE
Freedom and trade, volume III
*edited by Asif Qureshi, Hillel Steiner and Geraint Parry*

12 CAPITAL MARKETS AND CORPORATE GOVERNANCE IN JAPAN, GERMANY AND THE UNITED STATES
Organizational response to market inefficiencies
*Helmut M. Dietl*

# THE LEGAL AND MORAL ASPECTS OF INTERNATIONAL TRADE

Freedom and Trade
Volume III

*Edited by*
*Asif Qureshi, Hillel Steiner and Geraint Parry*

Proceedings of a conference to commemorate the 150th anniversary of the repeal of the Corn Laws

*General editors*
Geraint Parry and Hillel Steiner

Routledge
Taylor & Francis Group
LONDON AND NEW YORK

First published 1998 by Routledge
2 Park Square, Milton Park, Abingdon, Oxon OX14 4RN
605 Third Avenue, New York, NY 10017

*Routledge is an imprint of the Taylor & Francis Group, an informa business*



*British Library Cataloguing in Publication Dtata*
A catalogue record for this book is available
from the British Library

*Library of Congress Cataloging in Publication Data*
The legal and moral aspects of inernational trade : freedom and trade
volume III / edited by Asif Qureshi, Hillel Steiner, and Geraint Parry.
p. cm.
"Proceedings of a conference to commemorate the 150th Anniversary of the Repeal of the Corn Laws."
Includes bibliographical references and index.
1. International economic integration. 2. Free Trade. 3. Foreign trade regulation. 4. International trade—Moral and ethical aspects.
I. Qureshi, Asif, H. (Asif Hasan), 1956– . II. Steiner, Hillel.
III. Parry, Geraint.
K3823.L44 1998
341.7'54–dc21 97–30853
CIP

ISBN 13: 978-0-415-15526-7 (hbk)

# CONTENTS

# ABOUT THE EDITORS AND CONTRIBUTORS

**Brian Barry** Professor of Government, London School of Economics.

**Ulick Bourke** Partner, Clifford Chance, Solicitors, London.

**James Cameron** Barrister and Director of the Foundation for International Environmental Law and Development (FIELD) at the School of Oriental and African Studies, University of London.

**Simon Caney** Lecturer in Politics, University of Newcastle.

**Ian Carter** Research Fellow, University of Pavia.

**Anthony Carty** Professor of International Law, University of Derby.

**Avner de-Shalit** Senior Lecturer in Political Philosophy, Hebrew University of Jerusalem.

**John Hunt** Director, Trade Policy Division, Department of Trade and Industry, London.

**Peter Ingram** Senior Lecturer in Law, Queen's University, Belfast.

**Michael Johnson** Senior Consultant, Malmgren Golt Kingston & Co., Ltd., London; former Head of General International Trade Policy Branch and later of Bilateral Trade Relations Branch, Department of Trade and Industry, London.

**Peter Jones** Professor of Political Philosophy, University of Newcastle.

**Paul Krugman** Professor of Economics, Massachusetts Institute of Technology.

**William Lucy** Senior Lecturer in Law, University of Hull.

**Edmond McGovern** Barrister, Exeter.

**Owen McIntyre** Lecturer in Law, University of Manchester.

**David Milman** Herbert Smith Professor of Corporate and Commercial Law and Dean of the Faculty of Law, University of Manchester.

**Geraint Parry** W.J.M. Mackenzie Professor of Government, University of Manchester.

**Ernst-Ulrich Petersmann** Professor of European and International Law at the University of Geneva, legal adviser in the GATT/WTO (1981–95) and in the German Ministry of Economic Affairs 1978–81.

**Asif Qureshi** Reader in Law, University of Manchester.

**Hillel Steiner** Professor of Political Philosophy, University of Manchester.

**Bhaskar Vira** Waste Management International Research Fellow, Oxford Centre for the Environment, Ethics and Society, Mansfield College, University of Oxford.

**Jonathan Wolff** Reader in Philosophy, University College London.

# GENERAL EDITORS' PREFACE

*Geraint Parry and Hillel Steiner*

The three volumes of *Freedom and Trade* consist of papers arising from a multidisciplinary international conference held at the University of Manchester in 1996 to commemorate the 150th anniversary of the repeal of the Corn Laws in 1846. The papers, along with commentaries, are published in three volumes, each self-contained and each devoted to one or more of the disciplines represented at the conference. One volume, edited by Andrew Marrison, is devoted to *Free Trade and its Reception 1815–1960*, a second, edited by Gary Cook, to *The Economics and Politics of International Trade* and the third to *The Legal and Moral Aspects of International Trade*, for which the editors are Asif Qureshi, Hillel Steiner and Geraint Parry. Professor Frank Hahn's plenary address to the conference appears in the volume on *The Economics and Politics of International Trade*. The volume on *The Legal and Moral Aspects of International Trade* also includes the papers of a panel of distinguished scholars representing each of the major disciplines involved who were invited to speak on 'The Feasibility and Desirability of Global Free Trade'.

The repeal of the Corn Laws in 1846 was an event of enormous significance in the history of international trade, in the development of institutions of international regulation, in the realignment of political parties and interests in Britain and in the emergence of new modes of political action through mass politics and single-issue interest groups. It remains an event which promptly conjures up the economic, political and moral sentiments surrounding the idea of free trade and its confrontation with the policy of protection. This significance can safely be affirmed even though, as so many chapters in these volumes attest, the nature of this significance remains hotly debated by leading world scholars in every intellectual discipline which is touched by this still controversial measure. Was the real impact of the repeal substantive or symbolic? It would clearly be mistaken to dismiss it as *merely* symbolic since symbols can be of the utmost importance not merely in history and politics but also in economics. No measure to regulate trade has ever given rise to so much contention at the time and since. It is also a suggestive indicator of the geopolitical situation at the time that this was not an international agreement such as GATT but a unilateral legislative action by one economically hegemonic state.

A return to the subject of 'Freedom and Trade' in 1996, 150 years after the repeal and as the new world economic order faces the uncertainties of the twenty-first century, is an intriguing experience. History never exactly repeats itself, either as tragedy or farce. Nevertheless many of the claims and counter-claims of the repeal period can readily be recognized in new guises in the present era. The campaign for free trade stemmed in part from a recognition of the growing interdependence of nations and the emergence of an ever more global market. This has now become the phenomenon which dominates not only international politics but also the domestic politics and economies of nations large and small. The international and the domestic are intertwined as never before. Within this new order economic liberalization may be the dominant ideology but many arguments, familiar from debates surrounding the repeal, make a re-appearance. Is liberalization a policy which in reality is designed to promote the interests of the present day economic hegemony? Is free trade of genuinely mutual benefit or is it a cloak for exploitation of various kinds? Will the new trading blocks and the new political communities which they have begun to create seek to revert to forms of protection? A distinctively new concern, not at the forefront of minds in the optimistic period of the repeal, is whether free trade is compatible with protection of the global environment.

These concerns have given new urgency to the search for authoritative institutions of international regulation. The emergence and influence since the Second World War of such institutions and agencies as the World Bank, IMF, and GATT must be counted as being among some of the most striking developments in the history of international politics and international law. The range and scope of these bodies have steadily grown and they have increasingly assumed political responsibilities in promoting policies which are of considerable future significance. It is not surprising therefore that, alongside these developments, there has been a growing interest amongst political theorists in the moral underpinnings of international economic and political policies. Many have turned from discussing the justice of domestic policy to examining the issues of fairness between nations, the legitimacy of interventions in the affairs of foreign countries and the proper limits to free international exchange.

The conference, which resulted in these three volumes, was entitled *1846 Freedom and Trade 1996: A Commemoration of the 150th Anniversary of the Repeal of the Corn Laws*, and sought to address this range of issues from the perspective of economic and political historians, international economists, international lawyers and political theorists. Whilst the repeal itself is the subject of many of the contributions, in others it serves as the peg upon which to hang discussions of the contemporary state of the international political economy. Moreover the conference was, it should be noted, a 'commemoration' and not a 'celebration' of the repeal. As many contributions indicate, the event still engenders strong views as to its intentions and its consequences. In each of the disciplines represented there have been important developments in the ways in which the repeal and later issues of freedom and trade are analysed. Innovations in the study of political parties and interests have permitted new examinations of the coalitions of groupings behind the repeal. Subsequent experience of mass politics allows scholars to see the campaigns of the Anti-Corn Law League as forerunners of the techniques of contemporary single-issue politics. In international economics we are, as Cook says in the introduction to the volume on *The Economics and Politics of International Trade*, still experiencing 'Corn Laws' debates, which may be conducted in different economic languages, but which can produce results just as paradoxical in terms of winners and losers as occurred 150 years ago. The remarkable revival in political theory over the last thirty years is now bringing new insights to questions of international justice, whilst lawyers are refining the instruments of international regulation in an arena traditionally dominated by the interplay of power politics. Finally, 150 years which have experienced decades of imperial rivalry, two world wars and forty years of Cold War tension have inevitably increased scepticism about the cherished beliefs of Cobden and other campaigners that free trade would usher in an unprecedented era of world peace and harmony. Cobden was President of the International Education Society which sought to promote the cause of European peace by establishing international schools in Britain, France and Germany. His views on trade were inextricably linked to his ideas on morality and on education. Cobden and the free-traders might therefore take some comfort if they could learn that, despite the intervening periods of scepticism and disillusionment, scholars are re-discovering the Cobdenite thesis and beginning to explore whether there is indeed a link between liberalization, democratization and peace between nations.

The conference and the volumes of *Freedom and Trade* have sought to address the range of issues which the original repeal of the Corn Laws raised, not only for its own time but in ways which have seemed of continuing interest and relevance. The conference was initiated and convened by Hillel Steiner and Geraint Parry of the Department of Government of the University of Manchester which was the main sponsor of the event. Andrew Marrison of the Department of History, Asif Qureshi of the Faculty of Law of the University of Manchester and Gary Cook, initially of the Manchester Business School and currently at the University of Derby were the convenors of the academic specialisms into which the conference and these volumes were divided. Professor Michael Rose of the Department of History at the University of Manchester and Professor Keith Tribe of the University of Keele made major contributions to the conference steering committee. The editorial team is also grateful to Routledge for its support and, in particular, to Alan Jarvis whose involvement extended to active participation in the conference.

That Manchester was the most appropriate venue for this event can hardly be doubted. The 'Cottonopolis' was where the Anti-Corn Law League was founded. The ideology and the interests of the major manufacturing concerns of the city entirely coincided. Indeed the statues of Richard Cobden and John Bright still prominently adorn the city centre. The movement's salience has been perpetuated in the name of the Free Trade Hall which has been Manchester's chief venue for political and cultural events until, somewhat ironically, it closed in 1996, to re-open as an hotel and conference centre. Perhaps this too has its symbolic quality since the closure and re-opening can be seen as part of the city's reinvention of itself as a different kind of commercial centre, responding to new terms of international trade in a global economy more complex than existed in 1846 but still one exercised by fundamental issues of freedom and protection.

## ACKNOWLEDGEMENTS

During the gestation and organization of the conference *1846 Freedom and Trade 1996* and the preparation of the three volumes of *Freedom and Trade* we have incurred many obligations. There is space only to acknowledge some of these debts. The Department of Government of the University of Manchester and its Manchester Centre for Political Thought sponsored the event. We are grateful for their support. The Dean of the Faculty of Economic and Social Studies, the Department of Economics and Professor Martin Harris, Vice-Chancellor of the University of Manchester, were instrumental in arranging for the crucial seed money to enable the conference to be organised. The Faculty of Law and the Department of History at Manchester provided funds and administrative facilities, as did the University of Derby. On behalf of the History and Policy Section, Andrew Marrison gratefully acknowledges the support of the Conferences and Initiatives Fund of the Economic History Society for a grant towards administrative and travel costs.

Mrs Rebecca Naidoo was an outstanding administrator in the preparatory period leading up to the organization of the conference. Ms Bernadette McLoughlin of the Department of Government provided invaluable administrative backing at all stages and particularly during the immediate conference period.

Hillel Steiner acknowledges the support of the Economic and Social Research Council and the Nuffield Foundation for the award of a grant to study issues of international justice which formed one of the conference's prime themes. Geraint Parry acknowledges the support of the Leverhulme Trust for an award to undertake research into nineteenth- and twentieth-century political thought.

Geraint Parry and Hillel Steiner
Department of Government,
University of Manchester
February 1997

# 1

# INTRODUCTION

*Geraint Parry, Asif Qureshi and Hillel Steiner*

This volume consists of two component elements. First, it includes the set of presentations made to a full plenary session of the conference. And second, it contains the contributions and discussants' comments prepared for the conference's Law and Political Theory workshop.

The multi-disciplinary nature of the conference provided an especially opportune and appropriate occasion to hold a common plenary session at which a panel of prominent representatives of each of the four contributing disciplines was invited to address the subject of: 'The Feasibility and Desirability of Global Free Trade'.

Accordingly, the presentations of Brian Barry (Political Theory), Paul Krugman (Economics), and Ernst-Ulrich Petersmann (Law) are reproduced here. (Regrettably, we were unable to include Deirdre McCloskey's historical contribution in this volume.) As the reader will quickly discover, there is by no means any consensus amongst the panellists in their views on that issue. Moreover, the lively general discussion provoked by their presentations bore ample witness to the presence of widely differing positions within, as well as between, these academic disciplines. The underlying reasons for this are, perhaps, not all that difficult to discern.

The campaign against the Corn Laws and in favour of free trade represented, from its inception, a moral as well as an economic programme. It claimed to offer to the British population a remarkable combination of economic improvement and social justice. By liberating trade, serious fetters on industrial growth would be removed and the injustice of the 'bread tax' on the very necessities of life abolished. More universally, free trade would bring about a new manner of conducting affairs between nations. The pursuit of narrowly conceived national advantage, by protection coupled with warfare, would gradually give way to an appreciation of the mutual advantages of international commerce in conditions of peaceful competition. It is thus entirely comprehensible that Cobden, in championing free trade, also conceived of it as an instrument for educative enlightenment and sought to promote it through the establishment of international schools in which pupils of different nations would learn together the virtues of international cooperation.

At the same time, protection, though castigated by free traders as a doctrine of short-sighted national interest, had, and continues to have its defenders, whose arguments similarly deploy moral considerations of undeniable significance. Protection, it has been urged, may be regarded as safeguarding those groups who are especially vulnerable to the fluctuations of world markets. It is seen as a means of providing less developed societies and industries with a breathing space in which to catch up with those first in the field. Equally important, it may sometimes be advanced as a necessary means for sustaining local ways of life endangered by powerful foreign and homogenizing influences. And increasingly nowadays, protectionism may be invoked to preserve valued aspects of the global environment.

These issues are all touched upon in a number of ways in the chapters devoted to political theory. And they are also central to the problems addressed by the international lawyers. What was distinctive about the Repeal of the Corn Laws was that it was a unilateral national measure, though one with significant international repercussions. In the present day, however, the typical approach to trade regulation is through the creation and development of international agreements and institutions. Thus as we enter the twenty-first century, it falls increasingly to a global community of negotiators to interpret the underlying principles and establish the detailed regulations of a new economic order which must seek to reconcile the liberalization of trade, in agricultural commodities and manufactures as well as services of an ever-changing nature, with the still deep-rooted desire for the preservation of domestic cultures and the growing recognition of the need for conservation.

The coupling together of Law and Political Theory in a single conference workshop was seen from the outset as being in the nature of a worthwhile intellectual experiment. Of course, the relation between scholarship in these two fields possesses a long historical pedigree: political and legal theorists have been addressing many similar questions for centuries. Our aim in this workshop, however, was to achieve some complementarity of analytical focus between the more practical concerns of lawyers and the characteristically abstract concerns of political theory. Evidently, questions about the desirability of certain institutions and policies cannot be satisfactorily answered in the absence of soundly distilled information about their feasibility. Conversely, whether and in what circumstances realistic prospects for trade liberalization ought to be pursued must depend upon coherent assessments of their relative merits – assessments that need to be anchored in a set of broader theoretical frameworks.

That said, the pairing of legal and political theory papers at each session confronted the discussants with the formidable challenge of bridging often very divergent ways of looking at similar phenomena. This task they discharged admirably, managing to draw illuminating contrasts and parallels even in those instances where the papers' perspectives differed quite markedly.

Some commentators on public affairs have dubbed the first Ministerial Meeting of the World Trade Organization (WTO) in Singapore[1] as being high on rhetoric but short on results. But rhetoric, one might suggest, can often be a prelude to achievement in the long run. There is thus some merit in mentioning that meeting, which was focused *inter alia* on further expanding and strengthening the system of international trade regulation, since this was also a central theme of the Law and Political Theory workshop. Indeed it is to the credit of the contributors that their chapters closely mirror and predict the concerns and outcomes of the Ministerial Meeting.

Simon Caney distinguishes two dominant theoretical approaches to the general question of what norms ought to govern states' dealings with one another in regard to trade as well as other matters: cosmopolitanism and realism. The former is universalistic and does not discriminate among human beings in taking a policy's impact on their respective interests as the measure of its justifiability. Realism, in all its various forms, rejects this as utopian and insists that national interest is the paramount consideration determining the moral obligations by which any state's policies can or should be judged. Caney carefully examines the three principal types of objection mounted by realists against cosmopolitanism and finds them unsuccessful.

John Hunt integrates a historical and political perspective with a significant breadth of realism. He rightly points out the influence of political structure on trade policy, and the need to create new disciplines, emphasizing particularly competition and investment. His realism leads him to suggest liberalization as an incremental process and not as an immediate fiat. One can but note his accurate prediction that the Singapore Ministerial Meeting would be a premature forum to launch another new round of negotiations for trade liberalization.

Owen McIntyre challenges some of the assumptions underlying Caney's dichotomy between the cosmopolitan approach and that of realism. He suggests that national interests can be realized through cosmopolitanism. Drawing on Hunt's paper, he illustrates the point by suggesting that the primary benefit sought by the Anti-Corn Law League was cheap food for the British consumer rather than any universal benefit for the world at large.

Peter Ingram argues that, historically, international law has been chiefly focused on adversarial features of interstate relations, and has not balanced this concern with one for the regulation of those extensive non-conflictual transactions that constitute and advance international economic interdependence. Indeed the voluntaristic character of international legal obligations, as well as the world's plurality of value systems, represent substantial obstacles to the adequate formation of such a regulatory framework. However, Ingram finds the development of international institutions along with the growth of their procedural powers – and the stake nations acquire in their continuing membership of such organizations – to hold out some promise of overcoming the longstanding problems posed by both voluntarism and the purely formal equality of states.

Ulick Bourke emphasizes the strengthening of multilateral disciplines. He advocates the direct applicability of international trade norms in national systems and interestingly calls for direct access, for private parties, to international judicial processes in the field of trade.

Responding to Ingram and Bourke, William Lucy queries the plausibility of any strongly unified explanation of developments in international law, and suggests that the notion of 'trust' may have an important role in understanding aspects of interstate cooperation.

Jonathan Wolff contends that, in so far as the moral case for freer trade rests on (various conceptions of) the desirability of competition, it may be weakly grounded. These several conceptions are each identified and subjected to critical assessment. Wolff argues that, although it may be true that competition advances social utility, neither that consideration nor any other of these conceptions precludes the possibility that competitive exchanges are exploitative. And he therefore concludes that competition and the trade deregulation that may be needed to bring it about must, to be justifiable, be accompanied by systems of compensation for those who would otherwise be the resultant losers.

Ernst-Ulrich Petersmann offers a detailed exposition of the relationship of trade and competition rules. His perspective on competition rules is defined in terms of access to markets. As such, competition policy is conceived both in terms of governmental as well as private anticompetitive activities. Petersmann, however, points out the need for strengthening the competition rules as they relate to private activities. He explains how the seeds for integrating such rules have to some degree already been sown in the international regulation of trade – particularly the WTO. Petersmann concludes by advocating a progressive integration of competition rules in the WTO system through, initially, the establishment of a WTO Committee on Trade and Competition. Thereafter, it is suggested, a subsequent WTO round of trade negotiations should integrate competition rules into the WTO code. Parallel to this effort, Petersmann advocates a Plurilateral Agreement[2] on Trade and Competition.

Despite their diverging assessments of the merits of international competition, Ian Carter argues that several of the caveats respectively offered by Wolff and Petersmann imply significant points of convergence on the kinds of circumstance in which liberalized trade is warranted.

Avner de-Shalit outlines four types of international exploitation and contends that, as standardly interpreted, both Marxist and liberal theories of exploitation provide deficient explanatory accounts of them. However these theories fare better when revised to include consideration of the autonomy-eroding effects of inferior bargaining positions. De-Shalit thereby draws attention to the possibility that free trade between rich and poor nations may be exploitative, by virtue of fostering manipulation of the latters' preferences through the displacement of their indigenous cultural values.

Michael Johnson aptly describes the General Agreement on Trade in Services (GATS) as 'work in progress' and, in that context, traces the influences which led to its establishment. Some of these resulted in limited market access commitments, in a list of exemptions from the most-favoured-nation (MFN) standard and the postponing of negotiations for liberalization of trade in parts of the services sector. Further, he highlights some of the difficulties in the current structure of GATS: for example, the problem of quantifying commitments in the services sector and identifying market access problems. Finally, in looking to the future, he notes the difficulties of defining a subsidy in the services sector and of formulating a safeguard agreement.

David Milman concludes that exploitation is indeed a common theme between what de-Shalit explains and what Johnson examines in the field of trade in services, the former being concerned with constructing a viable theory of exploitation and the latter with the operation of practical *realpolitik* in the field of trade in services. But Milman observes that the new GATS has some way to go before it can be assessed in terms of equity and exploitation.

Bhaskar Vira explores the substantive conflict between economic deregulation, such as trade liberalization, and environmental regulation. Acknowledging both the strength and limitations of the efficiency argument for deregulated trade, he argues that economic growth by itself is insufficient to mitigate the environmental impact of much human activity. The fact that both environmentalists and free trade advocates support full cost internalization does not imply invariable compatibility between their positions since, in some circumstances, optimal environmental policies must include quantitative controls on resource extraction and product and technology use – controls which directly affect the volume and composition of international trade.

James Cameron comprehensively surveys recent developments in the international trade and environment debate – particularly in the context of conflicting interests in trade and the environment. This is done by considering *inter alia* some GATT/WTO cases and the agenda of the WTO Committee on Trade and the Environment. Essentially he advocates the balancing of trade and environmental concerns in the WTO forum. He is firmly of the view that there need to be changes in the WTO code: for example, by the amendment of Article XX of the GATT,[3] and through a presumption of compatibility between national measures conforming to multilateral environmental agreements (MEAs) and provisions of the WTO code. He concludes by noting the need for some demonstrable success at the Ministerial Meeting in Singapore.

Strongly endorsing central points in the accounts offered by Vira and Cameron, Brian Barry argues that trade-restricting measures must have a role to play in the economic system of any society that seeks to balance considerations of consumer satisfaction with those of producer satisfaction and environmental protection.[4]

Asif Qureshi focuses on the trade-related aspects of international taxation. He traces fiscal sovereignty under General International Law and under the GATT/WTO framework in the light of the trade-distortive effects of taxation. He concludes by making a proposal for a WTO code of conduct on the trade-related aspects of international taxation.

Reflecting on Qureshi's chapter, Anthony Carty draws attention to the German conviction that perpetual peace requires consideration of not just the removal of trade barriers but also effective political structures.

Hillel Steiner claims that, although it seems certain that some kinds of international trade are morally undesirable and that persons ought not to engage in them, this fact is insufficient to justify their enforced restriction on grounds of justice which requires that they be legally permitted. Identifying several broad types of morally objectionable trade, he argues that legal restriction of only one of them – trade with regimes that countenance domestic rights violations – can be so justified and may, perhaps, be morally mandatory.

Edmond McGovern supplies an interesting exploration of how standards and technical regulations can operate as barriers to trade. In particular, he considers the existing opportunities within the WTO system to deal with the capacity of national technical regulations and standards to create problems for international trade. Four strategies are identified for dealing with standards and technical regulations from the perspective of liberal trade: namely, non-discrimination, control of trade-restrictive regulations, harmonization and integration, and procedural and institutional improvements.

Commenting on Steiner's and McGovern's papers, Peter Jones finds moral consequentialism to be the normative approach underpinning the EC's and WTO's official ideology and its capacity to accommodate important social values threatened by free trade – a capacity which is absent in rights-based conceptions of justice.

## Notes

1 Held in December 1996.

2 That is, an agreement binding only on the parties to the agreement.

3 Article XX lists the general exceptions to the GATT prohibitions against the imposition of trade-restrictive measures.

4 Barry's comments on the papers by Vira and Cameron are incorporated in his plenary panel presentation, pp. 12–25.

2

# THE FEASIBILITY AND DESIRABILITY OF GLOBAL FREE TRADE

*Ernst-Ulrich Petersmann, Paul Krugman and Brian Barry*

## I Is global free trade desirable and feasible?

***Ernst-Ulrich Petersmann***

I have been asked to stimulate the general debate on this subject by a few personal ideas. Let me just mention three problem areas on the long and winding road to global liberal trade.

First, global liberal trade is desirable because it enhances not only economic consumer welfare but also individual freedom and peaceful cooperation among countries. Empirical research into the relationship between economic freedom and economic growth of 102 countries over the period 1975–95 has confirmed that the more economic freedom and open markets a country had, the more economic growth it achieved and the richer its citizens became.[1] It is also no coincidence that liberal trade regimes, like European integration law and the GATT/WTO Agreements, have more effective systems for the protection of the rule of law and for the peaceful settlement of disputes than most other international organizations. This seems to confirm the long-standing emphasis in political philosophy (e.g. of I. Kant and D. Hume) and economic theory (e.g. of D. Ricardo and A. Smith) that the mutual gains from voluntary international trade, and from an international division of labour based on liberal rules, offer the most important means to overcome the 'Hobbesian war of everybody against everybody else' through peaceful cooperation, even if people and governments act as self-interest utility-maximizers. Yet, 'free trade' must not be confused with *laissez-faire* liberalism. The GATT/WTO world trade and legal system is still in need of more effective international rules limiting 'market failures' (such as private anticompetitive business practices) as well as 'government failures' (such as protectionism), and promoting the supply of agreed 'international public goods' (such as protection of the environment and sustainable development).

Second, there is no convincing reason why liberal trade should be feasible only in the context of regional free trade areas and customs unions but not on a global level. The democratic task of governments to maximize the individual preferences and equal rights of their citizens requires them to pursue the objective of global liberal trade. Yet, just as liberal trade and democracy were achieved in the national context through painful social learning processes and revolutionary changes of authoritarian political regimes, global liberal trade and the necessary 'constitutionalization of discretionary foreign policy powers' will require revolutionary changes of international law and institutions. As long as governments continue to be perceived as benevolent dictators, and their discretionary foreign policy powers are viewed as a magic black box and 'executive prerogative', international relations will continue to be dominated by power politics and protectionism for the benefit of 'rent-seeking' interest groups. It is no coincidence that the success of European integration law, such as the progressive achievement of a single market based on individual market freedoms and competition rules protected by independent courts, was largely a function of the progressive constitutionalization of national foreign policy powers through Community law principles that are largely identical with the basic principles of national constitutionalism: rule of law; primacy of constitutional rules over post-constitutional policy-making processes; horizontal and vertical separation of powers; limitation of all government powers through inalienable human rights; 'necessity' and 'proportionality' requirements for all governmental restraints of individual rights; democratic participation in the exercise of government powers, and principles of social justice. The worldwide GATT/WTO legal system includes an increasing number of similar legal guarantees (e.g. of intellectual property rights and access to domestic courts) and constitutional restraints on foreign trade policy powers (e.g. non-discrimination requirements, prohibitions of non-tariff trade barriers, mandatory third-party settlement of disputes). But the actual achievement of global liberal trade will require a much higher degree of 'constitutionalization' of discretionary foreign economic policy powers.[2] Even in the EC, we have so far failed to establish an effective liberal 'foreign policy constitution' preventing protectionist abuses of the EC's discretionary trade policy powers.[3]

Third, the goal of worldwide liberal trade also raises new economic policy issues that have been discussed in the context of regional integration for many years. For instance, to what extent does global liberal trade require the harmonization of divergent national competition, investment, labour, environmental and social regulations? The strength of GATT law derived largely from the fact that the legal ranking of trade policy instruments (such as subsidies, tariffs and non-tariff barriers) was largely consistent with the economic theory of optimal intervention and the requirement of democratic accountability. But there is no equivalent economic consensus on the optimal ranking of domestic policy instruments in fields such as competition, investment, labour, environmental and social law. The 1994 WTO Agreement has followed the model of EC law by limiting protectionist abuses of domestic policy instruments through prohibitions of 'unnecessarily trade-restrictive measures' (such as technical and sanitary regulations and standards, professional qualification and licensing requirements) and requirements of mutual recognition or harmonization of equivalent standards. But we are still far away from an agreed economic and political theory on how to deal best with the increasing number of proposals to harmonize divergent national regulations inside or outside the WTO.

## II

### *Paul Krugman*

Let me begin by making the observation that free trade is not some sort of remote goal, a vision of the unattainable. The fact is that over the past fifty years the world has moved from a highly protectionist, segmented global market to something that is not all that far from free trade. Tariffs on manufactured goods are now very low in the advanced countries – less than 5 per cent on average – and have come down a long way even for developing countries, as many of them have leapt onto the neoliberal bandwagon. True, there are still important non-tariff barriers in some areas; agricultural trade is still highly restricted; and service trade liberalization has barely begun. Still, if we represent the late 1940s level of trade barriers as 100, and utter free trade as zero, we are currently at something like 10 or 15 – we have in fact moved most of the way to free trade already.

Let me be a bit more concrete. If you look at the estimates that the US International Trade Commission makes of the consumer cost of domestic protection – how much our own trade barriers raise costs to consumers – you find that the number is down to less than half of one percent of GDP. And two-thirds of that cost comes from only one sector: apparel. It is only a slight exaggeration in the case of the United States to say that we already have free trade in everything but clothing.

It is still an important question whether we can continue to reduce the scope of protection. Particularly interesting is whether the growing technical possibility for international trade in services will materialize into a comparable growth in the actual amount of such trade; for at least right now many of the services that might be traded, from insurance to telecommunications, are subject to national regulations that explicitly or implicitly close the market to foreigners. But the crucial question, it seems to me, is not whether free trade can progress but whether we can – or should – sustain the trade liberalization the world has already achieved.

A few years back there was a widespread conviction that the free-trade system had passed its peak – people like Lester Thurow were proclaiming that the GATT was dead, that soon the world would fragment into giant rival trading blocs. As it happened, none of that worked out as the doomsayers supposed. The Uruguay Round did, in the end, produce a decent though not wonderful agreement. The great trading blocs are nowhere to be seen – NAFTA seems to have been the end of a trend, not its beginning. And the whole premise of that sort of rhetoric, which was the idea that the major industrial nations were in a quasi-military rivalry for world markets, has to some extent been discredited. Obviously I would like to take some personal credit for that, since I have waged a campaign to convince people that the whole idea of national 'competitiveness' is junk economics. But the apparent triumph of the American-style open economic system over the more closed European and Japanese models is surely the main reason that rhetoric about the 'war for the twenty-first century' has subsided.

The big threat to free trade now is quite different: it is the sense of many people in the advanced world that competition from low-wage countries, countries that now have some access to Western capital and technology, is undermining our standard of living.

Unlike the nonsense about 'competitiveness', this fear has some real foundations. For one thing, it is certainly true that something about the world has changed. As late as the mid 1970s it seemed to be a fact of life that developing countries, no matter how low their wages, could not compete with the accumulated advantages of the rich countries in manufacturing. (Does anyone remember the New International Economic Order, which centered on demands to raise the price of primary products?) But since then some combination of factors – lower transport costs, better communications, a more favourable political environment with the fall of Communism – has tipped the balance, and so countries that used to earn their foreign exchange by selling jute and coffee now earn most of it by selling shirts and sneakers.

It is also without doubt true that this new kind of trade has had some adverse effect on less skilled workers in the advanced countries. Somewhat surprisingly, this does not seem to be a matter of labour versus capital: in the United States, where the changes in income distribution have been most marked, the share of wages and benefits in GDP has hardly changed. But there has been a sharp increase in earnings inequality. And at least some of that is due to Stolper–Samuelson effects: because we export airplanes to the Third World and import sneakers in return, the demand for skilled labour is higher and the demand for unskilled labour lower than would otherwise be the case, and so the real wages of the unskilled are lower than they otherwise would be. I have written extensively on this subject, worked quite a lot with the numbers, and arrived at the conclusion that the volume of this trade is just not large enough to be the main source of the changes in income distribution. But still, there is a kernel of truth to the concerns of the anti-globalization forces.

That said, it is also important to realize that this kernel of truth lies at the center of a large blob of nonsense. Many of the critics of North–South trade seem to believe that it is devastating not only to the distribution of income within advanced countries but to the aggregate income of those countries – that, as one of the World Competitiveness Reports from Davos (that wonderful font of pretentious idiocy) put it, 'the problem of wealth creation in the so-called industrial countries has become acute ... the *raison d'être* of many countries is at stake'. This is the competitiveness misconception all over again: the mistaken belief that world trade is a zero-sum game, the failure to understand that new entrants into the world market expand that market just as much as they expand productive capacity.

There is also what I regard as a particularly shameful aspect of the anti-globalization movement: the persistent claim that globalization takes place at the expense not only of workers in advanced countries but at the expense of those in the developing countries too. This is an easy case to make if you are prepared to be a bit intellectually dishonest. All you have to do is describe the low wages and ghastly working conditions of labourers in factories producing shirts and shoes for the West; then declare how terrible a crime it is that multinational corporations do such things to their workers, and demand a stop to such trade. What you do when telling this kind of story, of course, is carefully to omit mentioning the even worse wages and working conditions that people endure outside the new export sectors of these countries – conditions to which we would once again condemn these workers if we shut off the trade that now exists.

In fact, if we are asking the question 'Should we have free trade?', the compelling moral argument for that trade is, in my mind, the benefits it conveys to desperately poor workers in the Third World. For the fact is that export-led growth has been a huge benefit to the working populations of countries like Indonesia, Thailand, and Malaysia. If you look at the current conditions of those workers, this may seem hard to believe: they seem so terrible compared with First World standards that you assume they must have got worse. But these are or were desperately poor countries. I have recently done some research on Indonesia, a country which is often used by anti-trade exponents such as William Greider as an example of exploitation. Indonesia is indeed a miserable place, with a corrupt and brutal government. Around one child in three under the age of five is underweight, the result of inadequate nutrition. But hard as it may be to realize, the current state of Indonesia is a huge improvement on the recent past. Back in the mid 1970s, the days of the New International Economic Order, more than half of those children were malnourished; average caloric intake per capita has increased by more than a third. In fact, the actual progress of Indonesia and of other countries around the Pacific Rim has vastly surpassed the wildest hopes of those who used to call for massive foreign aid, global raw material cartels, and all that. Yet the same sort of people – indeed, often the very same people – are those who are most vociferously opposed to the new form of North–South trade.

So to the question, should we try to sustain and extend the relatively free trade regime we have achieved, my answer is an overwhelming yes – yes not on cold-blooded economic efficiency grounds, but on the grounds that globalization has done more good for more human beings than anything else in the last few decades.

But there is still the other question: whether or not we should have free trade, will we actually manage it?

It is surely important here to point out that the naysayers have been proved very wrong so far. The GATT was supposed to be dead; instead, it and the WTO are very much alive. Despite ferocious opposition, NAFTA went through, and the predicted economic and political disaster for its American sponsors has not happened, even though Mexico's economy has been pummelled by financial crisis. Populist, anti-trade politicians from Pat Buchanan to James Goldsmith have made a lot of noise, but have not actually had much influence on elections.

Still, it remains true that a liberal trading system is a fragile thing. It is always easy for politicians and for that matter journalists to blame mysterious and evil global forces for everything that goes wrong in an economy. When you have the combination of growing world trade, especially trade with low-wage countries, and serious economic problems at home, you have the makings for a serious political backlash against the open economy.

Surprisingly, the United States seems at the moment not to be the natural home for such a backlash. Our economy is in relatively good shape; the last two or three mega-tomes denouncing the global economy have sputtered out well short of the best-seller lists. And oh yes, America is relatively well endowed with belligerent economists prepared to defend free trade in public. For the moment, at least, the majority opinion in the United States (in so far as we think about it at all) is that globalization is on balance a good thing.

What worries me is Europe. The woes of the continental European economy do not need repeating. What is noticeable is the absence of what looks to an Anglo-Saxon economist like rational analysis of these problems. Comparative advantage has never had much of a foothold in European minds. And in Europe – especially in France – pseudo-sophisticated intellectual tracts denouncing the global economy routinely make the best-seller lists, in a way that they never have in the English-speaking world.

So should we have free trade? Definitely: for all the stresses it causes, it is a vast human – not just economic – good thing. Will we have it? Doubtful: the age-old tendency to blame problems on trade is as strong as ever, and there is a lot of blame to go around.

## III Is more international trade better than less?

### *Brian Barry*

> 'Contrary to the usual ideas free trade breaks down in theory, but protection when you try to apply it. ... However, I wouldn't say as much outside this room!'
>
> J.M. Keynes in a Cambridge tutorial, February, 1929.[5]

Both of the preceding sections of this chapter raise in an admirably clear form the question of the value of international trade. The way in which the WTO is set up presupposes that freedom of trade is virtually a moral imperative, and that the desire to restrict it can arise only from unworthy motives. Yet, as both writers show, if the demands of free trade are pressed beyond a certain point they interfere with the pursuit of national objectives whose legitimacy it is hard to dismiss.

In this commentary, I hope to contribute something to the debate opened up by Petersmann and Krugman.[6] To make my initial question about the value of international trade more specific and tractable, let me replace it by another. Let us stipulate a constant amount and distribution of welfare (in the economists' sense of preference-satisfaction) from the consumption of goods and services and then ask: is it a better state of affairs if a larger rather than a smaller proportion of those goods and services come from outside the country in which they are consumed?

Let me offer an answer in two parts, dealing separately with cultural goods and others. In the case of cultural goods, then, I suggest that it is desirable if some proportion comes from outside the country, even if the amount and distribution of welfare is unaffected. (This is, in technical terms, an ideal-regarding as against a want-regarding judgement, but I feel sure that it is one that many people would make.) At the same time, it seems absurd to imagine that more cultural imports are better than less without limit. It must therefore be within the proper scope of government to limit the scale of cultural imports if there is a real danger that they will seriously weaken the vitality of domestic cultural production.

What exacerbates this danger is the fact that the cost of making television programmes can easily be recouped within the vast US market, thereby making it profitable to sell them on to other countries for whatever the market will bear, however little that may be. Inevitably, there is no possibility that television programmes made in another country for consumption within that country can even begin to come close to competing on price with US imports. I believe therefore that it is legitimate for governments to impose rules about the minimum proportion of domestic content in television programming and if necessary other media as well. This was a matter pressed by the French government in the WTO negotiations, and I wish they had attached as much importance to it as they did to securing a market for French rapeseed oil.

It is, of course, perfectly true that any such restrictions carry with them the danger of being used by the government as a cover for censorship of content, but a government bent on that will find ways of doing it anyway. So long as the limits are purely quantitative and it is left to those doing the importing to choose, within those limits, what should be imported, I do not see that any real danger to freedom arises. And in return for the restriction on imports, what can reasonably be hoped for is a substantial increase in the diversity of cultural goods available to those who live in the country concerned.

It may, of course, be said that a government keen to promote indigenous cultural products can do so by subsidizing them and that this is a preferable approach to that of imposing quantitative restrictions on cultural imports. There are two points to be made about this objection. The first is that, to the gung-ho enthusiasts for free trade, subsidies to domestic production are just as much anathema as limits on imports, since they are equally ways of giving an 'unfair advantage' to domestic producers. As a number of papers at the conference showed, such metaphysicians of the market are actively at work within the WTO, and their counterparts have notoriously been busy for years within the European Community trying to strike down any efforts by governments to tilt the so-called level playing field. So far, admittedly, neither of these sets of doctrinaires has (as far as I know) complained officially that the Arts Council funds British creators and performers and that the BBC commissions new work almost exclusively from within the UK. But extrapolating from current trends suggests that complaints about the discriminatory use of taxpayers' and license-payers' money are only a matter of time.

The second point is simply that, because of the peculiar economics of American film and television (mentioned above), a government might have to spend a very large amount indeed on subsidies before it could render it profitable to show home-produced material rather than American material sold at knock-down prices. Even allowing, therefore, that subsidies have a place, the sensible conclusion to be drawn is that quantitative import restrictions have a place as well. Nothing but pure dogmatism can, I suggest, lead to the answer that the latter must be ruled out as a legitimate policy instrument.

As far as other goods and services are concerned, I find it very hard to imagine that, if the amount and distribution of welfare are held constant, a situation in which a larger proportion of goods and services come from outside the country is superior to one in which a smaller proportion does. As Bhaskar Vira says (Chapter 11, pp. 147–62), there is a position according to which restrictions of trade reduce freedom and that is in itself a significant count against them.[7] Obviously we can define 'freedom' so that this becomes a necessary truth, since any restriction on freedom of trade is a circumscription of liberty. But how important is this kind of liberty?

Concretely, suppose the brand of some good that I regard as offering the best value for money happens to be a domestic one. Does it really matter whether or not there are a number of foreign brands also available in the shops? A natural reason for replying in the affirmative is the fear that, if the foreign goods were to vanish from the shelves, it might not be long before the domestic product became less good value for money. For the lack of foreign competition might enable the local manufacturer to put up the price or allow the quality to slip, or both. But this makes freedom a purely instrumental value: the real concern is for welfare (that is to say consumer satisfaction), and free trade is merely a means to it.

Once we have reduced the question to one of welfare, it becomes an empirical matter whether in some specific case the overall amount and distribution of welfare is made better or worse by freedom of trade. If, for example, import controls enabled the economy to be run at a much higher level of activity, the deterioration in the value for money offered by goods might be overwhelmed in the welfare calculation by the welfare gains from reduced unemployment and the far greater volume of production. I am, let me make it clear, treating this as a hypothetical case – though I do at least wish to insist that it is not fanciful for some historical contexts. The point of it here is simply to illustrate that, to the extent that freedom of trade is conceived as having only instrumental value, it must always be an open question whether some particular set of rules to regulate it is welfare-enhancing in comparison with all the conceivable alternatives.

The distinction I have been drawing between the ethical significance of cultural and other goods was made – in a far less nuanced form – by John Maynard Keynes in a speech on 'National Self-Sufficiency' that he gave in Dublin in 1933: 'Ideas, knowledge, art, hospitality, travel – these are the things that should of their nature be international. But let goods be homespun whenever it is reasonably and conveniently possible; and, above all, let finance be primarily national.'[8] Qualifying the first half of Keynes's exhortation, I have suggested that a phenomenon only slightly developed in the early nineteen thirties, American 'cultural dumping', can validly be opposed by appropriate government action. A further qualification is in order with respect to travel. We can surely deplore politically motivated attempts by governments (such as those constantly made from 1945 on by the US government) to tell their citizens to where they can and cannot travel. But we must take account of a development that was even less conspicuous in 1933 than 'cultural dumping': mass tourism. I suggest that the threat posed by the growth of cheap mass tourism justifies vigorous and extensive action by the government of a country to control its impact. Even from the crassest commercial point of view, it is remarkably stupid to allow whatever it was that was distinctive about a place to be engulfed by the heedless expansion of the tourist industry. But even if that were not so (and perhaps it is not invariably so), it would always be a legitimate objective of government to preserve existing ways of life from destruction by mass tourism.

On the other side of the picture, I believe that it is essential to be less cavalier than Keynes was about the possibility that there may be real welfare losses from keeping out foreign goods by freeing the domestic producers from competition. Experience in countries with highly protected domestic markets suggests that the negative effects on welfare are liable to be cumulative. The problem that tends to be especially recalcitrant is that firms are liable to settle for a quiet life, taking advantage of the lack of foreign competition to shun the pain of innovation. The contrast between the West German and East German economies at the time of re-unification is the most vivid illustration of the pathological effects of assured markets. Allowing everything that plausibly can be allowed for the effects of Marshall Aid from America versus the exploitation of East Germany by its corresponding Great Power, the Soviet Union, there has to be something perverse about the economic system of a country that inherited the People's Car (the Beetle) and finished up thirty-five years later with the Trabant.

Why did Keynes wish goods to be homespun whenever reasonably or conveniently possible? With almost half the period since the repeal of the Corn Laws having now elapsed since Keynes's lecture, it is interesting to ask how the arguments he put forward in it against free trade stack up today. Keynes's support for protectionism is decidedly unfashionable. But does that mean it was mistaken?

Keynes advanced four reasons for looking askance at international trade. The first was not so much an argument against free trade as a counter-argument to the traditional case for it. More precisely, Keynes maintained that this argument was less strong in 1933 than it had hitherto been. Thus, following the logic of Keynes's argument, it could be that free trade had been the right policy for Britain in 1846 but was no longer on balance advantageous over eighty years later. The traditional argument that Keynes had in mind was the Ricardian appeal to comparative advantage: some countries are naturally better suited to producing certain things than others, and two countries with different characteristics can both benefit from trade. Ricardo's illustration of the thesis involved corn and wine. Robert Skidelsky tells us that 'wine did not agree with [Keynes] and he drank it sparingly', adding that neither Maynard nor Lydia 'cared enough about food or drink ... to give them much thought or time'.[9] Nevertheless, I take it that Keynes would have had to admit that reducing everybody in the country to the consumption of British wine would be to carry the 'homespun' principle a bit too far. What he did claim, however, was that 'most modern mass-production processes can be performed in most countries and climates with equal efficiency' and that it was 'perhaps' true of 'agricultural products also' that the economic cost of national self-sufficiency was dubiously sufficient to outweigh 'the other advantages of gradually bringing the producer and the consumer within the ambit of the same national, economic and financial organisation'.[10]

Leaving aside the (as yet unstated) advantages to be weighed against the cost of national self-sufficiency, what should we make of Keynes's argument that that cost had diminished? If he was right then, has he continued to be right? It seems to me that, on the ground on which Keynes took his stand, he must be judged to have been right at the time, and triumphantly vindicated by subsequent developments. The rise of the Asian 'tigers' illustrates more clearly than any piece of evidence available to Keynes in 1933 (except perhaps the rise of Japan as an economic power) how exportable manufacturing technology is. If the only argument for free trade were Ricardian comparative advantage, it would have little application to anything except tropical agricultural produce and certain geographically concentrated raw materials.

However, if we hark back to a greater and subtler economist than Ricardo,

Adam Smith, we can identify a force that has since 1933 increasingly worked in the opposite direction and become ever more important. For Smith, the key significance of the extension of markets was that it enabled the division of labour to be driven further by making it profitable to carry out manufacture on a larger scale than would otherwise have been possible and hence reducing unit costs of production. I suppose that the most dramatic illustration of this trend since 1933 is provided by the car industry. At that time, both Britain and the United States had a number of completely independent car companies, manufacturing all their own major components. Today, if we exclude car firms that are franchise operations for other companies, there is only a handful of car companies in the whole world. The implication is that national car companies have almost become things of the past: even the American giants, Ford and GM, are international. I do not claim to understand why it takes so many hundreds of millions of pounds to design and tool up for, say, the production of a new gearbox. But anybody who remembers the experience of fighting to get a British Leyland car out of one gear into another will be inclined to agree that one country (at any rate when that country is Britain) cannot go it alone in the manufacture of gearboxes, and *a fortiori* the manufacture of entire vehicles.

Even where the scale of efficient production is not larger than the bounds of a country, the same forces are at work to ensure that, if there was no effective foreign competition, the amount of competition arising from a multiplicity of domestic manufacturers would generally be a great deal less than in 1933. Hence, if there are (as I have suggested) cumulative losses from lack of competition, the costs of national self-sufficiency in this respect would be significantly greater nowadays than Keynes could have anticipated.

Nevertheless, it is impossible not to be struck by the justice of Keynes's original observation that there is little underlying reason for most manufacturing to be carried out in one place rather than another. To a remarkable degree, the countries of the European Union have similar economies (the country with the most dissimilar economy in western Europe, Norway, has done well by staying out), and the main effect of the liberalization of trade among them has been to increase the ease with which they can sell goods of the same description to one another. To adapt Mark Twain, we may say that they make a living by taking in one another's washing machines.

What brought home to me the questionable rationality of all this was seeing a very large, heavy lorry laden with bricks making its way up the country from one of the channel ports. Large parts of Britain (and especially the more populous parts) are more or less built on clay. We surely cannot have lost the technology of making bricks adequate for any reasonable purpose. So why are we importing them? Keynes did not mention the environmental damage (both local and global) created by the sheer transport of goods over long distances as an argument against international trade. When Keynes gave his lecture, the greenhouse effect, though conjectured long before, was not a live issue; far more transport of heavy goods was by rail as against road than now; and lorries were not the behemoths that a supine Ministry of Transport has allowed on our roads. Perhaps if road transport were made to pay its full cost – local, in the destruction of roads and amenity, and global in its contribution to global warming – the gratuitous movement of near-identical goods over long distances would be greatly reduced. This would have the advantage of reducing the amount of international trade substantially while still retaining the threat of competition if the domestic producers fell too far short of what foreign firms in the same line of business could do.

Second, 'Keynes stated bluntly that free trade, combined with international mobility of capital, was more likely to provoke war than keep peace.'[11] Chris Brown nicely documented the amazingly naive optimism of many leading nineteenth-century free traders about the inevitable peace-creating tendencies of free trade.[12] In relation to these fantasies, Keynes's nay-saying represents a welcome breath of scepticism. At the same time, however, I have to say that Keynes's argument for his proposition seems to me distinctly thin. All that he had to suggest was that minimizing 'economic entanglement between nations' would reduce the 'strains and enmities' that were otherwise liable to arise.[13] But a defender of free trade might respond that, while it is tautologically true that complete autarchy would eliminate conflicts (so long as no country simply wished to rob another), complete autarchy is impossible. In the real world, countries cannot be totally self-sufficient: in northern climes the goods may be homespun but the cotton will have to be imported.

Given this necessary interdependence, it is plausible that an international regime in which countries can be assured of having access to raw materials by simply paying the going market price for them will be less liable to economically motivated conflict than one in which access depends on political control of territory. Keynes suggested that 'the ownership of national assets by foreigners' had led to war in 1914.[14] But this seems to me a misleading way of talking about what was really going on, which was colonialism.

The 'scramble for Africa' among the European powers from the 1880s onward, and the struggle for control over resources and markets in other parts of the world in the period up to 1914, were indeed potent causes of rivalry and conflict. But the driving force behind all of this territorial aggressiveness was the conviction (flowing from the nature of the existing international system) that if a country wanted access to, say, chrome or copper, it had better have political control of the part of Africa in which they were to be found. Thus, it seems to me that Keynes misdiagnosed the economic causes of the First World War. The Kaiser's ambitions for a 'salt water' empire led to the naval rivalry between Germany and Britain that undoubtedly contributed to tensions between them in the years before 1914. But what fuelled this ambition in turn was the quest for secure sources of raw materials and dependable access to foreign markets. Detaching access from political control – which is in essence what free trade does – must surely reduce the perceived advantage of possessing colonies and thus take some of the heat out of at any rate one source of international conflict.

Keynes's third argument for national self-sufficiency seems to me more robust and indeed to have far more resonance today than it could have had when Keynes put it forward. 'We each have our own fancy. Not believing we are saved already, we each would like to have a try at working out our salvation. We do not wish, therefore, to be at the mercy of world forces working out, or trying to work out, some uniform equilibrium according to the ideal principles of *laissez-faire* capitalism.'[15]

What was for Keynes in 1933 a speculative dystopia has now become, to an alarming extent, our contemporary reality. Survey mankind from China and Peru and there is no mistaking the convergence on a single economic model. No doubt much of this convergence can be accounted for by the extraordinary way in which political leaders all round the world have embraced the market and all its works, even in cases (such as Russia) where the result has been a catastrophic decline in the average standard of living and, even more, in universality of access to basic essentials such as food, housing and medical care. But this cannot explain all moves towards convergence, such as the forced abandonment of the 'Swedish model' which many people (including me) saw as the most promising way forward.

Those who deplore the pressure to conformity and those who applaud it agree that it arises above all from the extreme mobility of capital. Keynes's dictum – 'above all, let finance be primarily national' – could scarcely be more comprehensively flouted than it has been by the massive movement in recent decades towards the complete liberalization of capital flows. Unless it is to cut itself off from the rest of the world, a country must be attractive to capital or its economy will grind to a halt. Even if its government has no ambitions to create a net capital inflow, and has no desire for foreign finance as such, it must still ensure an internationally competitive return on capital or risk the flight of domestic capital. This is obviously an enormous constraint on the development of diversified economic systems.

The fourth of Keynes's targets was, one might say, Thatcherism *avant la lettre*. With our quest for cheap food at all costs having brought about endemic salmonella in chickens and BSE in cattle, Keynes's words show an almost uncanny prescience. 'We have until recently conceived it a moral duty to ruin the tillers of the soil and destroy the age-long traditions attendant on husbandry if we could get a loaf of bread thereby a tenth of a penny cheaper.'[16] Everything else had been sacrificed to 'this Moloch and Mammon in one', but, Keynes said: 'Today we suffer disillusion, not because we are poorer ... but because other values seem to have been sacrificed ... and sacrificed unnecessarily. For our economic system is not, in fact, enabling us to exploit to the utmost the possibilities for economic wealth afforded by the progress of our technique ... leading us to feel that we might as well have used up the margin in more satisfying ways.'[17] What Keynes had in mind specifically by these remarks he had already made clear a little earlier in his speech: 'with what we have spent on the dole since the War we could have made our cities the greatest works of man in the world.'[18]

I profoundly sympathize with the thrust of this part of Keynes's lecture – here reproduced only in fragments, which destroys much of its rhetorical force. Lytton Strachey, challenged for his refusal to take part in the First World War, responded 'I am the civilization for which you are fighting.' On the same lines, those of us in 'unproductive' occupations that contribute to the flourishing of the arts and sciences should stop apologizing for our existence or trying to justify it within the 'productivist' paradigm and should insist that a large part of the measure of a successful economy is its providing the material basis for the grandest achievements of civilized life. Back in 1933, when the British GDP per head was a fraction of what it is now, Keynes was poking fun at the idea that we could not "afford" the highest standards of achievement ... because they do not "pay". How much more grotesque it is to be told now by the leaders of both major political parties that we still cannot 'afford' to spend money on the collective pursuit of the activities that raise mankind above the beasts![19]

However, before getting too carried away, we must ask exactly what all this has to do with the evils of free trade. The link in Keynes's mind is fairly clear. For if (his third point) universal free trade must lead every country eventually to 'some uniform equilibrium according to the ideal principles of *laissez-faire* capitalism', the result must be to turn 'the whole conduct of life ... into a sort of parody of an accountant's nightmare.'[20] But is the connection as tight as Keynes's argument requires?

We are, of course, assured by the government (in very much the terms derided by Keynes) that maintaining and enhancing the country's 'competitiveness' entails that we cannot 'afford' high standards of environmental protection, worker safety or job security. Yet all that can validly be said about these things is that if we want to have them we cannot also enjoy quite so many consumer goods as otherwise. If we are willing to pay for them, we can have any standards we want. (What is much more plausible is that countries can have different standards only if they can equilibriate their balance of payments through adjustments in the exchange rate; but it calls for little effort to imagine what Keynes would have thought about a single currency yoking together diverse economies at a permanently fixed parity.) Similarly there is no imperative arising from free trade that prevents a country from providing itself with whatever cultural goods it chooses to pay for. The point is simply enough made by pointing out that in other member states in the European Union – our most immediate sources of competition – the proportion of the national income that goes in taxes is anything from a half more to double the proportion in Britain, and that in most the arts and sciences are far better funded.

Keynes's assumption of a tight connection between free trade and the 'accountant's nightmare' nevertheless still has force if we bear in mind that, once the chosen environmental and worker-protection standards are in place, the implication for free trade must be that the government can do nothing about the content of the goods and services that get produced. If, for example, tough air and water standards make some highly polluting process unprofitable, because it can be carried out more cheaply in some other country or countries with laxer standards, there is nothing to be done about it.

Keynes himself had rather expansive notions about the range of occupations that the government should act to keep alive. National self-sufficiency, Keynes argued in a broadcast talk a year before the Dublin lecture, in 1932, 'promised a "well-balanced" or "complete" national life, allowing English people to display the full range of their national aptitudes in mechanical invention and in agriculture, as well as preserving traditional ways of living.' Thus, there must be heavy industry: 'I wish to see the blast furnaces of the north-east coast to roar again and ships of British steel sail out of the Clyde.' And there must be a healthy agricultural sector, for there is a type of Englishman that 'needs as his pursuit in life the care and breeding of animals and contact with the changing seasons and the soil.' Any additional cost would be worth it: 'To say that the country cannot afford agriculture is to delude oneself about the meaning of the word "afford". A country which cannot afford art or agriculture, invention or tradition, is a country in which one cannot afford to live.'[21]

Keynes's wish to freeze the pattern of production not merely as it was in 1933 but rather as it had been twenty years before seems rather quixotic, and it must be doubted that there is really any specific 'need' to be a steelworker or shipbuilder that could conceivably justify the cost of keeping the blast furnaces and the shipyards working at full capacity. But the loss of jobs of the general kind provided by those industries is another matter. We clearly suffer from a serious lack of jobs in which people in the bottom half of the distribution of intelligence can take pride, and Keynes was surely right to insist that the satisfactions of the consumer must be traded off against the satisfactions of the producer, rather than the former being somehow assumed without question to be more important.

Agriculture is the sphere in which Keynes had the most indubitably strong case for saying that production must not be seen as a mere undifferentiated contribution to the consumption of goods and services. The way in which agriculture is conducted (and the extent to which it is conducted at all) has an immense influence on the whole appearance of the countryside, and makes an enormous difference to the pleasure that can be taken in it both by those who live in it and those who live in the cities. We have, unfortunately, made all the mistakes that Keynes pointed to and are still continuing to make them in assuming that we cannot 'afford' to impose planning controls on farm buildings, protect all the remaining hedgerows by preservation orders, or insist that footpaths must not be ploughed up. Nor have we introduced the restrictions on the use of pesticides and fertilizer that would prevent agriculture from being one of the major sources of pollution. The fundamental error has been not to treat agriculture in Britain as an amenity first and a source of food only second.

To the zealots of free trade, the determination of the industrial countries to exempt agriculture from the world market is a source of uncomprehending fury. Yet it is clear that, as with cultural goods only far more so, achieving the desired ends by means of subsidy alone would be prohibitively expensive and in any case an unnecessary drain on tax revenues when there is the alternative of making the domestic consumer pay a bit more for food by placing a tariff on imports.

In the same vein, it is perfectly legitimate (indeed admirable) for a government, acting on behalf of its citizens, to require livestock animals to be reared and kept in humane conditions – to live in the open air, to have room to move about naturally, and so on. This again will of course raise the price of meat. But whereas a government cannot reasonably insist that agricultural imports should have been grown in conditions that are as careful of local amenity as those imposed on domestic production, it is perfectly legitimate to demand that all meat sold in the country must conform to the same standards of humane rearing and slaughtering, regardless of its origins. To treat such demands as responses to 'psychological spillovers', as Vira does in his chapter,[22] is to miscategorize and trivialize them. The point is not merely to gratify the 'tastes' of domestic consumers but to carry through consistently a moral view about the way in which animals should be treated. If we are concerned in Britain about the welfare of animals, it would be very odd to say 'but only the welfare of animals reared in Britain'.

There is no reason why human beings should be exempted from the same kind of concern. If we think that child labour and the suppression of trade unions is wrong, our government should be able to block imports produced under unacceptable conditions. The efforts of a number of governments (including the British) to keep such issues out of the WTO and kick them over to the ILO are a barefaced attempt to give them to a relatively weak and ineffectual body rather than one that will, unless something is done to stop it, outlaw all such legitimate concerns of citizens and their governments about the conditions under which goods are produced. James Cameron's chapter shows just how far advanced this process already is.[23]

I have so far left on one side what was no doubt for Keynes the most important element in his critique of economic orthodoxy: its willingness to accept high levels of unemployment as beyond the control of governments. Indeed, it is clear that what precipitated Keynes's sympathy for protectionism was the persistence of large-scale unemployment in Britain since the return to the gold standard at the old parity in 1925 and the international spread of mass unemployment after the crash of 1929. For Keynes, as we have seen, the main evil of unemployment was the wasted opportunities for betterment that it represented. But in addition there are at least three other reasons for regarding unemployment as a great evil. These all reflect Keynes's concern for the welfare of producers and not only consumers. One is the way in which full employment shifts the balance of power in favour of the employee, and forces employers to treat their workforce with some consideration. The second is the amply documented contribution that a secure job makes to mental health and, conversely, the way in which the risk of falling into depression is multiplied by the experience of unemployment. The third is the function of regular work as a socializing agency: the correlation of crime and general social dysfunction with unemployment is too clear for there to be any doubt about its reality.

Where does free trade fit into the picture? What is, I take it, clear is that any country taking Keynes's advice and 'us[ing] up the margin in more satisfying ways' than paying a lot of people to be unemployed would have to introduce tight controls on capital movements and on imports that would bring it into immediate conflict with all the world's major international economic institutions. Not only socialism in one country but even full employment in one country is now out of reach.

But must freedom of trade create the endemic high levels of unemployment that we have in the world today? That is a problem for the economists, and the main remark I have to make is that I am sorry they do not seem to have put it top of their list of priorities. However, since I have built these comments around Keynes let me end with his later thoughts about the international order. It is something of a commonplace nowadays for people to say: 'we need a new Bretton Woods agreement.' But there is no point in a new Bretton Woods agreement in the absence of a new Keynes to suggest what its content should be. Lacking a new Keynes, we could do worse than return to the old Keynes and go back to a crucial feature of the draft for the Bretton Woods agreement that was eliminated from the final version. This was the demand that balance of payments disequilibria should be regarded as the responsibility of creditor countries at least as much as debtor countries.

> Under the Keynes plan, the Clearing Union ... could *require* a surplus country whose credit balance exceeded half its quota to carry out such measures as the stimulation of domestic demand, the appreciation of its currency, the reduction of import barriers, and the making of international development loans.[24]

If this were tweaked so that the pressure was disproportionately on creditor countries at times of international recession and disproportionately on debtor countries in an international boom, it would offer some hope of bringing an element of rationality into the management of the world economy. As things stand, I have to confess to being deeply puzzled by the unprecedented frenzy of enthusiasm for the market – this 'Moloch and Mammon in one' as Keynes described it – when it is becoming ever more apparent that it is incapable of delivering any of the things that one might ask of an economic system: equity, sustainability and efficiency. Both within and between countries, the rich get richer and the poor get poorer; there is nothing in the market mechanism to inhibit the destruction of the habitat of man and other creatures; and it cannot even bring about the effective deployment of the world's human resources.

## Notes

1 See J. Gwartney, R. Lawson and W. Block (eds), *Economic Freedom of the World: 1975–1995*, 1996. Of course, the empirical correlation between economic freedom and wealth does not prove causation, and the measurement of governmental restrictions on 'economic freedom' raises difficult normative and empirical problems.

2 Cf. E.U. Petersmann, 'Constitutionalism and international organizations', in *Northwestern Journal of International Law and Business 1997* (forthcoming).

3 Cf. E.U. Petersmann, 'The moral foundations of the European Union's foreign policy constitution: defining "European identity", and "Community interests" for the benefit of EU citizens', in *Swiss Review of International Economic Relations* (*Aussenwirtschaft*) 1996, pp. 151–76.

4 See chapter 8, 'The Need for Integrating Trade and Competition Rules in the WTO World Trade and Legal System'.

5 A.F.W. Plumptre, 'Maynard Keynes as a Teacher', pp. 247–53 in Milo Keynes (ed.), *Essays on John Maynard Keynes*, Cambridge: Cambridge University Press, 1975, quotation from p. 248.

6 I am grateful to the editors for allowing me to incorporate into this presentation material that was originally a commentary at one of the plenary sessions.

7 Bhaskar Vira, 'Environmental Regulation and Economic Deregulation: Is There a Conflict?', pp. 150– below.

8 Quoted in Robert Skidelsky, *John Maynard Keynes: The Economist as Saviour, 1920–1937*, New York: Penguin Books, 1994 [1992], p. 477.

9 Ibid., p. 218.

10 Ibid., p. 477.

11 Ibid.

12 Chris Brown, 'Sovereignty, Free Trade and Liberal Internationalism', 150th Anniversary of the Repeal of the Corn Laws conference, Manchester: 1996.

13 Skidelsky, p. 477.

14 Ibid.

15 Ibid.

16 Ibid., p. 478.

17 Ibid.

18 Ibid.

19 A good illustration of the way in which the political parties have subordinated the case for supporting the arts to the concerns of accountants is provided in what purports to be a *defence* of the Labour Party's commitment to the arts. Note the priorities expressed in Sir David Puttnam's letter to *The Independent* newspaper: 'New Labour's *Road to the Manifesto* identifies the economic significance of the arts, as well as their "enormous impact on education, leisure and the quality of life". They are, it says, "significant earners for Britain" and employ hundreds of thousands.' *The Independent*, 20 July 1996, p. 15.

20 Skidelsky, p. 477.

21 Ibid., p. 476.
22 Vira, p. 57 below.
23 James Cameron, ' "What Now?" Trade and Environment: An Overview of the Current Debate', pp. 163–79 below.
24 Richard N. Gardner, 'Bretton Woods', pp. 202–15 in Milo Keynes (ed.), quotation from p. 210, emphasis in original.

# 3

# COSMOPOLITANISM, REALISM AND THE NATIONAL INTEREST

*Simon Caney*

How should states conduct their foreign policy? When, if ever, may a state engage in protectionist policies? Should wealthy states write off debts from impoverished states? Should states seek to reform currently existing forms of international economic cooperation and international organizations (like the United Nations, the World Bank, the OECD, the IMF, the EU and the WTO)? Should they discourage trade with regimes which repress their citizens and deny them fundamental rights? In order to answer these pressing questions we need to establish the general criteria by which one should assess the conduct of states. We need, that is, to address the following abstract questions: What weight should states give to the interests of people who are not citizens of their own states? Should they seek to advance the well-being of all human beings? Should their foreign policy be committed solely to the promotion of the 'national interest'?

Two approaches might be suggested to these questions. According to those who subscribe to a *cosmopolitan* approach, all human beings have political and economic rights which all states must respect. Many cosmopolitans argue that there should be global principles of distributive justice which require wealthy states to transfer wealth and resources to impoverished members of other states. States, that is, are bound not simply by negative duties requiring them not to murder or enslave members of other states: they are also bound, as a matter of distributive justice, to distribute wealth to the needy and destitute regardless of their citizenship or nationality.[1] Cosmopolitans might also argue that such transfers can also be justifed on humanitarian grounds as well as on the grounds that they are demanded by a correct theory of distributive justice.[2] In what follows I shall not, however, distinguish between these different types of obligation and shall refer simply to cosmopolitan obligations or cosmopolitan ideals.

A second approach is affirmed by *realists*. The latter are highly critical of cosmopolitan approaches to international politics, arguing that they are utopian and inapplicable given the power-dominated nature of international relations. Indeed, on some occasions, realists claim that the foreign policy of states should not be informed by any moral considerations.[3] Their more common position, however, is that states are under a moral obligation to further their national interest where this is understood to mean that they should promote the welfare of their citizens. According to realists, states are not morally bound by global principles of international distributive justice. States should be motivated, not by a concern for the interests of foreigners, but by a concern for the well-being of their own members. Thus at the end of his work *In Defense of the National Interest*, Hans Morgenthau enjoins us to 'remember always that it is not only a political necessity but also a moral duty for a nation to follow in its dealings with other nations but one guiding star, one standard for thought, one rule for action: THE NATIONAL INTEREST'.[4] Similarly, Stephen Krasner writes that states ought to pursue their national interest and accordingly argues that the United States should ignore 'Central America, most of Africa, Indo-China, and most of the other countries of the Third World' because they 'are irrelevant for the United States'.[5]

Realism is an extremely varied tradition.[6] Some like Morgenthau are sceptical of cosmopolitan ideals because they adhere to a pessimistic account of human nature. They adopt what Kenneth Waltz has termed a *first image* theory.[7] More recent realists like Krasner and Waltz himself base their scepticism about the success of cosmopolitan ideals not upon an account of human nature but on the structure of the international system. These structural realists (or neo-realists) affirm what Waltz termed the *third image*: their claim is that the structure of the international system impels states to pursue their national interest and to eschew cooperative policies.[8] Whatever their disagreement about the fundamental causes of the lack of international cooperation, however, all realists make the descriptive claim that states generally seek to further their national interest and the normative claim that they should do so.

Cosmopolitans and realists thus judge the desirability of institutions like free trade in very different ways. Whereas cosmopolitans consider the impact free trade has on all human beings, realists assert that states should judge the desirability of free trade in terms of its impact on the standard of living of its citizens. The aim of this chapter is to examine some prevalent realist defences of the claim that states should pursue the national interest and realist critiques of the cosmopolitan claim that states should be concerned with the standard of living of members of other states. The chapter examines first the realist argument that cosmopolitan ideals cannot be successfully implemented given the anarchic nature of global politics (sections I–III). It then considers the realist contention that a system in which states further their own interests results in a morally better outcome than one in which they adopt cosmopolitan ideals (section IV). Finally, it considers the familiar realist argument that attempts by states to aid non-citizens are necessarily unsuccessful if not counterproductive and hence that states should restrict themselves to the pursuit of their national interest (section V). None of these realist critiques of cosmopolitanism are, I argue, successful.

# I

Let us begin with what might be termed a Hobbesian argument – what I shall call the 'negative argument from anarchy'.[9] Many realists argue that the international system is akin to a state of nature in which the cooperation required for cosmopolitan ideals is absent and in which, therefore, states are allowed and indeed enjoined to further their national interest. Kenneth Waltz and Robert Art, for example, defend the pursuit of the national interest as follows:

> States in anarchy cannot afford to be moral. The possibility for moral behaviour rests upon the existence of an effective government that can deter and punish illegal actions. In anarchy, there is no government; hence there are no laws. ... If there is neither government nor laws, then there can be no concept of legal rights. States have a 'right' only to what they can achieve by their own efforts. No state has a legal or moral right to exist or to prosper, only the 'right' to do all that is in its power to do. In this sense, right does not mean legality, but rather the freedom to choose whatever is deemed most effective to attain a given end. The preconditions for morality are absent in international politics. Every state, as a consequence, has to be prepared to do that which is necessary for its interests as it defines them. Anarchy is the realm where all can, and many do, play 'dirty pool'.[10]

This argument is slightly ambiguous. Waltz and Art might be reasoning as follows:

### *Version 1*

1 Agents (states or individuals) do not have moral obligations to others if there is no coercive authority to enforce them.
2 There is no coercive authority, over and above states, which can ensure that states comply with duties to members of other states.
Therefore
C States are under no obligations to non-citizens and are entitled to pursue their national interest.

This defence of the 'national interest' and critique of cosmopolitanism fails, however, because its first premise is implausible. We do not standardly think that individuals are not subject to moral obligations simply because they cannot be enforced. Indeed, we have a strong intuition that some moral obligations should not be enforced (even if they could be). This last point even applies to claims about justice. A parent who always gives slightly more to one of his children than to another of his children is, we might say, acting unjustly but we would not necessarily say that laws should be implemented to compel him to treat them equally. (Although, if the injustice was severe we may well call for legal intervention.) Obligations, including obligations of justice, are therefore not necessarily obligations which can or should be enforced. Hence, to show that there is no world state which can enforce cosmopolitan obligations does not imply that there are no such obligations.

## II

These objections to Waltz and Art's argument succeed in undermining this first version but they do not really get to the heart of their argument.[11] On a more plausible interpretation of their argument, Waltz and Art are arguing as follows:

### *Version 2*

1 Cosmopolitan moral ideals are attainable only if states cooperate with one another.
2 States will not cooperate with one another.
Therefore
3 It is pointless for a state to adhere to cosmopolitan moral principles for this will achieve nothing.
Therefore
C States are under no obligations to non-citizens and are entitled to pursue their national interest.

Cosmopolitan moral principles require for their success a degree of international cooperation which, this argument maintains, will be absent. On this interpretation, the non-existence of a world state is significant because without one the cooperation required for the attainment of cosmopolitan ideals will, it is claimed, not take place. This argument is much more problematic for the cosmopolitan than the first interpretation of the Hobbesian argument. It is nonetheless unconvincing and I want now to examine some of its presuppositions.

One problem with the argument lies in its emphasis on cooperation. Premise (1) claims that no state on its own is able to bring about a world order that is acceptable from a cosmopolitan perspective. Cooperation is necessary to achieve this. This, however, does not imply that states on their own can do nothing for non-citizens. Cooperation may be required to create a just or nearly just world order. This should not, however, lead us to ignore the fact that each state on its own can achieve something. Furthermore, powerful states like the United States of America can effect considerable change on their own without any cooperation. The importance of cooperation should therefore not be overstated.[12]

A second problem with the 'negative argument from anarchy' is that even if cooperation between states is necessary for the realization of cosmopolitan objectives it is not clear that cooperation between states is unattainable. To see this, let us consider the reasoning underlying the claim that states will look after their own interests and abstain from cooperative ventures. The most lucid argument for this assertion is given by Waltz. He outlines two reasons. (a) First, he argues that states are concerned with their relative advantage rather than their absolute advantage. By this he means that states are concerned with their power in relation to other states. The reason for this is that their long-run survival depends on them not being overrun by other states: accordingly they seek to ensure that they are more powerful than other states.[13] He then argues that this concern for relative advantage means that they wish not to cooperate with other states. (b) Secondly, he argues that states are disinclined to cooperate with other states because if they do so they lose their independence and are reliant on the goodwill of these other states.[14] Consequently, Waltz concludes,

> In an unorganized realm each unit's incentive is to put itself in a position to be able to take care of itself since no one else can be counted on to do so. The international imperative is 'take care of yourself'! Some leaders of nations may understand that the well-being of all of them would increase through their participation in a fuller division of labor. But to act on the idea would be to act on a domestic imperative, an imperative that does not run internationally.[15]

Neither of Waltz's arguments, however, show that cooperation between states is impossible.

On (a), Waltz's assumption here is groundless. His claim appears to be that states are concerned with their long-run absolute advantage and hence with their relative advantage, but it is not clear why members of present states should be concerned with the power of future leaders of their state. Waltz's assumption here looks plausible only if we regard states as actors concerned with their long-run interests: but they are not. They are composed of individuals who may or may not be concerned with the power of those who will succeed them in power. Furthermore, as Robert Keohane has observed, the assumption that states seek to maximize rather than, say, satisfice is frequently unwarranted.[16] The assumption that states seek to maximize their self-interest (understood as relative advantage) is no more plausible than the assumption that individuals always seek to maximize their self-interest. However, (b) is also unpersuasive. Cooperation with other states need not make one more vulnerable and indeed when cooperation is mutually advantageous abstaining from cooperation with other states will damage one's interests.

Furthermore, recent work on international relations theory casts doubt on Waltz's pessimism concerning cooperation. Two important areas of research are relevant. First, as some have argued, hegemonic powers have the ability to create and maintain systems of cooperation between states.[17] The logic behind this argument (referred to as hegemonic stability theory) is very clear. Hegemons produce certain systems of cooperation because they have an incentive to do so and they also have the ability to do so and to secure cooperation from others. One popular example (given by both Krasner and Gilpin) is free trade.[18] Both argue, for example, that during the last century Britain occupied a hegemonic role which it used to promote and maintain free trade. Now this emphasis on the significance of hegemons has, of course, been criticized in various ways. Some claim that even if it were once true it no longer applies since the United States is no longer a hegemon. Others have argued that hegemons never possess the power attributed to them by this theory. Still others claim that whilst such hegemons have existed, they are not to be welcomed because of the way in which they have historically used their power.[19]

There is much to these criticisms but they do not damage one important insight in the argument, namely that some states because of their power can exert an extremely powerful influence over the affairs of other states. Even if the United States is no longer a hegemon, it is clearly more powerful than many states and given this is able to facilitate cooperation. Furthermore, the fact that hegemons have used their power in a malign way does not jeopardize the point being made, namely that they *can* act in a moral way and further cosmopolitan goals. Perhaps they have not done so in the past: perhaps they will not in the future. This does not entail that they do not have a duty to do so. 'Ought' implies 'can', not 'will' or 'has done'.

A second challenge to Waltz's pessimism concerning cooperation between states is posed by recent research on regimes.[20] The argument here is that even in the absence of hegemons, regimes can facilitate cooperation where '[r]egimes can be defined as sets of implicit or explicit principles, norms, rules, and decision-making procedures around which actors' expectations converge in a given area of international relations'.[21] Two reasons for such cooperation are suggested by Robert Axelrod and Robert Keohane. First, they point out that cooperation can evolve when the actors are not engaged in a one-off game but there is prospect of future contact. Where interaction takes place over time much research suggests that actors learn to cooperate and defection by one of the parties becomes less likely. Given the iterative nature of international politics, then, cooperation is possible.[22] Secondly, cooperation is more likely to evolve if fewer actors are involved. Building on analysis by Mancur Olson, Axelrod and Keohane argue that monitoring other states' behaviour and applying sanctions is easier the smaller the group. They then argue that much international politics – like, for example, the G-7 meetings or the OECD – involves the interaction of a small group of states.[23] Thus Waltz's very strong claim that cooperation between states will not occur is implausible. Both hegemonic stability theory and regime theory show that cooperation between states can and does take place. The second premise of Waltz's argument in defence of the national interest is implausible.

## III

At this point, a realist might respond that even if cooperation between states is possible I have not shown that states would cooperate in the pursuit of cosmopolitan ideals. The cooperation outlined above is simply, the argument goes, cooperation by states motivated by their own national interest. This third (and most powerful) version of the 'negative argument from anarchy' thus runs as follows:

### *Version 3*

1 Cosmopolitan moral ideals are attainable only if states cooperate with one another.
2 States will not cooperate with one another in the pursuit of cosmopolitan ideals (although they might cooperate in order to promote their own national interest).

Therefore

3 It is pointless for a state to adhere to cosmopolitan moral principles for this will achieve nothing.

Therefore

C States are under no obligations to non-citizens and are entitled to pursue their national interest.

According to this argument, even if a state is committed to international distribution it cannot rely on the cooperation of other states. Cooperation in the pursuit of global ideals will not occur. Therefore no state is subject to a duty to pursue cosmopolitan objectives because the requisite cooperation will not be forthcoming from other states.

This third version of the argument is, of course, right to observe that much cooperation is motivated by such self-interest. Three points, however, can be made against it. First, as even the most hard-nosed realist accepts, not all state behaviour is motivated by the national interest. Kenneth Waltz, for example, explicitly accepts this. He writes, for example, of US involvement in Vietnam that, 'We surely did not fight for profit or out of necessity. States, and especially the major ones, do not act only for their own sakes. They also act for the world's common good'.[24] As many have observed, much state behaviour is motivated by habit, convention and ideological commitment as well as self-interest. Given that states sometimes act along altruistic lines and given that self-interested cooperation is possible, it seems highly likely that altruistic cooperation is also possible.

Secondly, the fact (if it is a fact) that the cooperation I described on pages 30–1 above is motivated simply by self-interest does not entail that only this type of cooperation is possible. Consider hegemons and the most powerful states generally. If they choose to do so they can facilitate cooperation along ethically acceptable lines by withholding benefits from those who do not comply with basic ethical norms and by rewarding with investment and aid those who do comply with basic ethical norms. The cooperation required to further cosmopolitan ideals does not therefore require altruism on the part of all states. Altruistic hegemons can induce cooperation that benefits the starving and weak in the world by offering inducements to other self-interested states. Now, of course, powerful states rarely, if ever, do this but this does not show that they should not. As I argued earlier, 'ought' may well imply 'can', but it does not imply 'will'. One implication of this argument is that powerful states are – in virtue of their power – under an obligation from which weaker states are exempt.

Thirdly, the point made earlier (in response to the first version of the 'negative argument from anarchy') bears repeating. States may need to cooperate to realize fully cosmopolitan objectives. They can, however, achieve much on their own without cooperation – particularly in the case of the most powerful states (like, for example, the United States, Canada, Germany and Japan). The third version of the 'negative argument from anarchy' therefore fails to persuade.

At this stage, it is perhaps worth summing up the conclusions of the first three sections. I have argued against the 'negative argument from anarchy' that:

(a) cosmopolitanism does not require a world state (and that therefore the first version is unsuccessful);
(b) states, acting on their own, can further cosmopolitan ideals without co-operation with other states;
(c) the realist arguments for thinking that inter-state cooperation is impossible are unpersuasive;
(d) we have good reason to think that inter-state cooperation which furthers cosmopolitan ideals is possible.

The 'negative argument from anarchy' (in all of its versions) therefore has not established that states ought to further their national interest nor that they can disregard the interests of non-citizens.

## IV

The three arguments examined in sections I–III are primarily negative. That is, their emphasis is on the failings of cosmopolitan ideals rather than the virtues of the national interest. Some realists, however, like Hans Morgenthau in his book *In Defense of the National Interest* have relied on similar premises to the 'negative argument from anarchy' to produce a more positive defence of the national interest. Morgenthau begins by noting a disanalogy between, on the one hand, the relationship between individuals within a state and, on the other hand, the relationship between states in the international system. In the former, individuals can act altruistically because the state will protect them. In the latter situation, however, this is not the case. If one state acts altruistically, it lays itself vulnerable to exploitation by other states: such a policy is therefore an action of 'national suicide'.[25] Thus whilst 'individual egotism' is reprehensible, 'national egotism' is not.[26] Morgenthau then goes on to argue that promoting the national interest is not simply not reprehensible: it is the morally best option. His claim is that, given the anarchic nature of global politics, the interests of states (and thereby presumably the interests of their individual members) are best protected if each looks after their own interests. No supra-state authority exists to protect the interests of states and thus:

> In the absence of an integrated international society, in particular, the attainment of a modicum of order and the realization of a minimum of moral values are predicated upon the existence of national communities capable of preserving order and realizing moral values within the limits of their power.[27]

Therefore a 'foreign policy derived from the national interest is in fact morally superior to a foreign policy inspired by universal moral principles'.[28] This might be called the 'positive argument from anarchy' since it draws attention to the merits of states pursuing their own national interests. Morgenthau's suggestion is that the national interests of all states are best protected if each pursues its national interest. It is akin to a common line of reasoning in individual ethics that claims that the *summum bonum* is best achieved if each strives to further her own self-interest.

This defence of the national interest must, however, also be severely qualified. First, why should we value a state of affairs in which the national interest of each state is protected? What *summum bonum* is being promoted by Morgenthau's system of national egotism? Perhaps Morgenthau's suggestion is that this scheme best benefits the members of these states. The national interest thus has an instrumental value. It is, however, extremely doubtful whether a generalized system of national egotism really is advantageous for all human beings. One problem is that not all human beings belong to states and those who lack a state are therefore left unprotected by Morgenthau's proposal. In addition, a central flaw in his line of reasoning is that, in many cases, states are less able to help their own citizens than are other states. The state of Bangladesh, for example, can do less to aid its own citizens than can say the government of the United States. A scheme under which each state pursues its own national interest will therefore not be much comfort to the inhabitants of Bangladesh. Furthermore, under such a system the more powerful states will be able to overrun the less powerful. So even if states have the incentive to improve their citizens' standard of living they may well lack the ability to do so and the ability to prevent other states from damaging the interests of their own citizens.[29] Contra Morgenthau, a system of generalized national egotism will not necessarily be the best of all possible worlds.

An additional problem with Morgenthau's argument lies in his assumption that acting on altruistic grounds is tantamount to 'national suicide'. It is tautologically true that if one state assists another rather than itself then it will be worse off than if it had assisted itself. Assisting another, however, does not necessarily amount to an end to one's existence: it is therefore hyperbole to call it national suicide. Morgenthau's point is that if one always acts on altruistic grounds one leaves oneself open to economic domination by another or military conquest. This, however, need not be the case. Extremely powerful states can, for example, assist others without jeopardizing their power. As one structural realist – Stephen Krasner – points out: 'Great power removes the usual restraints on central decision-makers. Very powerful states escape some of the consequences of the inherently anarchic nature of the international system. For them it is not a Hobbesian world because there is no opponent that can threaten their core interests'.[30]

Morgenthau's argument thus relies on a Manichean view. Either states simply promote their national interest, in which case the national interest of each is protected: or they simply act on altruistic lines thereby exposing themselves to domination by others. The truth is that states can act on altruistic lines without rendering themselves vulnerable to domination by others. Morgenthau's claim that an international system in which each state advances its own national interest would benefit everyone is thus unpersuasive.

## V

Realists have given other arguments against cosmopolitan ideals of international redistribution and in this section I want to consider what might be termed the 'argument from impotence'. The latter maintains that cosmopolitan principles sanctioning redistribution are doomed to failure because wealthy states are incapable of assisting needy states. This claim is advanced by most prominent realists.[31] As Stephen Krasner puts it:

> Analytically, realism is skeptical of the ability of states to influence domestic developments in other polities. Such efforts are likely to require considerable resources and wisdom, both of which are usually in short supply. Prescriptively, a basic admonition of realism is that states must guard their own resources.[32]

Realists defend their claim in a variety of ways.

(a) Sometimes, like George Kennan, they maintain that states do not know what the good is for members of other states. States, on this view, suffer from what might be termed *moral agnosticism*: they do not know what constitutes the good for people who do not belong to their own state. Kennan, for example, writes that we should 'have the modesty to admit that our own national interest is all that we are really capable of knowing and understanding'.[33] Such a radical position is, however, untenable. There are some goods – like for example, clean water, unpolluted air, protection from drought and flooding – which all cultures value.

(b) Perhaps Kennan's claim is not so much that outsiders do not know what the good is for other people but rather that they do not know how these goods can best be furthered. The problem with external assistance, according to this second version, is not moral agnosticism: rather it is what might be called *technical agnosticism*. The claim is that we do not have the knowledge and wisdom necessary to be able to help the members of other states. This is a common realist theme and Morgenthau, Kennan and Krasner argue that cosmopolitan policies tend to be based on illusion and will accordingly tend to be unsuccessful and even counter-productive. Now realists like Krasner are right to observe that cosmopolitan policies sometimes rest on misconceptions. (Like most realists he cites the example of Woodrow Wilson's commitment to national self-determination to support this.)[34] States often do not have enough information about the political economy of other states to arrive at well-reasoned policies but this is insufficient to show that they are unable to help. To sustain that conclusion the realist needs to show not just that outside states do not have enough information but that they could not have enough information. And this last proposition is highly implausible, especially in situations where the recipient state welcomes outside aid.[35]

(c) Krasner makes an additional point, suggesting that assisting other states is unlikely to be successful because it will require 'considerable resources'. This, however, shows not that assisting others will be impossible but that it might be expensive. Krasner's conclusion should be that assisting others is possible but potentially costly for wealthy states.[36] But then, for him to reject cosmopolitanism, he then has to show why the wealthy states should not bear these costs. He has not shown that assistance is impossible.

A final point to make about the 'argument from impotence' is simply that the most thorough research on the issue does not support its pessimism. In *Does Aid Work?* Robert Cassen and his associates argue that whilst aid programmes do face pitfalls, aid can and does work. They chronicle, for example, the positive impact that aid can have on development. Aid has assisted growth or at least prevented destruction in Bangladesh, Mali and Malawi as well as in India and South Korea.[37] In addition, it has improved the absolute standard of living of the poor in India, Pakistan, Brazil and Columbia and the poor have gained in both absolute and relative terms in Taiwan and South Korea.[38]

Realist scepticism about the efficacy of aid programmes is therefore simply not compatible with the facts.

## VI

It is time to sum up. Are realists right to dismiss the cosmopolitan claim that wealthy states have a duty to redistribute wealth to the poor of this world whatever their citizenship? This paper has argued that their rejection of cosmopolitanism is ill-grounded and that their defence of the state's pursuit of the national interest is unpersuasive. None of the three formulations of the 'negative argument from anarchy' establish that states do not have an obligation to promote the standard of living of those outside their political boundaries. Similarly, the 'positive argument from anarchy' fails to establish that a system of national egoism best promotes the interests of all human beings. Finally, none of the realist arguments establish that the adoption of cosmopolitan ideals is necessarily unsuccessful and their scepticism is contradicted by the evidence.[39]

## Notes

1 See, for example, Brian Barry, 'Humanity and Justice in Global Perspective' and 'Justice as Reciprocity', both in Brian Barry (ed.), *Liberty and Justice: Essays in Political Theory Volume 2*, Oxford: Clarendon, 1991; Charles Beitz, *Political Theory and International Relations*, Princeton: Princeton University Press, 1979; Onora O'Neill, *Faces of Hunger: An Essay on Poverty, Justice and Development*, London: Allen and Unwin, 1986; Thomas Pogge, *Realizing Rawls*, Ithaca and London: Cornell University Press, 1989; and Henry Shue, *Basic Rights: Subsistence, Affluence, and U.S. Foreign Policy*, Princeton: Princeton University Press, 1980. For an analysis of contemporary theories of international distributive justice including cosmopolitan theories, see Chris Brown, *International Relations Theory: New Normative Approaches*, London: Harvester Wheatsheaf, 1992, pp.155–92.

2 See Barry, 'Humanity and Justice in Global Perspective' in Barry, op. cit.

3 See, for example, George Kennan, *Realities of American Foreign Policy*, London: Oxford University Press, 1954, pp.47–9; and Robert Art and Kenneth Waltz, 'Technology, Strategy, and the Uses of Force' in Robert Art and Kenneth Waltz (eds), *The Use of Force: International Politics and Foreign Policy* second edition, Lanham University Press of America, 1983, p.6.

4 Morgenthau, *In Defense of the National Interest: A Critical Examination of American Foreign Policy*, New York: Alfred Knopf, 1951, p.242. This passage suggests that the *only* criterion which should influence a state's foreign policy is its national interest. On other occasions, however, Morgenthau recognizes that states are bound by some very minimal negative moral obligations and may not treat non-citizens in certain ways (i.e. murdering, torturing or enslaving foreigners). States, that is, must observe some negative rights.

5 Krasner, 'Realism, Imperialism, and Democracy: A Response to Gilbert', *Political Theory*, 1992, vol.20 no.1, p.44. See also ibid., pp.49–50.

6 For two important discussions of the normative claims made by realists see Beitz, op. cit., part I and Marshall Cohen, 'Moral Skepticism and International Relations', *Philosophy and Public Affairs*, 1984, vol.13 no.4. Neither Beitz nor Cohen discuss the normative

claims advanced by structural realists. In Beitz's case, his work *Political Theory and International Relations* was published either before the publication of the major works of structural realism – as in the case of Gilpin's *War and Change in World Politics*, Cambridge: Cambridge University Press, 1981 and Krasner's *Structural Conflict: The Third World Against Global Liberalism*, Berkeley: University of California Press, 1985 – or at the same time as them – as in the case of Waltz's seminal *Theory of International Politics*, Reading Massachusetts: Addison Wesley, 1979.

7 See Waltz, *Man, the State and War: A Theoretical Analysis*, New York: Columbia University Press, 1959.

8 *Second image* theorists explain the workings of the international system by appealing not to a theory of human nature or to the structure of the system but to the nature of states.

9 For Hobbes's own brief discussion of international relations see *Leviathan*, London: Dent, 1973, chapter 13 (p.65) and chapter 30 (p.189). See Donald Hanson, 'Thomas Hobbes's "highway to peace" ', *International Organization*, 1984, vol.38 no.2. See also Beitz's lucid critical discussion of Hobbesian approaches, Beitz, op. cit., pp.27–65.

10 Art and Waltz, op. cit., p.6.

11 See also Brian Barry, 'Can States be Moral? International Morality and the Compliance Problem', in Anthony Ellis (ed.), *Ethics and International Relations*, Manchester: Manchester University Press, 1986, p.68.

12 To employ a term created by Brian Barry, my point here is that it is inaccurate to assume that all state action designed to promote the standard of living of non-citizens is completely '*vulnerable* to non-compliance' by other states, Barry, ibid., p.72.

13 Waltz, *International Politics* pp.105–6.

14 Waltz, ibid., p.106.

15 Waltz, ibid., p.107.

16 Keohane, *After Hegemony: Cooperation and Discord in the World Political Economy*, Princeton: Princeton University Press, 1984, chapter 7.

17 See, for example, Lea Brilmayer, *American Hegemony: Political Morality in a One-Superpower World*, New Haven: Yale University Press, 1994; Gilpin, op. cit.; Charles Kindleberger, *The World in Depression, 1929–1939*, London: Allen Lane, 1973, pp.291–308; Kindleberger, 'Dominance and Leadership in the International Economy: Exploitation, Public Goods, and Free Rides', *International Studies Quarterly*, 1981, vol.25 no.2; Kindleberger, 'Hierarchy versus Inertial Cooperation', *International Organization*, 1986, vol.40 no.4; and Stephen Krasner, 'State Power and the Structure of International Trade', *World Politics*, 1976, no.3. Brilmayer's work which, unlike the others cited here, is primarily an essay in normative international political philosophy, provides an excellent discussion of the nature and moral significance of 'hegemony'.

18 See Robert Gilpin, *The Political Economy of International Relations*, Princeton: Princeton University Press, 1987, pp.85–92 and pp.124–7; and Krasner, 'State Power and the Structure of International Trade', op. cit.

19 On the ideological assumptions underlying hegemonic stability theory see Isabelle Grunberg, 'Exploring the "Myth" of Hegemonic Stability', *International Organization*, 1990, vol.44 no.4. From a very different perspective Waltz is also critical of states (especially hegemons) that seek to further cosmopolitan ideals. He writes 'States ... also act for the world's common good. But the common good is defined by each of them for all of us, and the definitions conflict. One may fear the arrogance of the global burden-bearers more than the selfishness of those who tend to their own narrowly defined interests', *International Politics*, p.205.

20 For a recent collection of essays on regime theory see Volker Rittberger with the assistance of Peter Mayer (ed.), *Regime Theory and International Relations*, Oxford: Clarendon, 1993. For criticism of the presuppositions and normative biases of regime theory see Susan Strange, '*Cave! Hic Dragones*: A Critique of Regime Analysis', in Stephen Krasner (ed.), *International Regimes*, Ithaca and London: Cornell University Press, 1983, pp.345–6.

21 Krasner, 'Structural Causes and Regime Consequences: Regimes as Intervening Variables', in Krasner, ibid., p.2.

22 Keohane, op. cit., pp.75–6; Axelrod and Keohane, 'Achieving Cooperation under Anarchy: Strategies and Institutions', in David Baldwin (ed.), *Neorealism and Neoliberalism: The Contemporary Debate*, New York: Columbia University Press, 1993, pp.91–4.

23 Keohane, ibid., pp.76–7; Axelrod and Keohane, ibid., pp.94–8. See Mancur Olson, *The Logic of Collective Action: Public Goods and the Theory of Groups*, Cambridge Massachusetts: Harvard University Press, 1971.

24 Waltz, *International Politics*, p.205. See also Robert Jervis, 'Realism, Game Theory, and Cooperation', *World Politics*, 1988, vol.XL no.3, pp.342–3; Morgenthau, *Politics Among Nations: The Struggle for Power and Peace*, sixth edition, New York: Alfred Knopf, 1985, p.249; and Waltz, ibid., pp.91–2.

25 Morgenthau, op. cit., 1951, pp.35–6.

26 Morgenthau, ibid., p.36.

27 Morgenthau, 'The Mainsprings of American Foreign Policy: The National Interest vs. Moral Abstractions', *American Political Science Review*, 1950, vol.XLIV no.4, p.854.

28 Morgenthau, ibid., p.854.

29 We should also be wary of assuming that states are, in all cases, greatly concerned to promote their citizens' welfare. States (especially non-democratic ones) do not always have a great incentive to further the standard of living of their citizens and their leaders may be more concerned with building up military power or 'prestige projects'. As Robert Ramsay argues in his analysis of the United Nations Conference on Trade and Development, leaders of LDCs often have not pushed for increased transfers: see 'UNCTAD's Failures: The Rich Get Richer', *International Organization*, 1984, vol.38 no.2. Of course, even if their concern is less than one might hope they might be more concerned about their own citizens than are the leaders of other states.

30 Krasner, *Defending the National Interest: Raw Materials Investments and US Foreign Policy*, Princeton: Princeton University Press, 1978, p.340. See also Waltz, *International Politics*, pp.194–5 and 205–206.

31 See, for example, Kennan, *The Cloud of Danger: Some Current Problems of American Foreign Policy*, London: Hutchinson, 1978, p.40: Krasner, op. cit., 1992, pp.49–50: and Morgenthau, op. cit., 1985, p.110.

32 Krasner, ibid., p.49: see also ibid., p.50.

33 Kennan, *American Diplomacy*, London: Secker and Warburg, 1952, p.103.

34 Krasner, op. cit., 1992, p.49.

35 For an additional consideration underlying the 'argument from impotence' see George Kennan's argument that all development depends entirely on the efforts of the members of impoverished states. Hence, outside states are powerless to help. He writes that 'what we can or could do to help the Third World is very little in comparison with its developmental needs. Development has to come, in overwhelming degree, from within, not from without', Kennan, op. cit., 1978, p.40.

36 See, relatedly, Robert Goodin's discussion of realism's use of concepts like 'possibility': Goodin, 'Commentary: The Political Realism of Free Movement', in Brian Barry and

Robert Goodin (eds), *Free Movement: Ethical Issues in the Transnational Migration of People and of Money*, London: Harvester Wheatsheaf, 1992, pp.252–4, especially p.253.

37 See Robert Cassen and Associates, *Does Aid Work?*, second edition, Oxford, Clarendon, 1994, p.23 and p.26.

38 Cassen, ibid., pp.39–40.

39 This paper was presented to the Conference on Freedom and Trade at the University of Manchester (March 1996) and to the Political Studies Association Conference at the University of Glasgow (April 1996). I am grateful to those present at both occasions and would particularly like to thank Brian Barry, Chris Brown, Theresa Callan, Avner de-Shalit, John Horton, Peter Jones, Owen McIntyre, Cornelia Navari, Andrew Reeve and Jo Wolff for their helpful suggestions and criticisms.

# 4

# PERSPECTIVES ON LIBERALIZING INTERNATIONAL TRADE

*John Hunt*[1]

Let us recognize that Cobden was right. It was his resolution rather than Peel's reluctance which could lay claim to the true parentage of the Repeal of the Corn Laws. And the Repeal will always stand as a grand policy shift to the unilateral adoption of non-discriminatory free trade. There can be many ways of being right, and circumstances vary. But whether or not Cobden was right for all times and places, the Repeal presents us with a paradigm of trade liberalization of a singularly compelling kind.

The development of political economy from Smith and Ricardo onwards points more or less clearly to the basic policy prescription for free trade and needs no exposition here. Recent refinements in terms of first- and second-best, and qualifications associated with technical development, scale economies, adjustment costs, time and uncertainty hardly detract from the continuing power of some of the most telling theorems of economic analysis.

Seen with hindsight in the light of subsequent decades of trade policy practice, some perspectives of time and place do seem worth highlighting however. It has often been remarked that Britain adopted free trade in circumstances of established world industrial leadership. Whether or not the gains from trade are such as to make free trade right for all, those gains are no doubt most apparent, and adjustment costs most easy to absorb, in economies with a good range of comparatively well-developed industries – and more easy in times of boom than recession. It is also often observed that British world political power was, in the mid-nineteenth century, about as extensive as any country's has ever been. What is less often noted is the particular relevance of the domestic British political context which we tend to take for granted; a unitary state with a strong executive resting on a winner takes all electoral system – even if with a very restricted franchise at the time. These external and internal political structures offered the possibility of comparative freedom from constraints for government to implement more or less rational trade policies for which there was widespread public support. In the mid-nineteenth century and since, in the UK and elsewhere, things have been a bit different, and they have given rise to some rather different focuses for trade liberalization.

Germany, then with a less developed industrial economy and a different intellectual tradition, produced, in the work of List, a policy analysis contrasting with that of Smith and Ricardo in that it also focused on the case for a period of protection aimed at fostering developing industries as much as on the case for eventual free trade. And although in the practice of trade policy there was an important contemporary German focus on liberalization, it inevitably subsisted against the background of long experience of a mosaic of principalities with overlapping jurisdictions as between themselves and the recently defunct Empire. So German trade policy did not have the universalist aspirations of British free trade policy in theory or practice. The Zollverein (customs union) which was the culmination of amalgamations of customs territories in Prussia and then much of Germany was neither unilateral, nor non-discriminatory, nor free trade; it was liberalizing within its geographical limits but heavily influenced by the prescriptions of List in its adoption of external protection. The Zollverein has often been cited as an antecedent of the EEC whose founding fathers saw it as such, though historians still debate its real effect as an engine for political as well as commercial integration – echoed by political debate on the larger political impact of European economic integration on European political structures today. It may be worth adding in that context that the same internal German experience of overlapping jurisdictions, shifting coalitions and constant political brokerage may make the experience of competing competencies and repeated compromises in trade (and other) policy within the European Union seem less foreign to German traditions than to our own.

Again, mid-nineteenth century and subsequent trade policy experience in the United States suggests some further broad contrasts in which domestic political structures seem crucial. The separation of powers between the Executive and Legislature, and the constitutional reservation of jurisdiction over commerce to the Congress, gave a rather different focus to trade policy formation from that in the UK. Unilateral the policy might be, but implementation by the Administration of a clear cut free trade policy was not an option. Loose party disciplines within Congress tended to give sectional producer interests a comparatively strong influence over the shape of liberalization or protection. And interest group politics, important everywhere, have remained an outstandingly important focus for trade policy in the United States, giving it for much of the nineteenth century, and parts of the twentieth, a strong protectionist bias.

These contrasts may serve to emphasize that political space for the adoption of rational trade policies is not to be taken for granted and may not always be available – not even for second best, let alone the best. On the contrary, political space has a tendency towards short supply, and the policy analysts' designs to move the universe cry out for a political place on which to stand. The special situation of the UK in the mid-nineteenth century seemed to have endowed governments with a comparatively good measure of room for manoeuvre. This no doubt generated in this country a comparative advantage in rational policy analysis. Let us hope that the effects of this persist and that we can draw down on this tradition in our more straightened current circumstances to help make the best possible use of the opportunities of the late twentieth century.

Even today proponents of unilateral shifts to non-discriminatory free trade should not entirely despair. Looking back very broadly through the 1980s, it is remarkable how many countries came to see their interests in economic efficiency as crucial in requiring tariff rates below the bound maximum levels to which they were committed by international agreements. And, in implementing the results of the recently completed Uruguay Round of trade negotiations, the EC unilaterally rounded up the cuts agreed in the interests of simplicity and efficiency.

These examples of unilateral liberalization are of course incremental and gradual. Cobden and the Anti Corn Law League set their sights on free trade and demanded immediate and complete abolition of tariffs. They did not get it; they settled for something phased in over several years. And they certainly did not see off protection in the UK, tariff or non-tariff, for good and all. We have to deal today with the same tension between ultimate objectives and immediate progress. The British Government is committed to working towards global free trade. But the real dilemmas clearly lie in the practical incremental steps that might be taken towards that goal. There is now a bewildering range of subject matter going far beyond classical forms of protection by way of tariffs and quotas, ranging from measures familiar in Cobden's time, like subsidies, establishment and investment restrictions, to newer fields, like government procurement practices and technical regulation, product standards, restrictive trade practices, and intellectual property rights. It seems doubtful whether any of these subjects is in reality very new: rather, the increased interdependence of the world economy, the integration of production processes and markets – all the developments we tend to sum up in the word 'globalization' – mean that trade policy cannot limit itself to a focus on the old classical measures of protection anymore. At the same time, we certainly should not underestimate the importance of the old staple of trade policy in the form of tariffs. It is tariff cuts which are calculated to produce the vast bulk of the economic stimulus of the recently completed Uruguay Round of trade negotiations. And it will be, on present plans, between five and fifteen years before the post-Uruguay Round cuts are fully implemented: we are not there yet, even though we can try to accelerate. Applied in these complex fields, tariff and non-tariff, liberalization does not have the same ring as a slogan as free trade. But it is progressive liberalization that we must be about, just like Cobden. Trade policy has to work by incremental process, not by immediate fiat. Commitments to free trade goals are important in marshalling political forces. But it is tangible progress in opening markets which is crucial, and more complex.

Anyway we have to recognize the limits of the paradigm of trade policy which is represented by the Repeal. Piecemeal unilateral liberalization will always have its part to play, but takes us only so far further forward. The UK and the world economy were better off following the Repeal but in the last analysis it was the policy of the second best. The UK and the world would have been much better off still if France, Germany, the United States and other countries had followed suit. Trapped by less fortunate circumstance, and by less enlightened traditions, they were disinclined to do so. To such realities unilateral liberalization as a systematic and comprehensive policy had little response. And when the UK later took up similar unilateral liberal policies again in the 1920s it was to run into comparable obstinate circumstances: unconcerted unilateralism as a general systematic policy proved unsustainable.

Cobden was himself to become very well aware of the limits of unilateral trade liberalization as a systematic policy. Across the Channel, the French market remained heavily protected by a combination of import bans, quotas and prohibitive tariffs whose liberalization he became increasingly interested in securing in the late 1850s. Contemporary trade policy is still struggling with dilemmas comparable to those he encountered.

French policy operated within the domestic context of a strong étatist political culture, a mercantilist intellectual heritage going back to Colbert, and, as the Emperor Louis Napoleon himself remarked to Cobden, a tendency to make revolutions rather than reforms. Most French commercial as well as landed interests were opposed to liberalization, but the French reformer Chevalier, who was a friend of Cobden, had the ear of the Emperor who was persuaded of the economic benefits and consequent potential popular appeal. Unilateral liberalization was effectively blocked by the opposition of entrenched interests, but treaty-making power rested with the Emperor, even though a treaty would in practice have to embody a balance of reciprocal concessions.

The prospect of a bilateral trade agreement posed a lot of questions for the liberalizers. Should the concessions be exclusive to trade between the two parties, i.e. preferential and discriminatory? Would such discrimination not in practice be as much a move away from free trade as one towards it? How would trade between the parties be distinguished from trade with third parties and how would the discrimination be enforced? Would the closer relationship forged between France and the UK be at the expense of relations with other countries not parties to the agreement?

These dilemmas were to some extent alleviated by the conclusion, not only of the celebrated Cobden–Chevalier Treaty of 1860, but by a subsequent series of bilateral negotiations resulting in comparable bilateral treaties between France and the German Zollverein, Austria, Italy and other European states – though not with the US where trade policy remained unilateral, and protectionist. Here were the elements of a second paradigm of trade liberalization in the form of a serial and discriminatory bilateralism.

Serial bilateralism was to have a notorious subsequent history in the 1930s. Against the background of generally high levels of tariff and quota protection introduced or intensified in conditions of world stagnation and slump at the end of the 1920s, the UK, France and Germany undertook selective bilateral negotiations to establish preferential tariff and quota treatment in their spheres of influence, in the British and French empires and Eastern Europe.

Few would now subscribe to the widespread US contention in the 1940s, espoused in particular by Secretary of State Cordell Hull, that these policies were a direct cause of the political conflicts culminating in the Second World War, though their role in exacerbating the political and economic disintegration of the global community in the 1930s was no doubt very important nonetheless. The British Imperial Preference system embodied in the 1932 Ottawa Agreements was, in Prime Minister Baldwin's phrase, aimed at 'keeping the sane forces of the world together'. But the problem was that every preference in favour of countries inside a special arrangement was a discrimination against those outside it, with an attendant set of market distortions; and the serial negotiation of successive arrangements could become self-defeating as new preferences diluted or neutralized previous preferences to other parties. Increasingly competitive global markets operated on the basis of relative rather than absolute price calculations, so preferential liberalization increased effective trade barriers to outsiders at the same time as decreasing them to insiders. Anyway the preferences tended to be of a piecemeal selective kind and were extended in the context of high protection against outsiders. The result appears to have been a distortion of trade and investment flows which tended to lock economic activity into established or arbitrary patterns rather than allowing it to adjust to increasingly competitive and growing American and Asian economies.

Current controversies over regional trade policy today have to address similar issues. They take place against a global background in which fluid security and monetary relations do not seem to offer the same structural stabilities as in the preceding Cold War era, and the formative importance of trade policy in foreign relations, multilateral and bilateral, may seem so much the greater. Of course, the global economy is now becoming ever more closely integrated and complex. The European Community has presented the world with a model of regionalism in practice which has probably created more trade than it has diverted – although a full evaluation of the impact of the Common Agricultural Policy would no doubt involve some heavy qualifications to that. Nonetheless, it is not the customs union model, with its internal free circulation, which tends to throw up current dilemmas, but rather the tendency to look for reciprocal preferences through free trade areas and other preferential arrangements; many of these do not cover all trade because they exclude a range of agricultural and other sensitive products and they restrict internal free trade through origin rules which impose their own bureaucratic and distortive costs. The real effects of such arrangements are thus likely to be complex.

Such preferential arrangements are a fact of life, in the Mediterranean, in Eastern Europe, in North America and elsewhere. Controlled so as to ensure that they genuinely create more trade than they divert for outsiders as well as insiders, and so that they do not become so ubiquitous as to undermine the general rule of non-discrimination, they no doubt have an important part to play. But they necessarily involve the introduction of new distortive effects on trade and investment along with liberalizing effects and tend to produce pressures for the extension of discrimination beyond tariffs to other regulations of goods, services and investment. They are thus to be considered as second best options, and the dangers that their accumulative impact would amount to a set of systematic discriminations against countries not covered by them needs to be taken into account.

Even back in 1860, many of these dilemmas appear to have been well understood and this gave rise to an important asymmetry in the Cobden–Chevalier Treaty. For whereas the French concessions under that Treaty were initially exclusive to the UK and only extended subsequently, with variations, to the other countries which concluded bilateral agreements with France, the UK concessions were by contrast extended *erga omnes*. What is remarkable, however, is that Cobden and his negotiating team took some care to limit these erga omnes concessions to those products for which France was the UK's most important supplier.

This approach was to be developed by US practice in the later 1930s. With some Latin American countries the US had begun to pursue a policy of serial discriminatory bilaterilism not in principle unlike the French policies of the 1860s. But this was progressively abandoned in favour of a serial non-discriminatory approach in which bilateral negotiations focused on products for which the countries concerned were each others' principal suppliers. Neither the limits nor the possibilities of this approach could however be fully explored before war, with its attendant economic controls, intervened.

The General Agreement on Tariffs and Trade still needs to be seen in its context as a reaction to the serial bilateralisms of the 1930s. It was developed through the Anglo-American wartime planning for the peace and in subsequent multilateral negotiation through the mid-1940s. This led to the development of the Havana Charter for an International Trade Organization of which the GATT trade barriers regime was to be only one part. Other parts were to have covered restrictive trade practices, investment, commodities and the like, but these parts did not come into being, primarily because the US Congress was not prepared to ratify. The GATT, apparently designed to be self-standing against this eventuality, survived on a provisional basis. This is not the occasion for systematic exposition of GATT provisions, but some features of the system as it developed in practice may be worth highlighting for their relevance to subsequent trade liberalizing possibilities and achievements.

First, the system was supposed to be multilateral and, in principle, global with a non-discrimination (most-favoured-nation) rule, subject only to limited exceptions. The exceptions permitted the continuation of existing tariff preferences though generally no new preferences, except for customs unions and free trade areas covering substantially all trade; discrimination in internal or border non-tariff regulations was not permitted. In practice, however, a number of new tariff preferences were introduced, notably by the recently formed EEC in the 1960s and 1970s under its arrangements for trade with countries in the Mediterranean Basin, former colonial territories of its constituent Member States in Africa, the Caribbean and Pacific, and more generally with developing countries. Although these arrangements and their subsequent development were highly controversial at the time, and along with other tensions threatened to put the continuation of the GATT system into question, they were tolerated as an adaptation of pre-existing preferential systems to the new circumstances following the formation of the EEC, and as presenting a limited if important set of departures from the core system. At the same time the core system was re-invigorated by a commitment to new and particularly ambitious multilateral negotiations under the Kennedy Round in the 1960s which was primarily aimed at alleviating trade diversionary effects arising from the development of the EEC's trade policies.

Second, the heart of the system was to be a series of rounds of tariff negotiations. These were to focus on a network of bilateral product-by-product negotiations between principal and substantial suppliers, with the implementation of non-discriminatory most-favoured-nation concessions only after the completion of the full network of negotiations. This formula, devised in the wartime planning, was intended to avoid the distortive and self-defeating aspects of serial bilateralism as practised in the 1930s, whilst embodying mechanisms to achieve reciprocity and so alleviate 'free rider' problems. The format of a round was supposed to allow scope for trade-offs between countries and products and to set a term to intensive networked negotiation. Successive GATT rounds have adapted this system so as to accommodate general tariff cutting formulae rather than simple product-by-product negotiation, to accommodate the occupation of a particularly large number of principal supplier positions from the 1960s onwards by the EEC as well as the US and to cover measures other than tariffs on goods. But the formula remains central to the GATT system and represents a third paradigm for trade liberalization – now multilateral, but still reciprocal.

Third, the GATT system was peculiarly dependent on, and adapted to, the internal constitution and the internationally dominant position of the US. The scope and length of successive rounds of trade negotiations was set by the parameters of successive negotiating authorities which the US Congress began delegating to the Administration in the mid-1930s. These negotiating authorities were themselves intensively negotiated within the US where interest group politics remained alive and well; liberalizing rein was often combined with protectionist leash, although the dominant world economic and political position of the US helped to make it more generally inclined towards trade liberalization in the latter part of the twentieth century, as the UK had been in the mid-nineteenth.

Fourth, and most generally, the system as it developed managed to strike a notable combination of forward-looking ambition with practical pragmatism. At the core, underpinning the arrangements for successive negotiating rounds, was a liberal rules-based system – one which on the one hand was highly qualified and tolerated compromise, but on the other hand entrenched achieved market opening results and locked governments into a multilateral negotiating process. Through the 1950s, the cuts in tariffs achieved in successive rounds have to be seen in the context of continuing post-war quota protection and limited currency convertibility; and successive rounds appeared to be running into diminishing returns by delivering smaller cuts. But by the end of the 1950s, European countries had liberalized the bulk of their quotas and moved to convertibility on current account so that tariff liberalization already secured and about to be undertaken stood out with renewed significance. At the same time as recognizing the importance of the large cuts in industrial tariffs subsequently achieved by the Kennedy Round in the 1960s, it has to be acknowledged that these were hammered out in the context of an increasingly protectionist Common Agricultural Policy being negotiated within the EEC, and of a protectionist and discriminatory quota regime for textiles imports from Japan and the developing world being introduced by the US and then the EEC as well. To some extent these policies were an extrapolation of the effective protection in place in the 1950s but still submerged behind post-war controls. Nonetheless, they were qualifications to the overall progress of trade liberalization over the coming decades. The GATT regime applied in principle to agriculture and textiles as to everything else, but it was to be many years before its disciplines could begin effectively to apply to these sectors.

The origins of the Tokyo Round of the 1970s are to be found not only in the first enlargement of the EEC to take in the UK, Ireland and Denmark, but also in the increasing strains on the US economy culminating in the suspension of the Bretton Woods gold exchange rate system and the temporary imposition of new tariff protection in 1971. As Treasury Secretary Connally put it 'we had a problem and we wanted to share it with our friends – just like we did our prosperity'. After this 'Nixon shock' came the 1973 'oil shock' when the OPEC cartel of producer countries trebled the price of the oil exports on which the industrialized countries were heavily dependent. The trading powers of the world stared into the abyss of a downward spiral of self-defeating protection, drew back, and continued negotiating another ambitious package of trade liberalization instead. But this achievement was again to be qualified by continued agricultural protection and intensified textiles protection with the so-called Multi Fibre Arrangement extending discriminatory quota protection from cottons to man-made fibre products. The UK, adjusting to the impact of the EEC internal market from 1973 onwards, and now one voice amongst nine Member States in influencing a Common Commercial Policy which was conducted by the European Commission, became for some years more equivocal in its pursuit of trade liberalization.

Nevertheless, at the end of the decade the Tokyo Round delivered a further series of industrial tariff cuts more extensive still than those of the Kennedy Round, and did much more besides. It was during the course of the Tokyo Round that the GATT system was effectively extended beyond the classical trade barriers represented by tariffs and quotas. The agenda was widened to begin covering in detail trade barriers presented by the thousands of internal regulatory measures imposed by modern governments in the form of product standards; by the reservation of government procurement markets to domestic and other favoured suppliers; by ill-disciplined governmental subsidies and commercial dumping coupled with potentially equally undisciplined countervailing and antidumping duties. New rules were negotiated building on the basic provisions of the GATT, but although the major trading powers subscribed to these codes of new rules, many developing countries did not. Through the 1970s the developing world tended to focus on securing 'special and differential' treatment to permit greater latitude for recourse to trade protection; and on the largely forlorn hope of securing economic benefits through the negotiation of new international commodity agreements. The Tokyo Round did not manage to solve the problem of increasing recourse by the US and the EC to 'grey area' discriminatory restrictions, in addition to those on textiles, to deal with surges of imports, notably from Japan and industrializing countries such as Korea, in sectors including steel, vehicles and consumer electronics: a selective safeguard clause legitimizing and disciplining these practices proved as unnegotiable as their effective abolition. And underlying this difficulty was an increasing problem over enforcement of the GATT rules: the US was becoming less able to use its hitherto dominant position to impose its own interpretations on other governments; and the increasing complexity of the system was giving rise to an increasing need for effective arbitration over its finer points.

Before the Tokyo Round was concluded there were already new initiatives to extend liberalization beyond trade in goods to new areas not covered by the GATT in the form of trade in services, investment and counterfeit products. These initiatives, together with interest in new negotiations to offset trade diversion arising from the second enlargement of the EC, lay at the origin of the Uruguay Round of the 1980s and early 1990s. Before that round got underway in earnest, however, there was a further partial relapse into piecemeal protection, mainly in the form of 'grey area' restrictions. Later frustration with the apparent stalling of multilateral liberalization appears to have been one of the factors promoting the new espousal of bilateralism and regionalism by the US which engaged on the negotiation of a new comprehensive free trade area with Canada – later to be extended to Mexico as the NAFTA. No threat of a systematic relapse into protectionism comparable to what threatened in the early 1970s seemed to arise however: the 1980s witnessed widespread shifts towards market policies in most parts of the world (not least the UK), and in the developing world as well as the developed.

The achievements of the Uruguay Round built on what went before. In terms of calculated economic impact the tariff cuts were, as has been noted, of predominant importance once again, but much more on top of these was achieved. New rules were established for trade in services and for safeguarding intellectual property rights, and liberalizing arrangements were laid down for agriculture and textiles. Basic GATT disciplines were to be applied in principle in all of these fields, though much of the value of what was set in place represented a framework for future negotiations as much as an accomplished liberalizing achievement: actual liberalization of services and agriculture was to be dependent in practice on future negotiations, and 're-integration' of discriminatory textiles quotas and introduction of intellectual property protection was to be phased in over a long transition. Nonetheless, the Uruguay Round did succeed in embodying the great bulk of its results in a Single Undertaking to which all governments subscribed – and this applied to the areas like standards, subsidies and antidumping disciplines (though not government procurement) to which the Tokyo Round had earlier developed GATT codes which had not been accepted by all governments. The Single Undertaking established a new World Trade Organization with a new dispute settlement system whose results could not be blocked by a losing party and which included a new commitment for governments to bring offending measures into conformity with adverse findings, with compensation or retaliation for any unreasonable delays. The degree of self-restraint which governments have thus undertaken to exercise under this new system is quite remarkable and without obvious precedent in international relations. How it is actually put into practice will inevitably be a litmus test of the success of the new WTO.

If the new WTO is indeed to succeed it will however have to do a lot more than implement the results of the GATT Uruguay Round and build up the new dispute settlement arrangements. If it is to match or surpass the earlier GATT system it will need to deliver comparable new contributions to trade liberalization, and in conditions of increasing complexity. One measure of these complexities may be the time taken by the last three GATT Rounds: the Kennedy, Tokyo and Uruguay Rounds were concluded some seven, ten and fifteen years after the conclusion of the previous round. But can the world trade system afford to wait for so long for a further liberalization? Arguably not: the pace of economic change seems to be accelerating and the ever-closer global integration of production and markets suggests that remaining trade barriers will impose correspondingly heavier penalties by way of market distortion, placing a greater premium on future trade liberalization. All this suggests a need to look for a new liberalization package nearer to seven years after conclusion of the Uruguay Round than fifteen.

Unfortunately, the difficulty seems as clear as the need. Not only does the agenda become ever-longer and the issues more complex in themselves. More important, the number of key players multiplies: no longer can the main work of negotiation be left to the US, the EC, Japan and Canada. The increasing importance of industrializing as well as developed countries, and of countries in transition from command to market economies, calls for their closer involvement in all aspects of the negotiating process: more concessions are needed from them; and more voice is expected by them. So more systematic preparation of the subject matter of negotiations seems to be called for, together with some adaptation of negotiating structures.

The prospective agenda seems fairly clear in outline. Investment issues were broached in the Uruguay Round but received limited coverage in the results: they would no doubt have to figure prominently in a new liberalizing effort. Other so-called new issues concerning relations between trade policy and competition rules, environment or social policies, important as they are, seem by contrast to offer little early prospect of new liberalization; in some cases rather the contrary. But in the services field, from financial services to telecommunications, from professional services to transport there is still a lot more scope for liberalization, as also in the extension of security for intellectual property rights. There similarly remains a lot of mileage to be made on non-tariff issues like standards and other regulatory matters, subsidies and government procurement disciplines – and not least the inclusion of the latter into the WTO Single Undertaking with the aim that in the future all WTO members would as a rule apply non-discrimination principles for government procurement, as for other trade. Simplification and harmonization of origin rules could make a valuable contribution in dealing with an increasingly problematic source of market distortions. And there is still a lot of scope and need for further tariff reductions on goods with more extensive coverage of bound commitments.

The temptation to retreat from the challenge is obvious. In the wake of the Uruguay Round as of previous trade rounds, governments, now released from their commitments to negotiate new liberalization, may be tempted into piecemeal unilateral protection prompted by trade disputes and sectional pressures. They may be tempted into new discriminatory regional arrangements of a kind which only offer trade creation at the expense of trade diversion. Or they may be tempted to give up the enterprise of global trade negotiating rounds altogether, taking the agenda issue-by-issue as the WTO system would in principle allow.

Within some important limits, some fragmentation of liberalizing negotiations might help to make them more manageable. Regional arrangements which are non-discriminatory on the lines of the 'open regionalism' being developed by a number of East Asian countries could make an important contribution to multilateral liberalization. Intensified inter-regional cooperation in the transpacific, transatlantic, and Europe–Asian contexts is likely to be crucial in preparing the way for future multilateral liberalization. Issue-by-issue negotiations may also succeed in preparing further progress. And anyway the first task for the WTO Singapore Ministerial Conference in December 1996 was to get intensive work underway, issue-by-issue, rather than to launch new negotiations as such.

It is nonetheless difficult to see how the world trade system will be able to secure important new liberalizing results without the trade-offs between countries, issues and sectors which only a global round of negotiations can offer. The global round was the centre piece of the old GATT and will surely need to be the centre piece of the new WTO. Governments do not need to decide whether or not to launch a new round immediately. But they will need to address the matter quite soon. The heirs of Richard Cobden would go for a new round.

## Notes

1 The views expressed in this chapter are personal, and not necessarily those of the DTI or the UK Government.

# COMMENTARY ON CANEY AND HUNT

*Owen McIntyre*

These two chapters consist of one of a general philosophical nature, considering the theoretical grounds for 'cosmopolitanism' and 'anti-cosmopolitanism', and the other concerning more specifically the British state's attitude over 150 years on questions of free trade.

Simon Caney, in considering the role of altruism in international relations, finds that there are no theoretical grounds for 'anti-cosmopolitanism'. As a lawyer it seems presumptuous to comment on the line of argument developed. However the dichotomy presented between a cosmopolitanist approach and that of the realists, does appear to be based on a series of presumptions worth considering further. First, is it not possible for a state to pursue its national interests through adopting a 'cosmopolitanist' approach? We must first of course question whether everything portrayed as an altruistic act really is. Gifts may not be given directly in exchange for favours or influence, but any great benefactor may expect to gain influence even if this is not directly sought. Carrots can be as much an instrument of power as sticks, and the powerful may prefer to disguise both under more pleasant sounding labels. Newly industrialized states may claim that developed states use concern for human rights and the environment as a means of disguising the attempted imposition on them of standards conspicuously lacking in Europe and North America, in the period of rapid industrialization.

However, cannot even genuine cosmopolitanism be in the national interest? Might not a state also consider that it is in the best interests of its citizens if they live in a peaceful and reasonably prosperous world and consider it worth making an effort to bring this about? This may be particularly true of small prosperous states, such as the Benelux and Scandinavian countries, who may obtain greater international influence and protection through encouraging international goodwill. However in an increasingly interdependent world is it not in the interests of most states that their citizens can go abroad to trade, be educated, work or even just go on holiday? Even if they stay at home, does not cosmopolitanism to some extent offer them some security? Were not the GATT and the Bretton Woods institutions, as John Hunt notes, reactions to the experience of those who had lived through the 1930s and the subsequent war?

In the area of international environmental policy it has long been recognized that activities in one state may have a direct effect on conditions in other states. These 'overspills' have been characterized as being either 'physical', 'economic' or 'psychological'.[1] In solving such problems cooperation and technical assistance may be the most cost-effective means of proceeding. Nor are 'psychological overspills' confined to the environmental field, in a world dominated by mass communications and a global media industry, the citizens of every state are increasingly aware of what is happening elsewhere, are concerned about it and in turn expect their governments to take action on their behalf. Citizens of a state can also more easily compare the policies and behaviour of their own government (domestically and internationally) with that of others.

States, with their concerns of 'national interest', are no longer, if indeed they ever were, the sole actors that require consideration. Clearly in a democracy, for example the United States, the re-election prospects of a government may be as important in some foreign relations policy decisions as 'rational' policy analysis. Those seeking to influence both the government and popular opinion may increasingly have interests beyond those of the state. In the environmental field many inter-state treaties have their origins in the work of non-governmental bodies such as the IUCN, while in the evolution of the world trading system the part played by various non-state actors, such as transnational corporations and various trade associations, cannot be overlooked.

This brings us to consider John Hunt's chapter which seeks to provide reassurance that the United Kingdom's espousal of free trade (despite the occasional lapses he notes) has been constant throughout the last 150 years. In part, he portrays this adherence to the doctrine as altruism. The world, he argues, may have been a better place if others, Germany, France and the United States, had followed suit earlier, but they did not. Cobden's Britain was the pioneer of global trade in manufactured goods and services and, at the time, it alone could have taken the initial first step in promoting free trade. Others joined as and when it became convenient for them to do so until, with the creation of the WTO, there appears to have been a final rush to join. The abolition of the Corn Laws, however, was only the last, and most controversial in a long series of unilateral free trade measures. Whatever the advantages of cheap food to feed the industrial masses, the Anti-Corn Law League was more than a mere self-interested economic pressure group. They at least believed they had moral right on their side. Yet was even this really 'cosmopolitanism', or was not the primary potential benefit the League sought, cheap food to the British consumer (and incidently their employers), rather than any universal benefit to the world at large? Indeed, perhaps, on this anniversary, we should note as much the 150 years of Britain's policy of cheap food (whether from home or abroad), with all its economic and environmental consequences, as the wider and less easily determined international consequence.

Schwarzenberger[2] notes that no international economic order can be stronger than the prevailing international political order, while from Cobden onwards free trade has been advocated to strengthen political stability. Some might argue that the GATT's origins lie as much with List and the Zollverin, with the United States taking the part of Prussia and free trade reinforcing political alliances, as with Cobden. Where the Zollverin went beyond Cobden, and where the GATT and more so the WTO has followed, was in recognizing the importance of institutions to reinforce the mutual dependence of the market. The importance of institutions in creating a market economy is now being recognized in the domestic context,[3] and this must apply equally to the global market. In this light, the free trade debate becomes less a debate over the virtues of 'cosmopolitanism' and the national interest, as a debate on what the interests of the nation are, and who should determine it. This choice is likely to be more influenced by the day-to-day restraints of the international order than by moral absolutes. Free trade may be morally right as Cobden thought, but whether or not this is so, it has reached its present pre-eminence in international decision making only through 150 years of gradual development of state and institutional practice – in short, through international law making.

## NOTES

1 See Blackhurst and Subramanian, 'Promoting Multilateral Cooperation on the Environment' in Anderson and Blackhurst (eds), *The Greening of World Trade Issues* (1992), p.247, referred to in H. Ward, 'Common but Differentiated Debates: Environment, Labour and the World Trade Organization', *International and Comparative Law Quarterly*, footnote 80.

2 G. Schwarzenberger, *Economic World Order? A Basic Problem of International Economic Law*, Manchester, Manchester University Press, 1970.

3 See e.g. J.-P. Platteau, 'Behind the Market Stage Where Real Societies Exist – Part I: The Role of Moral Norms', *Journal of Development Studies*, 1994, vol.30 no. 3, pp. 533–77; 'Part II: The Role of Public and Private Order Institutions', ibid., pp. 753–817.

5

# PROCEDURAL JUSTICE AND THE PROBLEM OF VOLUNTARISM

*Peter Ingram*

## International relations and the interdependence of states

For political philosophy, the problem of international justice has been most closely connected with problems of war and peace, national sovereignty and the rights of states. These are themes with origins which can be traced back to the just war theory of the Middle Ages. In the twentieth century, developments in moral philosophy have ensured that human rights have come increasingly to the fore; increasing attention is being paid to the rights of individuals in peace as well as war and to other humanitarian concerns, as thinking about the nature of domestic justice has been extrapolated to a wider international scale. As philosophers have become increasingly interested in the subject of global distributive justice, the real world of international relations has brought to notice problems in the allocation of natural resources and in environmental issues. These are clearly economic matters with major implications for the commercial life of states as well as the well-being of their citizens, but commercial relations proper rarely figure in philosophical thinking. True to form for the intellectual, perhaps, matters of trade are seldom considered.

Despite many possibilities for expanding the treatment of relations between states, the preoccupation with the problems that war presents has survived. Of course, it is right that war should figure largely in philosophical thinking: it is a constant threat to every other aspect of international life. However, its domination of the field for philosophers has precluded a balanced conceptualization of international affairs. By this I mean that one possible consequence of the centrality of war in philosophical thought is that non-military as well as military matters are too readily pictured in terms of actual or potential conflict. One recent writer has rightly observed: 'A theory which concentrates on condemning armed aggression is clearly insufficient.'[1] Nevertheless, she goes on to extend the negative image of conflict, in a familiar way, into political and economic areas, where states can 'interfere' in each other's affairs and have 'detrimental' effects on each other's populations.

Admittedly, the harm that states can and do inflict on each other is part of the reality of international relations, but it is hardly the whole of it. The effect of dwelling on negative features, from war to environmental pollution, is to portray states as, residually, adversaries who are necessarily opposed to each other. There is a consequence for theory in this approach: the focus of international law, and relations between states generally, is seen to be the prevention and resolution of disputes. Yet disputes need not be the focal point of international law any more than of domestic law. In a healthy system, disputes are at the margin, not at the centre. Domestically, to concentrate on deviance, disagreement and conflict – the stuff of criminal and civil cases before the courts – is to focus on malfunctions, whereas the first function of law is the positive guidance of the law-abiding. This holds true for the conduct of affairs according to law in the international arena too.

The reality of international life on a day-to-day level is found in the successful regulation of transactions that are not confrontational, whether they are those of states, businesses or private persons; these may involve finance and commerce, travel and communication, culture and education, and a host of other activities. Because it threatens these peaceful and productive activities, conflict (both military and nonmilitary) cannot be ignored. All the same, in a world where so many people benefit from international travel and trade, it is unfortunate that the willing adherence by states to multilateral agreements, their constructive participation in international conferences, and their membership and support of a large number of international institutions can often pass almost unnoticed. It is the flourishing of peaceful relations between states which today continuously affects the lives of ordinary people:

> In the absence of some system of international law, the international society of states [and, one might add, their citizens] could not enjoy the benefits of trade and commerce, of exchange of ideas, and of normal routine communication.[2]

There are many who would view developments on the nonmilitary side of interstate relations optimistically. One route to a peaceful and just world is surely for states to become economically more interdependent, and this is the natural consequence of free trade. Most people would believe intuitively that economic interdependence must encourage cooperation, fair play and peaceful relations among states in the same way that it does (one hopes) among individuals.[3] If we assume that the national interest of states is individual self-interest writ large, then states, like individuals, will want to increase their well-being as much as possible. They will realize that they cannot provide everything that they need or want by their own efforts, and, like individuals in domestic society, they will find it worthwhile to establish and maintain a system for exchanging their own products and services for those of others. Motivated by self-interest, states will develop institutions which will inevitably encourage a habit of cooperation between them. If self-interest, cooperation and justice are linked in a Rawlsian fashion, then justice will be a natural by-product of a world where international agents become convinced that they can benefit more from cooperative economic and political relations than they can from aggression or hostility. This will be so because each party will be predisposed to ensure the continued effective operation of the system, and to this end they will devise and agree on rules to police and control each other's behaviour.[4] If economic progress of this kind promotes a just society, then trade, along with commercial activities generally, should be just as much the concern of those who philosophize about justice and international relations as war and welfare already are, particularly since fruitful trade relations will have the capability of enhancing the welfare of ordinary people.

The realization of the importance of economic interdependence is not new. In the eighteenth century Kant assumed that one of the factors pushing the world towards peace was relations of trade: 'The spirit of commerce, which is incompatible with war, sooner or later gains the upper hand in every state.'[5] The power of money, he believed, was the most dependable of all powers under the state, and states would consequently be 'forced, without any moral urge' to promote peace and prevent war. With the nineteenth century, however, the international aspect of the development of trade acquired increasing economic and political importance – the Anti-Corn Law League was just one aspect of this. The Victorians' belief in progress was fuelled in part by their experience of an unparalleled expansion in international trade relations, a period when one would have thought that the benefits of a world system were becoming clear to all the industrialized and industrializing nations, if not to the colonized countries of the European empires. Economic progress encouraged optimism: John Stuart Mill, for one, held that '[i]t is commerce which is rapidly rendering war obsolete by strengthening and multiplying the personal interests which are in natural opposition to it', and believed that 'the great extent and rapid increase of international trade [is] the principal guarantee of the peace of the world'.[6] Trading nations should surely have been aware of the detrimental consequences for their prosperity of disrupting peace. Nevertheless, this era came to an end with the outbreak of the Great War in 1914 – a warning, perhaps, that no degree of trade and prosperity is ever likely to make war impossible. Today, although we may think that good commercial relations are a step in the right direction, few of us believe that they are bound to lead automatically to a peaceful and just world.

The twentieth century has been characterized as the century of total war. Even so, an approach to international affairs which is centred on stopping conflict but which thereby endorses a negative, adversarial understanding of interstate relations as grounded in potential if not actual hostility, is being supplemented by a more positive appreciation of the interdependence of state interests. In this century a large number of international institutions have come into being, in response to a great many developing technical and administrative needs; for example, some physical areas, like the sea-bed, Antarctica and space, have been internationalized and therefore need common supervision and control. Extensive regulation is needed for communications of all kinds: physical transport by air, sea and land, and telecommunications by cable and satellite. Many of the world's natural problems (including health, the environment, conservation of resources, and food production) are not limited by national boundaries. In addition, there is increasing recognition of the need for internationally organized assistance in economic development. In the area of trade and commerce, institutions like the World Trade Organization exist not only to control competition and rivalry but also to promote coordination and cooperation for the sake of providing greater benefits all round. I shall return to the significance of international institutions for the theme of this chapter – procedural justice – in my conclusion.

## International law, consent and obligation

International law, which formerly consisted of little more than the law of war, a rudimentary law of the sea, and diplomatic protocol, has now extended into more productive and peaceful areas of international relations. As has been suggested, the system is there to regulate and promote productive and cooperative activity, not just to prevent conflict or punish violators of sovereignty. But international law *qua* law has always been something of a problem for philosophers. Rules designed to foster cooperation are required to be fair, and therefore must be consistently applied to and followed by all members of the international community. Rules also – in this world, at least – need sanctions. H.L.A. Hart stated the familiar criticism of international law in *The Concept of Law*:

> [T]hough it is consistent with the usage of the last 150 years to use the expression 'law' here, the absence of an international legislature, courts with compulsory jurisdiction, and centrally organized sanctions have inspired misgivings, at any rate in the breasts of legal theorists.[7]

Indeed, Hart understated the problem. The absence of centrally organized administration and enforcement is not just a contingent deficiency which could eventually be remedied with some concerted effort on the part of states. On the contrary, it is underwritten legally and politically by both the familiar concept of sovereignty and a fundamental principle of international law, namely consent and an associated idea of voluntarism. Economic, political, diplomatic and military sanctions have all been used by the international community, but they remain exceptional and have to be individually approved; for sanctions to be made a routinized response to lawbreaking is unacceptable at the present time and unlikely in the future.

This is not the place to explore the concept of sovereignty. Suffice it to say here that 'sovereignty' incorporates the ideas of nonintervention and equality, which together entail the conclusion that there is no superior authority to the state except where the state itself chooses to submit to some other authority. States – whatever their size, wealth, population and power – are all sovereign equals under international law, have the same external capacities under law, and are deemed to possess the same internal authority and right to make use of power domestically. Whatever the realities of world affairs, sovereign states are formally, from the point of view of international law, all identical with respect to legal personality. On the foundation of absolute sovereignty is built the idea that all international obligations are the result of voluntary agreements between states, and there is much support in the documents and decisions of international law to bolster this understanding.

The principles of sovereignty and non-intervention imply that if states ought to be left alone, they can be, in other words that in principle they are self-sufficient. This may be correct in a formal political perspective, but obviously no state is truly self-sufficient today. Relations with the outside world are indispensable; they are both continuous and intensive, and affect everybody. But as it is between individuals within a state, so it is between states: such relations have to have a regular, ascertainable basis if they are to endure and develop. In short, relations have to be rule-governed. Under domestic law, both regularity and security are assured because we know not only what it is that people ought to do, and that they will (or can be obliged to) do it, but also that, if they do not do it, in civil matters there will be compensation available and in criminal matters punishment. If we are to have similar assurance internationally, we must be able to depend in like measure on the actions of states. For this to be possible, sovereignty has to be reconciled with law.

Any system of law can – indeed, must, in the long run – rest largely on voluntary adherence, but no system can entirely depend on it. Certainly, it cannot do so as a matter of principle, for the existence of legal obligation presupposes that those subject to law can be required to do something against their will if that need should arise. Leaving aside the difficult problems that may surround the assimilation of states to persons, there is one crucial difference in this respect between domestic and international fora. Within a state, legal obligations are binding on everybody and universally enforceable, although not always enforced in fact. It is generally accepted that a system which allowed people at their (not the state's) discretion to opt in and out of legal obligations as they saw fit could not survive. This would apply even if, say, the only opting out we were concerned with was the result of sincere objections on grounds of conscience or was a situation where citizens were required to give due notice of intended default. If the community reverted to Locke's rather than Hobbes's state of nature, a degree of regularity might remain, but its members would depend on each other's goodwill. The rule of law would no longer exist, and there would be no legal system. Even those who might want to keep to the old written rules could not realistically afford to do so. More significantly, from our point of view, it would be a state of affairs that would produce innumerable cases of injustice, since even conscientious repudiation of obligations can be selfishly self-regarding and heedless of the rights of others. Whatever we think about a doctrine of initial consent as the foundation of obligations, it is clear that continuing consent as the basis of a public system of obligations is not viable.

Superficially, it is just this theme of continuing consent which permeates international law. At the time of concluding an agreement, of course, a state may enter reservations to one or more of its terms; but while a treaty is in force it is still subject to termination, denunciation or withdrawal by any of the parties, under constraints which amount to little more than the requirements of courtesy. As far as any international organization is concerned, not only does a member have the practical option of leaving it because, crudely, it simply does not like it,[8] thereby ending its assent to the organization's rules, but also, while remaining a member, a state can assert the right to apply its own unilateral interpretation to the rules to which it has initially consented.[9] Generally, the practical application and enforcement of rules on a day-to-day basis is left mainly to sovereign states since there is no central international authority with its own agents to do this, with consequent disparities in interpretation and procedure.

Although international law is flawed not just by a doctrine which combines initial consent and continuing consent but by a practice which has given effect to this doctrine in many ways, the system – against the odds (one might think) – has not fallen apart. Indeed, there are those who would hold that the international legal system survives just because it is not based on the kind of obligation which characterizes municipal law. It seems always to have been assumed

> that lasting authority for law could be built only on the self-interest of states and that consent was the expression of the realization of self-interest. Consent was the basis of international law because it represented the willingness of states to obey the law and their awareness that their own interest could be maximized through obedience.[10]

Forms of consent must be carefully distinguished, however. In understanding international law there is a vital difference to be grasped between initial consent, which accounts for the validity of a law, and continuing consent, or voluntarism (as I shall henceforward refer to it), which maintains compliance. For standard consent theory, only initially is the obligation self-imposed; for voluntarism, the obligation is always self-imposed. Herein lies the crucial difference between international law and municipal law; the former is voluntaristic, the latter is not, for within a state compliance can be secured – or at least ought to be securable – by those in authority.

It is specifically voluntarism on which I wish to focus henceforward. Given its political assumptions, international law cannot but be voluntaristic: there is no superior authority and – what is equally significant – there is virtually no universality, since very little international law applies in exactly the same way to all states. Where it does, this is simply because all states happen individually to have given their agreement; and where they continue to comply, this is because each, individually, is willing to. Even the United Nations Charter applies only to members of that organization; although this makes it almost universal in fact, it is not so in principle. The theoretical position of customary law and *jus cogens* can be significantly (but perhaps not completely) discounted; in practice, much customary law has been incorporated into treaty law anyway, and although customary law is in theory universal, for each state its own interpretation of a customary norm is authoritative, which detracts somewhat from its universality. Admittedly, there remain some basic principles of international law which are held to be applicable to all states, with or without their consent and whether or not they are members of the United Nations; but this is little more than doctrine.

Obviously, on its face, a thoroughgoing voluntarism is destructive of the very idea of obligation, and therefore of rules and the security which rules provide. As the basis of compliance it falls easy prey to the hard-nosed realist who would argue that in the end a self-imposed obligation is no obligation at all. Of course, this does not entail that regularity of behaviour is impossible, but it will be a regularity brought about by some other cause than legally determined compliance. The paradigm of the self-imposed obligation is, of course, the promise: socially, we take for granted that a freely made promise is binding on the person who has made it and that persons who act in good faith comply with the obligations created by their promises. Whether this is a contingent rule about 'promises' or part of the meaning of the word 'promise' is a question which I shall not consider here. The counterpart of the 'rule about promises' in international law is, of course, the foundational principle of treaty law, namely, *pacta sunt servanda*, which many would hold to be the very basis of international law as founded on consent.[11] Is this maxim itself a (superior) obligation? Or is it – in accord with a common theoretical approach to international law which would derive law from practice by a process of induction – descriptive of state practice, or (more accurately) of the dispositions of those who act on behalf of states?[12]

Notwithstanding the point made about voluntarism, treaties represent two conjunct ideals for international law: they are a source of law, presenting (or intending to present) express and determinate obligations; and as the outcome of agreement, they maintain sovereignty, equality and consent in association with law and obligation. They satisfy substantively the requirements of consent theory, without voluntarism. However, incorporating the latter is a radical move: the obligations of a treaty are then, in a formal sense, always freely undertaken. A state's obligations under law are not voluntary, for they can be objectively determined; but its compliance is.[13] In a way, the ordinary citizen's compliance with domestic law is also voluntary, but (in the ideal case) the citizen exposes himself to direct and effective legal sanctions which it would be irrational to incur; the defaulting state almost always does not, even though its actions are more public than those of a private citizen. Furthermore, a rational calculation about the benefits of disobedience is politically more acceptable for states at the international level than for citizens domestically. Nevertheless, in practice (with the assumption of good faith) voluntary compliance with objectively determinable obligations presents few problems. Treaty obligations are overwhelmingly adhered to. Why, then, do states largely comply with law?

Of course, quite literally, states have themselves contributed to making the rules that oblige them, and they do so to serve their own interests. They are not obliged by someone else's rules. Their agreement to the rules is not merely nominal, and the claim that the rules are in their self-interest is not something of a fiction. It has been observed that '[s]tates are markedly reluctant to implement (1) multilateral treaties not based on reciprocity ... and (2) customary rules imposing duties which in actual fact operate "unilaterally" or "asymmetrically" '.[14] Reciprocity in the system is evident in both positive and negative ways. The act of recognition is the political, legal and diplomatic token of this: the obligation to comply is owed by a state to the international community in return for the latter's validation of its statehood. It is a condition of recognition that states agree (or are assumed to agree) to abide by international law; it is also a condition of membership of the United Nations.[15] The idea that the world community of states is some kind of a club can be stretched too far, but the analogy provides a better clue to the source of continuing obligation than standard accounts drawn from domestic law.

> Membership in the club confers a desirable status, with socially recognized privileges and duties and it is the desire to be a member of the club, to benefit by the status of membership, that is the ultimate motivator of conformist behavior.[16]

Coercion and compulsion of the kind that is formulated within and by a legal system are not directly present in international law, but there are effective political and economic pressures working to make states conform, which derive from the wider ambit of general inter-state relations beyond the purely legal.

## Justice, values and rules

Why is procedural justice important? Since moral debate began, people have disagreed about the content of justice. The position of the developing nations has brought new parameters into discussions of the international aspect of this age-old problem. As far as agreement on a conception of substantive justice is concerned, there are two deep-seated difficulties: first, demands are often made in the name of justice which challenge or threaten the international *status quo* because they cannot be reconciled with the entitlements which states are generally assumed to possess under law; second, in a world in which there are deep differences of opinion over both fundamental values and the principles of moral justification it is difficult to formulate the universal moral theory which an agreed conception of justice must have.[17] As Charles Beitz has pointed out, cultural differences 'are reflected in the structures of various legal systems and in the attitudes customarily taken by different cultures toward social rules, collective ideals, and the value of individual autonomy'.[18] Such differences do not represent alternative (but complementary) approaches, nor even merely divergent ones, but opposed and exclusive positions; for example, if its implications are followed through, collectivism cannot but be in opposition to individualism. In any case, the plurality of values in today's world has made people (even in the West) wary of a system of international justice which would impose a single-value system, predominantly Western in orientation, on societies whose own systems of values are at variance with those of secular Western liberalism in many ways.

A lack of consensus about values is a feature of the modern international system. In matters of war and peace the difficulty can seemingly be overcome: since nation-states are sovereign, they are to be left alone – with very limited exceptions – to manage their own internal affairs. Intervention is forbidden – unproblematically, because it is conceived of principally in terms of armed force; and war is forbidden except for self-defence (in which case, indeed, the principle of non-intervention has been, or is about to be, disregarded). But it was pointed out at the beginning that the adversarial understanding of international relations is incomplete, even when extended by analogy, and misleading. Since nations are interdependent, states can no longer exist in splendid isolation; a conceptualization of a world system which seems to assume that they can be is out of date.

Perhaps agreement on a substantive concept of justice will be attained across the world community (if only through the decline of competing conceptions), although it is clearly a long way off. The development of international institutions may contribute to the formation of a partial consensus, since it has been argued that states can be socialized into a particular pattern of behaviour by belonging to them.[19] However, progress towards full justice does not have to wait until the achievement of a moral consensus, even though the international system is in principle consensual, not coercive. In the international situation, where a substantive consensus on values is lacking but justice is still sought after, procedural justice comes into its own. Procedural justice can be easily criticized for supporting a brand of positivism which is insensitive to substantive questions of justice, for being indifferent to the moral content of the rules it supports, for focusing on concepts like due process which have little value without reference to the moral quality of the legal–political system in which they are found. But in a world where substantive agreement is not possible, insensitivity of an appropriate kind becomes a virtue.

The first task of law is to provide a regulatory framework for constructive action beyond the need to deal with conflict: the fact of conflict, after all, is evidence of the breakdown of law. A maximally efficient legal system which set perfectly rational rules for perfectly rational agents would have neither disputes to settle nor offences to punish; although there might be the need for courts to pass judgment on novel cases not clearly settled by pre-existing rules, its main point would lie in the content of its rules. Under real systems of law (leaving aside the possibility of simple wickedness) disputes come about through limited efficiency and limited rationality. The rules are not perfect, and complete agreement on the values which underlie them is lacking. Internationally, as nationally, commercial and other transactions between legal subjects lead to disputes. These disputes have to be settled peacefully and justly if relations are to continue and develop, and if this is to happen, there must be ways of achieving settlements – ways which all parties will accept, regarding them as fair. But as far as possible, a system should also be ensuring that disputes do not arise, that the positive regulatory function of law fails as seldom as possible. For this to happen, the system must appear not to be unjust to those parties subject to its laws; for its procedures to be workable, they must be realistic, not idealistic.

The flaw in the international system is clear. Recall that international law is a realistic system in so far as it is still largely based on the principle of effectiveness. Its rules significantly, if not entirely, derive from and reflect the actual practice of states. (I say 'not entirely' because states – or those who represent them – are, like individuals, ready enough to aspire publicly to a standard that is seldom or never reached.) However, true justice can hardly emerge under a system whose rules derive from practice that is not already normatively regulated. Rules that emerge without restraint from a situation where the various parties are widely divergent in power or wealth will inevitably formalize that divergence. There is no injustice in a natural state of affairs – a situation where one state is rich and another poor because the first has many natural resources and the second few – any more than there is injustice in the fact that one human being is strong and another weak. But injustice arises where that state of affairs comes to be validated as a norm. Consequently, although earlier I may have seemed dismissive of doctrine, in a limited way doctrine does have a part to play in international law, and in particular, that part concerning peremptory norms (*jus cogens*) which sets limits to the practice of states.

The possibility of a stable system emerging from economic cooperation depends on interactions between genuine equals (and not the nominal equals implied by the present conception of sovereignty). If one state has its raw materials exploited by a foreign multinational economically important for a second state, it may have no alternative but to agree to carry on being exploited, if it does not realistically have the option of refusing to continue to trade; but this is not the free consent of a true equal. Furthermore, to believe that agreed, mutually beneficial exchanges will by themselves see that cooperative behaviour is rewarded and uncooperative behaviour discouraged is – unfortunately – a naïve idea. It will not guarantee justice, for many kinds of inequitable systems which benefit all parties are possible; however beneficial the effects may be, a sense of injustice will remain. Ensuring a 'level playing-field', with just benefits for every party and for the system as a whole, requires the imposition of norms and continued regulation. A system where there are deep differences over substantive norms, and 'where individual members look after their own concerns to the detriment of any collective need, will not be a strong system'.[20] Indeed, it will be weak and unstable because it is unjust. But voluntarism is just such a system: it allows states – at the expense of the rules – to look after their own concerns in their own way whenever they believe it necessary or expedient to do so. Stronger states can afford to do this, weaker states cannot. If strong states often forgo such opportunities, this is as a result of good will, not legal compulsion.

Inequality between states in the international system creates many problems. As far as is possible, these must be resolved fairly, although many will not be – and some cannot be. Fairness is not just a moral desideratum; unfair resolution of problems may in the shorter or longer term be destabilizing, increasing the possibility of conflict. In a constructive way, getting procedures right is itself a contribution to resolving problems. The difficulties presented by the idea of universal substantive principles of justice have already been pointed out. But preceding even the application of substantive principles all the parties to a dispute must find themselves in a fair relationship, which, given the international community's commitment to the principle of sovereignty, must include genuine equality. The concept of equality is something on which all states agree. Equality before the law is as much a principle of international law and justice where the parties are states as it is one of domestic law where the parties are persons. But equality has to be striven for in circumstances where there is natural inequality; it cannot evolve just from the practice of states even in a genuinely consensual system.

## Voluntarism, rules and international institutions

International institutions have their origin in the nineteenth century, but until the second half of the twentieth century, there were relatively few of them. Existing institutions came under the aegis of the United Nations at its inception, but since then a much larger number of public or governmental international organizations have come into being through international agreement between states. If an organization constitutes a continuing association of states, is a distinct entity from its members, and has its own legal powers and purposes with an international scope, it meets the criteria for international personality. The functions of international institutions are various, and selectively distributed, but they include: the making of rules, by which definite requirements are laid down in relation to certain matters; the setting of standards, by which more general principles are formulated, which (with a greater degree of latitude and force than rules) state a desired general level of attainment; coordination of measures of many kinds between member states without control being sacrificed; and administration of common services. Internally, and in their relations with each other and with states, international institutions suggest legal frameworks within which some degree of justice may be attained. In particular, they offer scope for the development of fair procedures as the basis of a more genuine equality between those states which belong to them.

In relation to law *stricto sensu*, although the permitted extent and method of rule-making varies according to their individual constitutions, the power of many international institutions to make rules which extend beyond the internal functioning of the organization itself is of paramount importance. The present number and variety of institutions is making an increasing contribution to international law. Although no state is a member of all institutions, every state is a member of some; in consequence, state practice within and in relation to these organizations is an important element in the process of customary law formation. Many organizations are concerned with activities of a technical nature where constant changes render processes of making law by renegotiating treaties inappropriate. For practical reasons, therefore, they must necessarily engage in regulatory acts which are effectively of a legislative character. The rules they make are binding on all members, and complied with by them, as a matter of fact. In effect, pressure is exercised in some institutions by requiring acceptance of a decision if membership is to be retained. Failure to accept the binding force of a decision may result in a member choosing to leave or being expelled; once again we are referred back to the idea of a club! But it is seldom in a state's interests to abandon membership. Acceptance of majority decisions is becoming a regular feature of state practice, and the result is that this way of doing things is increasingly acquiring a normative character.

In this chapter there has been little direct treatment of procedural justice, but two points should be clear: this sort of justice requires, first, genuine equality, and, second, the absence of voluntarism. International law in its classic formulation guarantees neither; although committed to equality in principle, the fact that it has its basis in practice may hinder the development of justice because any natural inequality is perpetuated, while its commitment to voluntarism maintains a major obstacle to the achievement of an obligatory system. However, the increasing importance of international institutions, possessing legal personality, as a major feature of the politico-legal system of the twentieth and (in all likelihood) the twenty-first centuries may be provoking a major reorientation of international law. International institutions often, although not always, favour smaller and weaker states. The rules and procedures of many institutions ensure a degree of real equality between members that is lacking elsewhere in the international system, while the technical or administrative nature of many of the activities that international institutions have to deal with means that substantive justice is often (though by no means always) not a major concern. For lesser states, organizations represent 'a sort of safety net which is, on the whole, capable of averting major risks to their security and independence' – they 'allow them to have a say even in areas where naked force and military superiority alone would otherwise constitute the legitimizing factors'.[21] If this is so, the development of these institutions is a major step towards the establishment of a genuine equality between states and the attainment of justice.

How, finally, is the problem of voluntarism confronted? In the standard account of (domestic) law, compliance follows from obligation. In a common interpretation of international law – holding that law rests on state practice – obligation is consequent on the habitual behaviour of compliance. If compliance, as a practice, precedes obligation, and if it is dependent on the will of the state, then voluntarism remains. However, states have for practical reasons to remain members of organizations that cater to their interests. The great majority of international institutions can only work with and through the willing cooperation of member states, but they also provide benefits for their members, and therefore states comply because they want to retain their membership. Hence, continuing compliance with agreements and rules depends on the political and material interests of states, which are significant, not on legal sanctions, which are weak or non-existent. States may be free to choose, but their practical concerns may leave them with only one choice to make. To deepen the interdependence of states (as international institutions do) is therefore to strengthen that interlocking of individual and collective interests which makes compliance with the rules the necessary choice.

## Notes

1 Janna Thompson, *Justice and World Order: A Philosophical Inquiry*, London: Routledge, 1992, p. 12.

2 J.G. Starke, *Introduction to International Law*, 11th edn, London: Butterworths, 1994, p. 14.

3 The personification of states that follows, together with the attribution of intentions and desires to them, is partly a useful shorthand which should not mislead; but it is worth noting in passing that the easy substitution throughout of, for example, 'the representatives of states' for 'states' would not capture the way in which the structures of both states and the international system condition real human beings to behave in certain ways.

4 Cf. Thompson, op. cit., p. 41.

5 'Perpetual Peace', in Immanuel Kant, *On History*, Indianapolis: Bobbs-Merrill, 1963, p. 114.

6 John Stuart Mill, *Principles of Political Economy*, London: Longmans, 1909, p. 582.

7 H.L.A. Hart, *The Concept of Law*, Oxford: Clarendon Press, 1961, p. 209.

8 Both the United States and the United Kingdom have withdrawn from organizations in the past; until 1997 the British government under the Conservatives considered further withdrawals. (Similarly illustrative of the nature of much international law is the way in which the UK has recently seen fit to review its commitment to the European Convention of Human Rights.)

9 See P.A. Tharp (ed.), *Regional International Organizations: Structures and Functions*, London: Macmillan, 1971, p. 5.

10 William D. Coplin, *The Functions of International Law: An Introduction to the Role of International Law in the Contemporary World*, Chicago: Rand McNally, 1966, p. 17.

11 Since the customary norms of treaty law have been codified in the Vienna Convention on the Law of Treaties of 1969 it is perhaps plausible now to argue that the obligations of a treaty are more akin to those of a contract than a promise.

12 Even the principle *pacta sunt servanda* has been made a positive rule, by being codified in Article 26 of the Vienna Convention, but a customary norm has to remain to avoid the circularity of self-reference.

13 Cf. Thomas M. Franck, *The Power of Legitimacy Among Nations*, New York: Oxford University Press, 1990, p. 196.

14 Antonio Cassese, *International Law in a Divided World*, Oxford: Clarendon Press, 1986, p. 17.

15 UN Charter, Arts. 1 and 4.

16 Franck, op. cit., p. 38.

17 Cf. Thompson, op. cit., p. 11.

18 Charles R. Beitz, *Political Theory and International Relations*, Princeton, N.J.: Princeton University Press, 1979, p. 17.

19 See Clive Archer, *International Organizations*, 2nd edn, London: Routledge, 1992, p. 170.

20 Archer, op. cit., p. 163.

21 Cassese, op. cit., pp. 409–10.

# 6

# LIBERALIZING INTERNATIONAL TRADE

## What is today's choice of weapons?

*Ulick Bourke*

Responding to an invitation from the Emperor of France in 1859, Richard Cobden undertook the last great work of his life: the negotiation of substantial tariff reductions with France. It was done unofficially but when the negotiations were concluded, Cobden received official instructions and powers to conclude the Treaty. 'When the secret came out', as the Dictionary of National Biography puts it, 'it roused violent excitement among the French Protectionists, and Cobden fought with them a strenuous battle for many months.' How times change!

Cobden based his life and career on his independence, his oratory and his persistence. He achieved remarkable things.

I propose here to consider the extent to which we are prepared today to achieve great things in liberalizing international trade. What are the means at our disposal? Are we capable of making good use of them? This is a good time to do so. We are at the outset of the post-Uruguay era. The first new WTO panel case has been heard. What is the path that lies ahead? And what use will we make of it?

### The pace of legal development in the European Community

It is useful to start with the European Community and draw the contrast between the way in which it has created a single market despite the fact that every Member State has its own deeply entrenched interests that it seeks to protect, before going on to considering whether Uruguay does, indeed, provide a means of effective trade liberalization. It is appropriate to draw this contrast because March 1996 saw the *Factortame III* and *Brasserie du Pêcheur* Judgments.[1] They follow *Francovich*,[2] but Francovich itself was simply the further development of cases going back to the 1960s – *Van Gend and Loos*,[3] *Costa and Enel*[4] and others.

What do these cases tell us? They deal with two issues of direct and obvious importance in the construction of the Common Market: *direct effect* coupled with the notion of *direct access* through Article 177 of the Treaty. Both have had an extraordinary influence upon the construction of the single market.

*Van Gend and Loos* established the doctrine of direct effect of Treaty Articles which were clear and precise, unconditional and 'legally perfect'.

*Costa* made it clear that Community law must have priority over national law, and *Defrenne*[5] showed that direct effect applied not only when national law was inconsistent with the Treaty, but also when positive obligations had been placed upon the Member States.

*Francovich* gave a right to an individual to claim damages against a Member State which had caused loss by reason of its failure to implement a directive. *Factortame* and *Brasserie du Pêcheur* establish a broader right to damages for a serious breach of community law by a Member State.

In *Factortame*, this right is established notwithstanding the fact that the UK Parliament had passed legislation contrary to the provision of community law in question (the right of establishment). In *Brasserie du Pêcheur* damages were awarded for an import ban, contrary to Article 30, in circumstances where a Judgment had already been delivered against the Member State concerned, Germany. What is remarkable about these Judgments is that they are broad in scope and open the way to litigants to push the frontiers of community law further forward rapidly.

In the ministerial rhetoric that surrounded *Factortame* in particular, it was not much emphasized that the right to recover damages extended to any breach of Community law which was serious and that it might be retrospective to a point which, whilst not fully defined, started where the Member State in question should have known that the national law was inconsistent with the Treaty.

There is not much doubt about when this point was in the case of *Factortame* – the time of the passing of the Merchant Shipping Act. In the case of Germany, it was made clear that the national judge, in assessing damages, was not limited to the date of the Judgment concerning beer, which was 1987. The judge could go back – and might well do so in the circumstances – to that other alcoholic liquid, *Cassis de Dijon*,[6] in 1979.

Why are these cases relevant to the liberalization of international trade? It is because the potent combination of *direct* effect and the *direct* access of individuals to the European Court via a national court, and the obligation imposed on Member States by Article 5 of the Treaty to cooperate, ensures that the means available to create a single market are powerful.

1987 – the date of the Judgment in the German beer case, and of the Parliamentary Session in which the Merchant Shipping Act was introduced – was also the year in which the Court gave judgment in the insurance cases concerning Germany, France, Ireland and Denmark.[7] Those Judgments, which, in truth, were compromises, nevertheless made it clear that Article 59 which provides for freedom of services across frontiers, means what it says. Insurance must not be confined to national markets behind protected frontiers.

An insurer today, secure in the backing given by the *Brasserie du Pêcheur* and *Factortame* Judgments and having, one might hope, the strength of a Spanish fisherman or a French brewer, would have been able to crack open his markets much more quickly. And he would have been immeasurably assisted by lawyers keen to pursue lucrative damages cases.

So much for the European Community. Let us turn to the World Trade Organization and consider whether this now provides the means, or will in the future provide the means, whereby world trade can be further liberalized in a shorter rather than a longer time.

## The WTO and the Uruguay Round

No one need doubt the achievements of the GATT. The statistics of the growth of world trade are there for all to see. However, the vast scope of the Uruguay Agreements, bringing in textiles, agriculture, services and intellectual property for all WTO members and the host of smaller agreements between a reduced number of participants, such as Government Procurement, is a huge step forward on the substantive side. But the WTO's members, all sovereign governments, and, more particularly, the wider business community and its lawyers, have to make it work. The key to this is the Understanding on Dispute Settlements. What role will this play?

## The Dispute Settlement Procedure

The Dispute Settlement Procedure is remarkably improved. It is compulsory for members to use it. Unlike its predecessor it proceeds at all levels unless there is a consensus that the case should not proceed. Thus the panel is to be constituted unless there is a consensus against it; its report is to be adopted unless there is a consensus against it; it may be appealed and the ruling of the appellate body must be followed. Sanctions for non-compliance with a panel ruling will have to be adopted. There is a formal body – the Dispute Settlement Body – in charge of this process and there are seven judges of high standing in the appellate body set at the pinnacle of the system. So much so good. Nevertheless there is a problem. A Rolls Royce or a Mercedes is not much use unless the ignition works. In this case the ignition key is held by the members of the WTO but it is not always they who wish to ride in the car. The keenest passengers are those whose commercial interests the Uruguay Agreements are designed to secure and protect – traders of goods, providers of services, owners of intellectual property rights, agricultural interests and so forth.

If these interests want the key to the car, they have to plead with their government for permission to take it out for a spin. In the case of the European Union it is worse than that. In most cases – and it is a complicated matter where the line is drawn – it is necessary to approach one's own government *and* the Commission. The Member State government may consult with a range of people. Consultations then take place within the Commission – in DG 1, at 'cabinet level', with Commissioners and finally in the legal service. Supposing one has surmounted those hurdles, it remains necessary to put the matter before the Member States as a whole in the 113 Committee.

How easy it is for one party in the process – government, Commission official, Commissioner, legal services or Member State – to find a reason for inaction such as: 'If we take that course of action it may prevent us defending ourselves against similar arguments in the United States'; 'If we annoy such and such a government today, they will not make concessions to us in our negotiations with them on, say, copper'; 'This is not in the overall interest of the European economy' or, finally, 'We are doing rather the same ourselves, so it would be embarrassing to raise this question'. Gary Horlick, a well-known Washington lawyer with long experience, rightly says in an article in *The Journal of World Trade Law*[8] that 'any Government ... does not want private parties to have anything to do with international law'. That is the spirit which those who wish to make use of WTO systems must overcome.

Is there a remedy for this problem of access? Unless there is progress there is a risk that the Dispute Settlement Procedure will not be effective. The further result of this will be that the vast commercial interests which are the principal beneficiaries of the multinational trading system, may lose interest or, at least, enthusiasm. That would not be surprising. It is not as though the World Trade Organization and its benefits are the everyday topic of discussion in boardrooms throughout the land.

Like Cobden, we should never give up. There are ways forward and I will deal with three of these briefly. First, there are chinks of light in the admission of private parties to the Dispute Settlement Procedure itself. Second, direct effect and direct access are still controversial and it may be that we shall benefit from some degree of historical inevitability. Third, the European Community has provided an instrument which opens up a process by which commercial interests may gain access to the system.

## Admission to the Dispute Settlement Procedure

First, the chinks of light. The first point here is clear. Once the process is started it has every prospect of working and this gives huge encouragement to persistence. The old system gave no such encouragement. One could win a case hands down and yet achieve nothing. This was as true for the members of the GATT – the Sovereign States – as it was for commerce and industry. Pieter-Jan Kuijper, head of the WTO unit in the legal service of the Commission, points out in an article on the New Dispute Settlement System[9] that the existence of the appellate body gives greater authority to panel decisions. The appeal process will be helpful in avoiding decisions which are unacceptable either politically or legally. Kuijper cites four recent cases which were unsatisfactory in political and legal terms and caused major problems for the US and the EC respectively and which an effective appeal system might have avoided – the two tuna/dolphin cases for the US, and Oilseed and Airbus for the EC.

Second, there is at least a possibility of the involvement of private parties in the system itself. A panel now has the right to seek information and technical advice from any individual or body which it deems appropriate. It may also seek information from any relevant source and may consult experts to obtain their opinion on certain aspects of the matter. Both of these new provisions are contained in Article 13 of the Understanding. A panel may also, on 'a factual issue concerning a scientific or other technical matter ... request an advisory report in writing from an expert review group'. These are not automatic rights but they are opportunities for the real interests to play a part in the procedure and to influence them – in other words, limited access.

What is not yet clear, however, is whether private parties can get their own lawyers admitted to the system. Argument before the old GATT panels was conducted by diplomats and civil servants with private lawyers, however skilled, advising on briefs and preparatory arguments but hanging around in the corridors (metaphorically at least) when it came to presenting arguments to a panel. That needs to change if only because it gives larger WTO members with substantial bodies of diplomats and long experience an advantage over newer and smaller members. I should perhaps add that both the UK Government and the European Commission at all levels – D. G 1, cabinet level and legal service – make serious and constructive efforts to coordinate cases with outside lawyers.

There are encouraging noises too in respect of transparency in the publication of panel reports at an earlier stage and even of press releases where issues have been settled short of a panel. It is up to the relevant commercial interest to use these opportunities and to their lawyers to make sure that they do so. If not used, they will be forgotten.

Finally, certain of the new agreements provide for limited 'local' review at the level of national courts. Each of the antidumping and subsidy codes, the Government Procurement Agreement and, most important, the Trade-Related Aspects of Intellectual Property Rights (TRIPS) Agreement, provide that WTO members should ensure that their judicial systems recognize the rights created by the multilateral agreements in their national law. This has always been done, so far as the European Community and the United States are concerned, in relation to the antidumping and anti-subsidy codes but the explicit recognition by national courts of rights arising from the agreements or codes will place great pressure on national and EC courts to recognize the origin of the law and to interpret their national law, so far as possible, to give effect to the WTO 'acquis'. In the case of TRIPS there are, moreover, huge commercial interests dependent on implementation of intellectual property law as provided by the Agreement and although the Government Procurement Agreement applies only to twenty-three countries, there should be plenty of opportunity for unhappy tenderers to consider action in the relevant court.

In these respects therefore the Dispute Settlement Procedure is much improved and provides some encouragement to those who wish to protect their interests. Admission to the system is not entirely closed.

## Direct effect and direct access

As to direct effect and direct access, the matter would seem to be much clearer. The Council of the European Community, following a US precedent at the end of the Tokyo Round, took care to insert in its decision approving the Uruguay Agreements, a recital to the effect that the Agreements were not intended to have direct effect. After some debate the recital settled reads:

> Whereas by its nature, the Agreement establishing the World Trade Organization – including the annexes hereto, is not susceptible to being directly invoked in Community or Member State Courts ...

It seems clear enough. One can only observe that the value of an agreement is much reduced if those intended to enjoy its principal benefits have no way of invoking them.

Then there is the *German Bananas*[10] Judgment where the idea of direct effect was firmly rejected because, the Court said, the WTO Agreements and in particular the Dispute Settlement Procedure did not have the characteristics of unconditionality and legal clarity required for direct effect in EC Treaty cases (the *Van Gend and Loos* case) or arising in other international treaties where the European Court had granted direct effect such as in *Kupferberg*.[11] Pieter-Jan Kuijper accepts this but rather daringly comments that 'when reading these paragraphs [i.e. those paragraphs describing the flexibility of the WTO Agreements] of the Banana judgment, one wonders if the court has ever read anything of dispute settlements beyond the text of Article XXIII'. He goes on to note that the WTO system does permit, at least in theory, easy withdrawal from the organization (thus indicating lack of unconditionality) but, whilst concluding that there should not be direct effect, discusses seriously whether 'there might be sufficient reason for the Court to change its view of the direct effect of the GATT after the entry into force of the WTO'. It seems likely, nevertheless, that the court will maintain the line it took in *German Bananas* for the time being.

Yet one wonders if that is the end of the story. Cobden, given the chance, would not have allowed it to be so. In the first place the installation of an effective and compulsory Dispute Settlement Procedure, reinforced by an appellate body of distinction and the means of enforcement, coupled with the very permanence of GATT/WTO (which, after all, pre-dates the European Union), begins to look more and more unconditional, clear and precise and legally certain. How realistic, for instance, is withdrawal from the WTO system following an adverse panel report? In the second place the commercial pressures involved in the GATT, GATS and TRIPS are so vast that they are not going to be held back easily. Moreover the gradual basis on which a change might be made is well established.

First, national law is likely to be interpreted so as to be consistent with the international obligations assumed under the WTO. Second, there is likely to be jurisprudence which reinforces this, sustained both by judgments in the courts of WTO members and in panels and by appellate body decisions, which will gain increasing authority. Then there is text book doctrine and parallels from other legal systems (the EC system itself, for instance, and NAFTA). There are, moreover, distinguished academics – Professor Petersmann is the leader of them – who will support this development. The jealous guardianship of this area of international law by WTO members may therefore be challenged by powerful economic interests. This has, after all, happened already in the Community – as evidenced by the clashes between private and state interests over State monopolies (under Article 90 of the Treaty of Rome) and over State subsidization contrary to commercial interests under Articles 92 and 93.

Direct access, as opposed to direct effect, does seem more remote. The Dispute Settlement Procedure has no equivalent of Article 177 of the Rome Treaty. The gap has been filled, however, so far as the European Community is concerned by a new regulation, the Trade Barrier Regulation,[12] which requires separate examination.

## Access to the WTO system via the Trade Barrier Regulation

The Trade Barrier Regulation of 1994 has its origin in the 'New Commercial Policy Instrument' which dates from 1984. The intention of this Regulation was to provide a way by which Community industry could establish, by means of a Community procedure, that it had been injured by an illicit commercial practice contrary to the ordinary rules of international law. It was an ineffective instrument in that it was used to demonstrable effect only once – by the Dutch company, AKZO, in a matter relating to patent litigation procedures in the United States. One difficulty was that the cases had to be brought by 'community industry' which meant that the better part of an entire industry within the European Community had to be lined up behind the complaint. This was not always an easy task. Moreover, it was necessary to prove that the commercial practice complained of was 'illicit' and that the industry had been 'injured' – again, requiring substantial proof.

The Trade Barrier Regulation, which has been heavily promoted by the Commission, significantly softens these conditions. In the first place, the term 'illicit commercial practices' has been replaced by the more neutral and wide-ranging term 'obstacles to trade'. That provides a very much easier burden of proof for the complainant. Moreover, a complaint may now be made by a single community enterprise (i.e. a company or business) where the obstacle to trade has caused it any 'adverse trade effect' on the market of a third country (i.e. a country outside the European Community). This avoids the problem of lining up the major part of an entire industry. The requirement that industry must support the complaint, however, remains when the adverse trade effect is found on the market of the European Community itself. In both cases further assistance is given by the substitution of the term 'adverse trade effect' for 'injury' – again, a significantly reduced burden of proof is required. The Trade Barrier Regulation, procedures for which can be completed within, according to the Commission, three to seven months, is clearly an improvement on its predecessor.

Nevertheless, there remains the essential problem which has been the theme of this discussion. Suppose that a Community enterprise or Community industry has successfully established that it is suffering an adverse trade effect by reason of an obstacle to trade (for instance, a denial of a benefit under one of the WTO Agreements) – in other words has done everything required under the Trade Barrier Regulation. In that event, and if it has been impossible to persuade the offending country to remove the obstacle to trade or the adverse trade effect, the European Community may take measures against the offending third country. It may, for instance, start proceedings under the WTO's Dispute Settlement Procedure. It will, however, only do so if it is satisfied that this is 'in the interests of the European Community'. So we turn full circle. The WTO's Dispute Settlement Procedure – an effective instrument by which the business community can obtain the benefits of the WTO Agreements – is open to all, in theory, but the door may, in fact, be locked and can only be opened if a key is obtained from a member of the WTO and permission to use the system granted.

There are signs that this may change but it has not changed yet. The Trade Barrier Regulation provides a means by which a business or an entire industry may prove that, if it is admitted to the system, it has a good case. Nevertheless, despite this proof, the European Community will only admit it to the system if it is satisfied that it is 'in its interests' to do so.

We are back to Cobden. The means by which trade may be liberalized and improved are there but the governments still hold the key. Can they be persuaded to exercise the political courage necessary to allow the system to be operated effectively in the interests of the business community?

At the end of his greatest speech in the House of Commons, Peel found Cobden's arguments unanswerable. This is not the case between industry and government at the present but there will be occasions when governments will have to accept that the WTO is not its private reserve.

## Notes

1 Joined cases C-46/93 and C-48/93, *Brasserie du Pêcheur SA* v *Germany*, and *R.* v *Secretary of State for Transport ex parte Factortame*; unreported. Judgment of the Court, 5 March 1996.

2 Joined cases C-6/90 and C-9/90, *Francovich* v *Italy* [1991] ECR I-S357.

3 *Van Gend en Loos* v *Nederlandse Administratie der Belastingen* [1963] ECR 95.

4 Case 6/64, *Costa* v *ENEL* [1964] ECR 585.

5 Case 80/70, *Defrenne* v *Belgium* [1971] ECR 445.

6 Case 120/78, *Rewe-zentral AG* v *Bundesmonopolverwaltung für Branntwein* [1979] ECR 649.

7 Case 252/83, *Commission* v *Denmark* [1986] ECR 3713;
Case 220/83, *Commission* v *France* [1986] ECR 3663;
Case 270/83, *Commission* v *France* [1986] ECR 273;
Case 205/84, *Commission* v *Germany* [1986] ECR 3755;
Case 266/84, *Commission* v *Ireland* [1986] ECR 3817.

8 Horlick, G. 'The US-Canada FTA and GATT Disputes Settlement Procedures', *Journal of World Trade*, 1995, vol. 29 no. 2, pp. 6–15.

9 Kuijper, P-J. 'The New WTO Dispute Settlement System: the Impact on the European Community', *Journal of World Trade*, 1995, vol. 29 no. 6, pp. 49–71.

10 Case C – 280/93, *Germany* v *Council* [1994] ECR 4973.

11 Case 104/81, *Hauptzollamt Mainz* v *Kupferberg* [1982] ECR 3641.

12 Regulation 3286/94, the 'Trade Barriers Instrument', *Official Journal of the European Communities*, L/349 of 31.12.94.

# COMMENTARY ON INGRAM AND BOURKE

*William Lucy*

These two chapters are very different in focus and emphasis. Ulick Bourke provides an informed sketch of the developments within the European Union and the world trade system that push toward free trade. By contrast, and in addition to a host of other arguments, Peter Ingram challenges and seeks to reconceptualize what he takes to be the dominant conception of international behaviour in both international law and legal philosophical thought. A detailed comparison of the two chapters would, therefore, be akin to comparing chalk and cheese. However, despite the many differences between them, both chapters can be sensibly discussed together because they are united in providing cautions against two common but rather different mistakes. The two mistakes often ensnare those who think about both the nature of law in general and the moral and political basis of any particular segment of law.

The first mistake is, in Roberto Unger's beautifully elaborate prose, 'a daring and implausible sanctification of the actual'. He explains the mistake thus: 'it would be strange if the results of a coherent, richly developed normative theory were to coincide with a major portion of any extended branch of law. The many conflicts of interest and vision that lawmaking involves, fought out by countless minds and wills working at cross-purposes, would have to be the vehicle of an immanent moral rationality whose message could be articulated by a single cohesive moral theory'.[1] Many who involve themselves in the task of attempting to unearth or reconstruct the point, purpose or value of any body of law often unwittingly fall victim to this mistake.[2] They assume that, for example, some coherent moral or political vision underpins the regime of workplace regulation or of national or international trade law and they might elucidate that vision by reference to notions such as individual rights, justice and efficiency. The problem with ascribing such 'an immanent moral [or political or economic] rationality' to any body of law is that it runs contrary to just about everything we know about law creation and enforcement in the modern state. We know, for example, that bodies of law are often created that have little more than symbolic effect since no provisions are made for enforcement or, if they are, enforcement is incomplete because of lack of resources and related factors.[3] Sociologists of law have taught these and related lessons for a good long time and, while their claims are made solely in relation to law created within the modern state, there is no reason to suppose that what is true of the law-creation process here is untrue of the law (and treaty- and convention-) creating process at the international level.

Falling victim to this mistake engenders nothing but disappointment when one examines and attempts to unearth the moral, political or economic vision of, for example, the WTO Uruguay Agreements or the EU provisions on the single market. One might argue that some conception of justice and of efficiency animate such agreements and regimes of law. The problem that arises with arguments such as these is that the agreements, conventions and laws in question seem designed to rule out non-state participation and therefore seem to thwart the values they might be thought to uphold. Bourke describes this situation as it arises within both the WTO and EU provisions vividly: it is akin to having a car but being prohibited access to the ignition key. (This baleful situation is also lamented by Ernst-Ulrich Petersmann in his essay in this volume.) Those most in need of access seem least likely to get it. But if we have assimilated the lessons sociologists of law have taught us about the processes of law creation – and we assume that those lessons can be generalized from the context of law creation within the nation state to law creation at the supra-national level – then Bourke's conclusion should not surprise us. The creation of virtually inaccessible but otherwise excellent regimes of legal regulation – the legal equivalent, as Bourke says, of a Mercedes or a Rolls Royce – might not be expected but should certainly not leave us in a state of shock.

The mistake Ingram cautions against in an ambitious and wide-ranging chapter is that of taking for granted a conflictual model of individual and state behaviour. Within the international context, such a model regards states as utterly self-interested and only just capable of refraining from the use of force in order to achieve their ends. Accepting this model means that lawyers' and philosophers' conception of international behaviour is fixated upon – as international law historically has been – the laws relating to armed conflict and intervention. The agenda for international law, in this view, is simply one of developing all possible means to reduce the likelihood of inter-state conflict. Ingram points out, quite rightly, how odd a view this is: we do not, for example, seek to base our understanding of segments of domestic law on such a conflictual model. Ingram also suggests that the sheer enormity of instances of everyday cooperation between states about matters of trade and international politics make such a conflictual model misleading. I am sure that this is right but Ingram's call for a reconceptualization of the model for international behaviour has a significant lacuna. For lurking at the back of his discussion is a concept he neither names nor analyses, namely, trust. This notion, on some analysis, is surely a key to understanding the massive number of instances of cooperative behaviour between states and hence the fulcrum of Ingram's reconceptualization. An understanding of international law and behaviour accommodating this notion would indeed be welcome and important. It is a job that Ingram has hinted at in his chapter and which need not be started in an intellectual vacuum since the notion of trust has recently begun to occupy philosophers, historians, sociologists and (to a lesser extent) lawyers.[4] The notion seems to offer intriguing possibilities and prospects within the context of international behaviour and law.

Perhaps the most ambitious and intriguing aspect of Ingram's chapter is his attempt to establish a link between the often messy and confusing notions of sovereignty, procedural and substantive justice. The former requires formal equality within the international community and that notion is, of course, closely connected to procedural justice. Ingram's bold claim is, however, the alleged connection between the latter and substantive justice: as he says, 'this sort of [procedural] justice requires ... genuine equality'. This claim raises a host of questions. True, Ingram tells us that international institutions may already recognize such a connection but this does not establish that the connection must or ought to be made. In fact, there are some who would argue – not implausibly – that notions of formal equality and procedural justice must for some purposes be kept completely distinct from substantive accounts of equality and justice. Ingram does little to refute this type of argument other than to suggest that the world is such that formal equality does not guarantee substantive equality. But, then, there are few who would disagree with this.

## NOTES

1 R. Unger, *The Critical Legal Studies Movement*, Cambridge, Mass.: Harvard UP, 1986, p. 9.

2 Neil MacCormick provides an august example: see p. 112 of his essay 'Natural Law and the Separation of Law and Morals' in R. George (ed.), *Natural Law Theory*, Oxford: Clarendon, 1992.

3 The sociological literature on the creation, enforcement and invocation of law is immense: for a starter see R. Cotterrell, *The Sociology of Law: An Introduction*, London: Butterworths, 1992, pp. 53–6, 245–72.

4 See D. Gambetta (ed.), *Trust: Making and Breaking Co-operative Relations*, Oxford: Blackwell, 1988; R. Kramer and T. Tyler (eds), *Trust in Organizations*, Thousand Oaks, Calif.: Sage, 1996. Lawyers are, of course, more than familiar with the notion of trust but rarely think about the idea in anything other than doctrinal terms. An exception is R. Cotterrell, 'Trusting in Law: Legal and Moral Concepts of Trust' (1993) *Current Legal Problems* 75.

# 7

# THE ETHICS OF COMPETITION

*Jonathan Wolff*

## *I*

Exchange is one thing, economic competition another. Exchange is possible without competition; and economic competition (of sorts) is possible without exchange. Put exchange and competition together and, roughly, you get the free market. There are many philosophical discussions of the free market; a sizeable number about free exchange; but – aside from in the context of consequentialist defences of the market – who this century has had much to say about economic competition?

This need not be a surprise. Not every concept, not even every important concept, bears philosophical reflection. So why should it be rewarding for a philosopher to consider competition? Well John Stuart Mill, summarizing the socialist case writes:

> Morally speaking [the evils of individual competition] are obvious. It is the parent of envy, hatred, and all uncharitableness; it makes every one the natural enemy of all others who cross his path, and every one's path is liable to be crossed. Under the present system hardly any one can gain except by the loss or disappointment of one or of many others.[1]

In *On Liberty* he famously remarks:

> Whoever succeeds in an overcrowded profession, or in a competitive examination; whoever is preferred to another in any contest for an object which both desire, reaps benefit from the loss of others, from their wasted exertion and their disappointment.[2]

G.A. Cohen comments on a passage from Marx in *The German Ideology* in the following terms: 'What is a society of competition [in this sense]? It is a society in which people use their powers to get as much as they can for themselves, without regard to the needs of others.'[3]

From each of utilitarian, Kantian and virtue-based perspectives a case can be made that economic competition generates, at least, a prima facie wrong. First, and most obviously, damage to the losers is a cost to weigh in the utilitarian balance. Here is Louis Blanc, as presented by Mill, on those costs:

> What is competition from the point of view of the workman? It is work put up to auction. A contractor wants a workman: three present themselves. – How much for your work? – Half-a-crown: I have a wife and children. – Well; and how much for yours? – Two shillings: I have no children, but I have a wife. – Very well; and now how much for you? – One and eightpence are enough for me; I am single. Then you shall have the work. It is done; the bargain is struck. And what are the other two workmen to do? It is to be hoped that they die quietly of hunger.[4]

Second, the competitive individual has no regard for the sufferings of those who are beaten, and thus seems akin to Kant's 'flourishing man' who, while wishing no evil, does nothing to assist those he sees in great hardship. Kant maintains that while a society following a maxim of mutual indifference is possible, it is nevertheless impossible to *will* that such a maxim should be a universal law.[5] It is true that this example is often taken to be problematic. Nevertheless the point remains that from a Kantian perspective the competitive individual behaves no better than the indifferent individual. Indeed one should say that the competitive individual behaves with even lower moral worth, often being the cause (rather than merely the witness) of another's distress.

Finally, as described, the competitive individual seems very far from any ideal of the virtuous citizen. Competitive society first pre-supposes and then reinforces a very unattractive character type. If Mill and Marx are to be believed it encourages selfishness, envy, hatred and lack of charity. Even some comments of Nozick suggest that competitive behaviour can be a vice:

> Is there any important dimension along which it is inappropriate to judge oneself comparatively? Consider the following statement by Timothy Leary: 'It's my ambition to be the holiest, wisest, most beneficial man alive today. Now this may sound megalomaniac, but I don't see why. I don't see why ... every person who lives in the world shouldn't have that ambition. What else should you try to be? The president of the board, or the chairman of the department, or the owner of this and that?' *The Politics of Ecstasy* (New York: College Notes and Texts Inc., 1968), p. 218. There certainly is no objection to wanting to be as holy, wise, and beneficial as possible, yet an ambition to be the holiest, wisest, and most beneficial person alive today is bizarre.[6]

It would be a mistake to conclude that acting competitively is wrong: perhaps there are stronger counter-arguments. Yet we have enough to motivate the thought that competition in general, and economic competition in particular, is morally problematic. When Tesco opens its new supermarket at the end of my road, it will put many local traders out of business. What is the difference between that and theft or arson? A serious moral question, one might think. Yet opponents of competition are more often treated as misguided sentimentalists than as serious moral thinkers. Why?

Perhaps we have become so used to the idea that these private vices generate greatly outweighing public virtues that we take the moral argument against competition to have been answered long ago. This, then, is to see the case for competition to be made out in consequentialist terms, and the argument is surely impressive: competition keeps prices down, quality up, and facilitates efficient employment of resources. Thus the utilitarian case for competition seems strong. What more can be said in its favour?

One argument made all too often is that competitive free trade is required by a proper respect for liberty. Anti-competitive situations are those in which certain people are prevented from doing something they want to do and this, so it is said, reduces their liberty. Therefore freedom requires free competition. This argument, however, is seriously flawed. Few claim we should have the liberty to harm each other. It is not a restriction on my (legitimate) liberty if I am prohibited from burning down your business premises. Yet harm suffered in economic competition can be just as serious. What we want to know is why one of these harms is permissible and the other not. A simple appeal to liberty cannot possibly help.

A more promising defence of competition focuses on the relation between competition and exploitation. It may seem odd that there could be a defence of competition here, for the socialist argument, we have seen, is that competition leads to exploitation. However the libertarian response is that this is a serious over-simplification. Properly understood, the genuinely free market renders exploitation impossible. Is this claim plausible?

## II

First we need an understanding of exploitation. The key idea of exploitation is that of taking advantage of another's vulnerability, for your own purposes, without proper regard to the effect your behaviour has on the interests of the other. For clarity it is worth distinguishing two aspects of the paradigm case: exploiting a person's circumstances and exploiting that person. If someone is in a vulnerable position it is possible to exploit that position: their circumstances. If you are poor, needy, ignorant, or dependent, I can often use this vulnerability as a source of power over you. Yet this need not involve exploitation of *you*. Paternalism can involve exploiting a person's circumstances for his or her own good. I agree to feed and house you, but only if you – against your will – agree to join Alcoholics Anonymous. In acting this way I certainly exploit your circumstances, but my goal is your good, not mine. I may have been manipulative, but not exploitative.

Conversely, it is sometimes possible to exploit someone who is not in a vulnerable position, or, at least, not a vulnerable material or 'objective' position. Thus one can exploit another's infatuation, or weakness of character, however rich in material resources they may be. Typically, though, one is in exploitable circumstances if one is relatively poor, or needy, or lacks information others have.

How should we understand the idea of exploiting a *person*? The notion of using someone purely as a means to your own ends seems to come close to the intuitive thought. This is a perfectly general notion, in the sense that economic exploitation is one important category of exploitation, but it by no means exhausts the field. Exploitation within the family may even be a more common phenomenon. To use someone is to treat them as you might a tool or an instrument, as if they do not have ends or interests of their own. In a humane society, thought Marx, one person's need would generate a claim on the resources of another. In an exploitative society one person's need is turned to a source of another's profit.

To complete the analysis we must appeal to a normative element in exploitation. To exploit someone is to use them; at the very least to treat them less well than they ought to be treated. But how ought one to treat people? Clearly there are many different ways of specifying norms of acceptable behaviour, and these will generate differing theories or conceptions of exploitation. In the young Marx, for example, we find norms of human flourishing. A theory of exploitation built on such a basis might claim that one person exploits another when the exploiter uses his or her power to bring about a personally beneficial arrangement while being indifferent to the effect the arrangement has for the flourishing of the exploited person.[7] More commonly, theories of exploitation are built on fairness or justice norms. An exploiter uses his or her advantage to bring about a particular arrangement, and is unconcerned whether that arrangement is unfair or unjust to the weaker party.

The socialist case, we saw, is that typically workers are exploited because of their vulnerable position. Blanc argues that competition for jobs creates a vulnerability for those competing workers, which is then exploited by capitalists in paying low, exploitative wages. The obvious response, and one that Blanc himself anticipates, is that in a properly competitive economy no such thing can happen. If the employer was prepared to employ someone at the highest offered price, then it appears that profits can be made even when wages are high. Thus 'excess' profits can be made at the lowest wages, and so competing employers will bid up the price until some threshold – perhaps the point where wages equal marginal product – is reached. But at that point, so it is said, there is no exploitation. Thus in a fully competitive economy exploitation will not exist: competition, on this view, does not create exploitation, but, on the contrary, makes it impossible.

Linking competition and (lack of) exploitation in this way seems very attractive. That someone is exploited entails that they fall below a certain norm. But what norm? Well, why not 'what they would get in a perfectly competitive market in equilibrium'? That, surely, is what their labour is 'worth'. And this fits perfectly with the idea that, paradigmatically, exploitation is the consequence of differential bargaining strength. For in a perfectly competitive market no one has any more bargaining power than anyone else. Why? Because no one is bargaining. Prices are set by the market. One can then see exploitation as arising from collusive or forcible interferences with the market mechanism.

The anti-Corn Law movement provides an excellent illustration of this way of linking exploitation and competition. The argument is that protectionist laws prevented the market for corn, and thus for bread, reaching its equilibrium point, and thus led to the exploitation of those who relied heavily on their consumption of bread – the poor. The solution is to free up competition in the corn market, by ending protectionism. Free international trade eliminates the exploitation of the ordinary consumer by landed interests. It would be absurd – and churlish on this occasion – to deny the force of such an argument. Nevertheless, there are serious complications.

The bold case that the market makes exploitation impossible, has two stages:

1 The competitive market in equilibrium sets the appropriate norm as a benchmark for judging whether exploitation takes place.
2 A certain form of competitive market is likely, in the long run, to reach equilibrium.

From these two claims it would follow that the specified competitive market has a long-run tendency to eliminate exploitation.

The first claim is widely made. Consider, for example, the following from David Miller – specifically about market exploitation: 'It is generally speaking a necessary condition of A's exploiting B that, in the exchange between them, A does better and B does worse than each would under equilibrium prices.'[8] It is a necessary condition precisely because, in this view, the market equilibrium provides the exploitation benchmark.

Perhaps few people explicitly make the second claim – that there is a tendency for equilibrium to be reached – about any form of market, whether capitalist or socialist. But note that its absence, conjoined with the first claim, yields an argument that the market is near certain to lead to injustice, if not exploitation, rather than the conclusion that the market eliminates exploitation.

Now, it seems to me, and I shall argue, that both of these premises are false, for all known forms of competitive market. Let us start with the second premise. I said before that Louis Blanc anticipated the idea that a competitive market in equilibrium would remove exploitation. His reply, as recorded by Mill, seems to me to have the right form but the wrong content. Blanc suggests that the competitive anti-exploitation argument works only if demand for labour equals supply: there is no work shortage or labour shortage. But, he replies, population growth means that the supply of labour is always expanding. Therefore the market never reaches equilibrium, and so there is always a shortage of work, and thus a position of vulnerability for the workers.

Where Blanc is right, it seems, is to deny that the competitive market – particularly in its capitalist forms – will ever reach equilibrium. Indeed, according to Joan Robinson, Marx's main point of difference with classical economic analysis, and perhaps his most important insight, is the claim that there is no long-run tendency to equilibrium in the capitalist market.[9] Blanc was wrong, though, to think that population growth is the cause of disequilibrium: it is, of course, too long-term a phenomenon.

For Marx the key is that there is not only competition between workers, but between workers and labour-saving machines. This generates his theory of the industrial reserve army, and the employment cycle, which, on the face of it at least, sounds very plausible. Essentially whenever wages begin to approach (what non-Marxists would think of as) their equilibrium price, the capitalist turns to labour-saving devices to cut labour costs. But what one capitalist does they all do; this cuts the demand for labour, replenishing the industrial reserve army and lowering the price for labour: restoring previous levels of exploitation.

Perhaps Marx is wrong about the particular mechanisms at work (although to a non-economist he sounds convincing). Yet behind this objection is a quite general point. The very idea that a competitive market could reach a state of equilibrium seems almost self-contradictory, unless one has a very narrow view of what competition involves (essentially competition within a given level of technology). For competition, through innovation, means that the market will go through regular short-term 'shocks' which forestalls any long-term drift to equilibrium. After all, what state would the market be in at equilibrium? Would competition through innovation have stopped? Then we no longer have a competitive market in the sense we know.

My general claim, then, is that the very nature of a competitive economy precludes it from reaching the sort of equilibrium that would – on the theory in question – make exploitation impossible. This shows, I think, that the second step in the 'anti-exploitation' argument fails. The competitive economy has no tendency to equilibrium. What about the first step: that the competitive market in equilibrium provides the correct benchmark by which one can assess whether exploitation is taking place? Now, the practical impossibility of reaching equilibrium does not render this idea incoherent. Assuming a fixed level of technology, we can make sense of the idea of a market equilibrium at that given level of technology. So should we follow the suggestion of Miller, and assume that some sort of competitive market in equilibrium provides the correct benchmark: in other words the 'just price'?

It will be instructive to approach this by first asking the question of whether the *capitalist* market can provide acceptable exploitation benchmark norms. Note that, if such a thing is established, it is theoretically just as possible for labourers to exploit capitalists as capitalists to exploit labourers. Now, for some this might seem a *reductio ad absurdum* of the approach. But it is perfectly understandable when we realize that the claim that the capitalist market in equilibrium provides the right benchmark assumes that:

1 The given set of property titles that the capitalist market presupposes is legitimate.
2 There is no moral difference between earning a 'wage' on the basis of using or hiring out the property you own, and earning a wage on the basis of your labour.
3 There is no moral difference between earning a higher than average wage for your work on the basis of your possession of a scarce skill, and on the basis of your exceptional work or effort.

Perhaps it is obvious why these assumptions are necessary. First, any market presupposes a set of property holdings, and so any derived set of prices can be just only relative to that set of property holdings. If the underlying set of property holdings, or titles, is unjust, then any resulting set of prices will be infected with injustice.

Second, the market sets prices for all factors of production, as well as all other commodities. Capital, as much as labour, has its equilibrium price. If – through bargaining vulnerability – owners of capital receive less than the equilibrium price of that capital, then, on the theory in question, assuming that their capital is legitimately held, owners of such capital are exploited.

This point also generates the third assumption. Crudely we can say that the market price for a particular person's labour is a function of demand and supply factors for the type of labour it is, and for the care and productive effort with which the labour is applied. Typically, then, I can command a high price for my labour if I have a rare, and demanded, skill, or if I am a hard and effective worker. Now, to suppose that the market price, in competitive equilibrium, is the just price, is to assume that the factors which determine prices are morally on a par. On this view, morally, possession of a rare skill is just as deserving of a high price as enormous care and effort in performing work. Put so starkly, this seems a highly implausible claim, and is widely disputed. But it is necessary if we are to accept David Miller's claim that the market provides the appropriate benchmark for judging whether exploitation has taken place. Hence we must reject that claim, if we believe that, at least in certain cases, possession of a rare skill does not justify a higher income than that earned by those who do not possess it.

So my two primary objections against the view that any competitive market – including market socialism – could end exploitation are: first, even if the market in equilibrium provides the correct exploitation benchmark, there is no tendency to equilibrium in a competitive economy; and second, no form of market in equilibrium provides the right exploitation benchmark as no form of market can discriminate morally pertinent from morally arbitrary determinants of price.

The thrust of the argument so far is largely negative: there is no reason to believe that a competitive market will eliminate exploitation. This, of course, does not show that competition can be exploitative. That is the task of the next section.

## III

Does the claim that economic competition can be exploitative have any plausibility? In many aspects of life we appear to value competition for its own sake, and this value is appreciated even by those who do poorly. Thus those who come bottom of the sports league more often vow to do better the following year than give up entirely to lick their wounds, complaining of their maltreatment. For such people competition is valued as a way of giving an extra level of enjoyment and interest to their activity, and as an opportunity and motive to enhance their skills. After all, many people choose to engage in forms of competition for recreation, and often they are admired for doing so. Being competitive in these spheres might be seen as a way of respecting oneself, or as, in part, a way of living the good life.

No doubt some people view economic competition in the same light: perhaps many do, perhaps even those for whom losing means losing everything. But for others this would seem a vastly misleading romanticism of the economic world that they find themselves in. Before we could attempt to adjudicate this dispute we must recognize that there are several different types or styles of competition – or at least of ways of viewing competition – and before we can take the argument about economic competition any further it is necessary to make a number of distinctions.

What all cases of competition appear to have in common is that they involve a number of people (or groups, or teams) who engage in an activity in which there can be differing levels of achievement, normally measured on a scale (which will often be broadly correlated with some underlying trait, which the scale is designed to capture). The person, group or team performing at the highest level of achievement, as measured by the scale, is the winner, and is given some recognition, reward or prize.

Why do we have practices of competition? We can distinguish several types of cases:

1 *Pure lottery*: this might be thought to be the limit case of competition. A scarce resource is to be allocated, and a competition of pure luck is held as a means of fair allocation. Here there are just two levels of achievement

– win or lose – and achievement on this scale is not meant to reflect any underlying trait or ability.

2 *Weighted lottery*: again a scarce resource is to be allocated, and a competition is held in which differential efforts are possible. In such a case the competition is arranged so that someone who achieves best on a scale designed to reflect some underlying trait will be awarded the scarce resource. For example the competition might be designed simply to be responsive to effort, on the assumption that those who try hardest are those who most want the resource in question, and it is a good thing if resources go to those who want them most. A different example would involve trying to arrange distribution so that it is responsive to some trait thought to be deserving, for the value of rewarding desert.
3 *Pure competition*: competitive behaviour is considered desirable in itself, and so turns an activity of no value in itself into something of value.
4 *Constitutive competition*: an activity can only exist if it involves some sort of competition (chess, for example).
5 *Activity enhancement*: a competition for a prize is presented as a way of enhancing an activity already thought valuable in itself.
6 *Side-effect of award*: a weighted lottery is held for the external effects of awarding the reward to someone of a certain type.
7 *Side-effect of activity*: a competition is held for the external effects of people engaging in the activity that the competition draws out or encourages.

In any given case it may not be clear what the underlying rationale for the competition is, or it might be that it has several different rationales. Indeed even the most familiar and banal example repays analysis. Consider the example of a parent who, at 4.30 pm is asked to arbitrate a dispute between two children, who want to watch different channels on television at 5.00 pm. In the absence of a video recorder or second television the parent announces that whichever child has the tidiest bedroom at 4.55 pm will get to choose which channel to watch.

At one level this might be seen as an example of a pure lottery: designed solely to facilitate fair distribution of a scarce, indivisible, resource – possession of the remote control of the television. (This assumes that the bedrooms are equally untidy to start with, otherwise the competition is obviously unfair.) Yet it is more plausible to think that the competition is intended to be a weighted (or Solomonic) lottery. Assuming a fair starting point, and roughly equal tidying abilities it is likely that the competition will be won by whichever child has the more intense preference to watch their chosen channel. Intense preference is likely to be reflected in extra effort, which has a good chance of leading to a winning performance.

Furthermore, although the children may not view it this way, the parent also might have 'activity enhancement' in mind. Tidying up skills will be improved when they are applied towards an end other than a tidy room, and it might encourage the idea that acting in this way is to act virtuously. (It might of course, have the opposite effect: encouraging the idea that tidying up is so unpleasant it should only be done when there is a prospect of reward.) Finally, the idea of side-effect of activity obviously applies. By getting the children to act in this way, the parent's own burdens will be reduced. Thus many different goals are served by this example.

Side-effect of activity may seem a slightly obscure idea, so it might be helpful to examine some more examples. Consider a farmer who announces a ploughing competition, in order to get his field ploughed cheaply. Or a publishing company that sets a literary quiz involving questions largely about its own titles, as a way of encouraging sales to those wishing to take part.

In *On Liberty* Mill briefly discusses two examples of competition: competitive examinations and economic competition. If we take first the example of competitive examinations for, say, the civil service, we can see it as satisfying a number of goals. First, it is a weighted lottery, giving desirable jobs to those who put in the most effort or have the highest ability. Second, there is an all-important side-effect of award effect: it advances social utility to put certain public jobs in the hands of those with certain proven abilities. Third, there is an indirect side-effect of activity effect. Having such practices will increase the general educational level of those who plan to take part in them, for the benefit not just for the competitors but for society as a whole.

Suppose, though, that the practice had only the very last effect; that we announced certain competitions simply for the beneficial effects of the competitive activity for society as a whole. Suppose there was no particular reason to give the highest achievers the most desirable jobs, and that the process of preparing oneself to take the examinations was of no personal value, yet the practice of having many people preparing themselves in this way had a great social utility. In such a case, I imagine, we would feel somewhat uncomfortable about the practice. Those preparing for examinations – whether they win or lose – could rightfully think of themselves as exploited, as being used for the benefit of others, or treated purely as a means. The Kantian case against this type of competition – and the ploughing competition and the literary quiz – begins to emerge.

Is there an equal Kantian case against the 'tidying competition'? After all, 'side-effect of activity' was present there too. Is this exploitative? My feeling is that we might say that the parent was being opportunistic, but not exploitative. The reason for this judgement is that children ought to tidy their rooms, and we apparently have no objection to the idea of parents manipulating their children into doing what they ought to do. Thus in our earlier terminology: there is exploitation of circumstances but not of a person. But there are obvious limits. If we found that a mother and father managed, by setting competition after competition, to get their children to perform every aspect of housekeeping, while they spent the time in the pub, then we would surely have crossed the border.

Does it make any difference if one has not set the competition, but nevertheless finds oneself a beneficiary of others' competitive activity? Here, I think, one must escape blame entirely if not only one has not set the competition, but it is not in one's power to try to stop or change it. If, however, one has power of influence and declines to use it one cannot use this defence.

So we have the provisional result that a practice of competition which is solely or primarily valued for the side-effects of the competitive behaviour is prima facie exploitative. But we have seen one case where the presumption is overturned: where people are encouraged by the competition to do what they ought to do. It is also not exploitative if the beneficiaries lack the ability to control or influence the situation. Another mitigating exception that we have noted in passing is where engaging in the competitive behaviour – in that case preparing for examinations – was beneficial for the person so doing. Finally we should add that when the benefit accrues to a group, and the person competing is a member of that group then this form of competition, while still exploitative, is less so than other cases.

Why value economic competition? Clearly it is rarely, if ever, thought useful as a pure lottery: as an arbitrary, and thus fair, means of allocating scarce resources which cannot sensibly be divided more equally. Certain arguments, relating to desert, in effect appeal to the idea of the competitive market as a weighted lottery, rewarding perseverance, tenacity, enterprise and effort, and it is hard to deny that the competitive market at least sometimes has this effect. Whether possessors of such qualities intrinsically deserve to have more than those who do not is, of course, highly questionable. Furthermore, there can be little doubt that less noble characteristics equally have their place: a talent for flattery, duplicity, manipulation, deceit about one's own preferences and many other similar skills also find their reward in the market. Luck, too, plays a central role. Consequently several things must be shown by anyone wishing to use the weighted lottery defence of economic competition. First, that certain traits are virtues; second, that it is 'fitting' that these should be rewarded; and third; economic competition rewards the right traits. All of these claims, of course, are contestable.

The idea of 'activity enhancement' is also implausible as a defence of economic competition. To use this argument would be to claim that economic competition enhances an activity that is otherwise desirable in itself. Most producers, though, would surely prefer a monopoly position. Competition is seen as a fact of life, not a life enhancer. And as competition is not constitutive of trade the 'constitutive competition' approach mentioned previously fails to apply.

What about the instrumental justifications? The idea I called side-effect of award would require us to value economic competition because it is socially useful for the enterprising to have more money than the less enterprising. This claim, of course, is often made: the enterprising can make best use of resources, for the benefit of all of us. However, even if this is true, it is less important as a justification of economic competition than the type of argument referred to as side-effect of activity. This is the idea that the process of competitive action is of social utility, for it is this that keeps prices down and quality up. The strongest defence of economic competition is that setting people in economic competition is good for us.

Thus we largely value economic competition for the side-effects of having people engaging in competitive economic activity. I suggested above, though, that we should see such arrangements as prima facie exploitative: importantly *not* as a situation where the winners exploit the losers, but as a situation in which both winners and losers in competition are exploited by those encouraging them to take part in potentially damaging competitive behaviour. Both winners and losers are treated as means, although the winners (for the time being) might make little complaint (for the time being). In essence the surprising (and frankly counter-intuitive) conclusion is that economic competition is an activity in which consumers exploit producers.

This conclusion will be resisted by many. Who could seriously believe that I, and others like me, exploit the shareholders of highly profitable multinational corporations in virtue of the fact that we benefit from such firms' engagement in competition? Several points need to be made, though, before this position can be fully understood. First, by 'producers' I mean everyone involved in production, and not merely owners of capital; and all such people are potentially victims of consumer exploitation. Second, my argument is perfectly consistent with the claim that owners of capital exploit their workers in far more significant ways than consumers exploit anyone. Third, my target, at this point, is an unmodified competitive market in which there is no state provision or redistribution, and thus nothing to mitigate exploitation (this will be important later). Fourth, and relatedly, by saying that competition is exploitative I am not proposing that we eliminate it: the utilitarian case in favour is overwhelming. Nevertheless there are ways of modifying the competitive market to reduce or eliminate this exploitation. My claim is that, under certain circumstances consumers exploit producers by encouraging economic competition: it is a further question whether we are presently in those circumstances.

This further question, of course, is the interesting one. Do consumers presently exploit producers? The answer is: yes and no. It is vital to distinguish local and global aspects of the discussion. Whatever resistance we may have to the idea that consumers in an advanced society exploit producers in their own society, it is much harder to oppose the thought that consumers in advanced societies exploit producers in less developed ones. The low wages, hazardous working conditions and uncertain life prospects experienced by those producing goods for an overseas market are a direct consequence of practices of economic competition. As willing beneficiaries of such practices we are exploiters.

What makes us exploiters in the global case and generally non-exploiters in the local case? It would be easy to say that the difference is that in only one of the two cases are great harms caused to the producer. However, on my analysis of exploitation this is not quite right: exploitation is characterized by the exploiter's *indifference* to whether certain sorts of harm are suffered, rather than the fact of any actual harms. Thus the difference is that we seem to be largely indifferent to the plight of producers in less developed countries, while we are far less indifferent to the plight of producers in our own.

We can give this contrast more weight by considering the question of what justice requires of us. I cannot, of course, attempt a complete answer here, but as part of an answer I want to appeal to something I have argued for elsewhere, and call the 'weak equity axiom'.[10] The axiom is:

> If a change generates a surplus or profit, then those who are already relatively badly off should not be made worse off still as a result of the change.

It is worth comparing this principle with both the Pareto Principle, and the Maximin Principle. It could be viewed as a less demanding compromise between the two – entailed by them both – and thus should be widely accepted as a necessary (*not* sufficient) condition for the justice of a change.

The Pareto Principle tells us that no one should be made worse off by a change. The weak equity axiom attends only to those towards the bottom of the distribution. Unlike the Pareto Principle it does not rule out the possibility that those who are already rich should lose out from the change.

Maximin tells us that the worse off should be made as well off as possible. The equity axiom tells us only that we should not make the badly off any worse off, but not that we should improve their position.

I should repeat that this is not intended as a complete theory of justice: it is simply a necessary condition which I believe to be almost universally held, if almost never explicitly acknowledged. But in some cases it has powerful consequences. It requires us to redistribute the benefits of any scheme so that those towards the bottom of the distribution do not make a net loss from the operation of the scheme. Thus in the case of economic competition it requires us to compensate those who, already badly off, find themselves further losers as a result of competition: workers and small traders who suffer as others benefit. In other words, it is just the principle needed to stop 'the weak going to the wall' – often thought to be the main moral defect of a competitive system.

It is beyond the scope of this chapter to defend the weak equity axiom here. But one reason for introducing it is that our own situation seems to be that within our own society we take certain steps to apply something akin to the weak equity axiom, whereas on the world-wide scale we do not. And this has significant consequences for the analysis of exploitation. Recall my rough characterization of exploitation. An exploiter uses his or her advantage to bring about a particular arrangement, and is unconcerned whether that arrangement is damaging to the weaker party. To the extent that we accept the weak equity axiom in order (among other reasons) to protect people from severe loss in competition, then it is less true that we are indifferent to the plight of such people. Therefore we may no longer be exploiting them. Yet if we do not apply the axiom in our dealings with others it is more likely that we are exploiters. Thus although we generally avoid exploiting producers in our own society, we do nevertheless exploit producers in the developing world, for our reluctance to employ the weak equity axiom is symptomatic of our indifference and hence our exploitation.

It is interesting to note that the weak equity axiom provides not so much an economic safety net for producers (it does not speak to the plight of those who are badly off without being losers in the system), but a *moral* safety net for consumers. If we do not attempt to implement it, or any stronger principle, but willingly benefit from economic competition, then we are exploiters. But if we do implement the axiom, then we avoid being exploiters, at least in that respect. We are no longer indifferent to the plight of those whose actions benefit us.

From the arguments given it becomes clear that it is not enough to defend practices of economic competition by pointing to their great social utility. Economic competition, in some circumstances, is a practice by means of which consumers exploit producers, and consumers are also voters who have the power to modify the institutions within which competition takes place. Competition can be a form of exploitation, and those, particularly those towards the bottom of any distribution, who lose through exploitative practices have a claim in justice for compensation. And this is a claim we can afford to meet. If competition advances social utility, then social utility can be raided to compensate those who would otherwise do very badly.

This is a way of arguing that, although the social value of economic competition is considerable, there is no good argument for letting the costs and benefits of economic competition lie exactly where they fall. There may be good reasons for putting resources in the hands of the most enterprising and tenacious, but this is not also a reason for putting nothing at all in the hands of those who lack these skills. The utilitarian case for competition should be supplemented by Kantian practices in which we treat people as ends in themselves by making sure that no one unjustly suffers as a consequence of social practices which benefit others.[11]

## Notes

1 J.S. Mill, *Chapters on Socialism*, p. 233, in *On Liberty and Other Writings*, ed. S. Collini, Cambridge: Cambridge University Press, 1989.

2 J.S. Mill, *On Liberty* in *Utilitarianism and Other Writings*, ed. Mary Warnock, Glasgow: Collins, 1962, p. 277.

3 G.A. Cohen, 'Self-Ownership, Communism, and Equality: Against the Marxist Technological Fix', in his *Self-Ownership, Freedom, and Equality*, Oxford: Oxford University Press, 1995, p. 132.
4 *Chapters on Socialism*, p. 235.
5 I. Kant, *Groundwork of the Metaphysic of Morals*, in H.J. Paton (ed.), *The Moral Law*, London: Hutchinson, 1948, p. 86.
6 Robert Nozick, *Anarchy, State, and Utopia*, Oxford: Blackwell, 1974, p. 244n.
7 For an elaboration of this account of exploitation, see my *Exploitation*, University of London MPhil Thesis, 1985.
8 David Miller, 'Exploitation in the Market', in A. Reeve (ed.), *Modern Theories of Exploitation*, London: Sage, 1987, p. 162.
9 Joan Robinson, *An Essay on Marxian Economics*, London: MacMillan, 1964, pp. 11–12.
10 See my 'Integration, Justice, and Exclusion', in U. Bernitz and Par Hallstrom (eds), *Principles of Justice and the European Union*, Jurist forlaget: Stockholm, 1996, pp. 15–26; and 'Rational, Fair and Reasonable', *Utilitas*, 1996, 263–71.
11 I am very grateful to Veronique Munoz Dardé for her comments on drafts of this paper, and to the participants in the workshop on Law and Political Theory at the Freedom and Trade conference at the University of Manchester: especially Ian Carter and Hillel Steiner for their written comments.

# 8

# THE NEED FOR INTEGRATING TRADE AND COMPETITION RULES IN THE WTO WORLD TRADE AND LEGAL SYSTEM[1]

*Ernst-Ulrich Petersmann*

International state practice has approached international competition problems from at least four different perspectives:

- The *intellectual property law approach*, notably in the 1883 Paris Convention on Protection of Industrial Property, has focused one-sidedly on 'effective protection against unfair competition' (Article 10*bis*) without providing for international antitrust rules to protect freedom of competition and consumer welfare (e.g. against market segmentation by means of patent rights).
- The *competition policy approach* relies essentially on the extraterritorial application of domestic competition laws (notably of the USA and EC) to anticompetitive practices abroad and on legally non-binding multilateral guidelines (e.g. the 1980 UNCTAD Guidelines and 1986 OECD Guidelines) and a few bilateral agreements for the coordination of domestic competition laws. Many national competition laws provide, however, for the exemption of export cartels, import cartels or government-supported restraints of competition; and the divergencies among national competition policies continue to generate international conflicts, e.g. in case of conflicting merger-control policies, or 'blocking statutes' in response to extraterritorial enforcement of US antitrust law.
- The worldwide *trade law approach*, notably in the General Agreement on Tariffs and Trade (GATT) of 1947 and in the 1994 Agreement Establishing the World Trade Organization (WTO), has so far focused on the liberalization of governmental market access barriers and market distortions, including government-supported restrictive business practices such as voluntary export restraints or the granting of 'exclusive or special privileges' to private enterprises (cf. Article XVII of GATT). GATT/WTO law also includes consultation and dispute settlement procedures for

certain trade-restrictive business practices. The more ambitious *integration law approach* in the stillborn 1948 Havana Charter for an International Trade Organization, which combined liberal trade rules with comprehensive competition rules for restrictive business practices, has, however, so far not been implemented on the worldwide level.

- The *regional integration law approach* – notably in EC law, the EC's 'Europe Agreements', in the North American Free Trade Agreement (NAFTA), the Andean Common Market, and in the Australia–New Zealand Economic Cooperation Agreement – integrates trade and competition rules so as to protect international market competition and cross-border transactions against both governmental market access barriers (e.g. in favour of public undertakings and enterprises with privileged positions) and private distortions (e.g. in the case of trade-restricting patent misuse and anticompetitive licensing agreements). Moreover, the states involved also have domestic competition laws protecting the private rights of competitors and enabling parties affected by anticompetitive practices to submit their case to a domestic court for judicial review.

This chapter begins with a brief survey of the development from GATT's trade law approach to a new integration law approach in the context of the WTO (section I). It then discusses the need, as well as some recent proposals, for negotiating additional international competition rules in the WTO (section II). Section III summarizes the main policy conclusions.

## I
## From GATT's trade law approach towards an integration law approach in the WTO?

### *The GATT principles of national sovereignty and 'competition among rules'*

The 'GATT 1947' has provided the legal framework for the successful worldwide liberalization of tariffs and non-tariff barriers from its entry into force in 1948 until its termination by the end of 1995. The rules of GATT, such as the most-favoured-nation treatment (Article I) and national treatment requirements (Article III), primarily aim at the reduction of discriminatory market access barriers for traded products. They do not limit the sovereign freedom of GATT member countries to decide on their domestic policy objectives, and to use non-discriminatory domestic policy instruments (e.g. so as to correct market failures and supply public goods). The legal ranking of discriminatory trade policy instruments in GATT law is largely consistent with the economic and political ranking of trade policy instruments according to their economic efficiency and democratic accountability (cf. Table 8.1). There is, however, no corresponding consensus among economists and governments on the optimal ranking of domestic policy instruments, e.g. for limiting anticompetitive business practices (cf. Table 8.2). GATT/WTO law limits the use of domestic policy instruments by requirements of transparency, non-discrimination and judicial review (cf. e.g. Articles III and X GATT), prohibitions of unnecessarily trade-restrictive product standards, product-related production standards, professional qualifications and licensing requirements (cf. e.g. the WTO Agreements on Technical Barriers to Trade, Sanitary Standards and Trade in Services), and by procedures for the mutual recognition and harmonization of divergent national standards (cf. the WTO Agreements on Technical Barriers and Trade in Services). But these WTO rules leave governments large discretion to experiment with divergent domestic regulatory systems.

*TABLE 8.1* The public choice of trade policy instruments

| *Instruments of import protection* | *Economic ranking (efficiency)* | *Political ranking (parliamentary control)* | *Legal ranking (GATT)* |
|---|---|---|---|
| Border adjustment measures for non-discriminatory internal taxes and regulations | Optimal instrument for correcting *domestic* distortions | Non-discriminatory measures subject to legislation | Allowed (note to Art. III GATT) and not subject to countermeasures |
| Production subsidy | First best (production distortion) | Direct budgetary transfers subject to legislation | Allowed but possibly 'countervailable' and 'actionable' (Arts. VI, XVI:1, XXIII GATT and 1994 Subsidy Code) |
| Import tariff | Second best (production and consumption distortion) | Transparent taxes, goverment revenue and protection rents subject to legislation | Allowed subject to tariff bindings (Arts. II, XXVIII) and safeguard clauses (e.g. Arts. VI, XIX) |
| Import restrictions<br>• global quota<br>• country quotas | Third best (additional distortions of price competition; private protection rents *in lieu* of tariff revenue; legal insecurity) | Less transparent, administrative distribution of market shares and protection rents to importers and foreign exporters | Prohibited subject to GATT's safeguard clauses (e.g. Arts. XI, XII, XVIII–XXI) and non-discrimination requirements (e.g. Arts. XIII, XX) |
| Voluntary export restraints (VER) | Fourth best (additional transfers of quota rents abroad, additional legal insecurity) | Non-transparent transfers of protection rents at home and abroad without parliamentary and judicial control | Prohibited (Art. XIII GATT) with only temporary exceptions (1994 Safeguards and Textiles Agreements) |

*Table 8.2* Illustrative list of anticompetitive business practices regulated by competition policy

**Horizontal restraints** 'Hard core cartels' among firms in an oligopolistic market (e.g. on price fixing, output restrictions, market division, customer allocation, collusive tendering) and other anticompetitive cooperation between firms selling competing products. While 'naked' cartels tend to be prohibited, the anti- and pro-competitive effects of other horizontal cooperation need to be balanced (e.g. based on a 'rule of reason', individual exemptions or group exemptions).

**Vertical restraints** Distribution strategies between manufacturers, suppliers or distributors such as tying (the sale of one good is conditioned on the purchase of another good), exclusive dealing (the seller requires the buyer to purchase products only from the seller), territorial restraints (the seller requires the buyer/distributor to resell the product within a limited geographical area) and resale price maintenance (the seller requires the buyer to resell the product only at a specified price). While resale price fixing tends to be generally prohibited, the pro- and anticompetitive effects of other vertical restraints need to be evaluated (e.g. misuse control).

**Abuses of intellectual property rights** Technology licensing arrangements abusing the monopoly-like position of IPR holders e.g. through non-competition clauses (e.g. 'grantback': the licensee is required to assign inventions made in the course of working the transferred technology back to the licensor) or non-contestation clauses (the licensee is prevented from contesting the validity of the IPR or other rights of the licensor). IPR abuses might be subject to the general competition rules on horizontal and vertical restraints.

**Abuses of market dominance** Dominant firms accounting for a significant market share (e.g. of 40 per cent or more) may attempt to monopolize a market, e.g. through excess prices, price discrimination, predatory low prices, refusal to deal or vertical restraints. Rules against the abuse of a dominant position may be conduct-oriented (e.g. a general prohibition against monopolizing and foreclosure of competition) or result-oriented (e.g. prohibition of predatory pricing only if the losses can be recouped).

**Mergers and acquisition policies** Horizontal, vertical or conglomerate mergers may reduce competition or increase efficiency. Merger policies may be designed to ensure the contestability of markets by preventing a monopoly (price-setting by a single seller), monopsony (price-setting by a single buyer) or oligopolistic market power. But acquisition policies may also be used for industrial policy purposes.

**Public undertakings and enterprises with special privileges** In view of their market power (e.g. financial independence), they may be required to behave according to market principles (Art. XVII GATT, Art. 90 EC). Exclusive trading rights and monopolies may be prohibited (Art. 37 EC).

The border adjustment rules in GATT Article III (as clarified by the interpretative note to Article III) allow a member country to extend non-discriminatory internal product taxes or other product regulations to imported products, for instance so as to prevent or 'internalize' consumption externalities in the importing country (such as health risks and environmental harm). GATT's border adjustment rules also allow a member country to exempt exported goods from such product taxes or product regulations in the exporting country based on the assumption that the exported goods will be subject to the product taxes and product regulations in the importing country ('destination principle').[2] By contrast, GATT's border adjustment rules do not allow a member country to subject imported products to domestic process and production methods (PPMs) if they are not incorporated in the products themselves. This 'country of origin principle', and the resultant 'competition among diverging national production regulations', are likewise consistent with the economic theory of optimal intervention, according to which domestic market failures (such as production externalities) should be addressed directly at the source (i.e. in the country of production). As production factor endowments, environmental absorption capacities and national values differ from country to country, different PPMs in an exporting country are no sufficient justification for trade restrictions in an importing country.

The freedom of each GATT member country to decide on its domestic regulations (Article III) and on the level of its import tariffs (Articles II, XXVIII), and to apply safeguard measures against injurious imports (Articles VI, XIX, XX), enables each country to protect national public goods (such as a 'conservative welfare function' so as to protect import-competing industries against wide-spread unemployment caused by low-priced imports). These GATT rules clearly recognize the right of each country to accord more importance to legitimate national public goods other than liberal trade. But GATT's unconditional most-favoured-nation treatment obligation also requires each country state to respect the equal domestic policy autonomy of other GATT member countries; PPM-based countermeasures discriminating against foreign products are therefore prohibited.

The 'domestic policy autonomy' of GATT and WTO member countries is based on the political and economic assumption that differences between national regulatory systems (e.g. PPMs) may be legitimate for many reasons (such as different production factor and resource endowments, environmental absorption capacities, preferences and opportunity costs). Also national competition laws and policies differ among countries, for instance regarding the use of per-se-prohibitions (e.g. of horizontal cartels and certain vertical restraints), rules-of-reason with rebuttable presumptions (e.g. for abuses of market power), or requirements to balance pro-competitive and anticompetitive effects (e.g. of mergers). The institutional frameworks of national competition laws (e.g. more private law suits before trial courts and fewer administrative investigations in the USA than in the EC), the available legal remedies (e.g. civil claims of 'treble damages' and criminal sanctions in the USA, but not in the EC, in addition to 'cease and desist' orders), and the effective enforcement of the 'law in the books' also vary considerably among jurisdictions. As international 'competition among regulatory systems' may be sub-optimal if there are cross-border externalities or 'international public goods' involved, GATT/WTO law provides for generous safeguard clauses (e.g. in Articles VI, XIX-XXI) enabling governments to protect themselves against dumped, subsidized or otherwise injurious imports.

### *GATT's trade law approach: why GATT's focus on governmental market access barriers was justified*

Two characteristic features of GATT law, and of the successive 'GATT Rounds' of multilateral trade negotiations, have been the priority given to the liberalization of governmental market access barriers, and the progressive extension of the scope of GATT rules not only to all trade policy instruments (i.e. government measures discriminating against imports or exports), but also to internal policy instruments (such as non-discriminatory technical regulations and standards). This GATT approach, and the WTO as a negotiating forum for future negotiations on the reciprocal liberalization of governmental market access barriers, continue to deserve priority for at least two reasons:

1 Government-supported market access barriers appear to be relatively more important than private market access barriers. Hence, the gains from further liberalization of e.g. tariffs, non-tariff border measures, technical regulations and standards, rules of origin, contingent protection like antidumping and countervailing duties, government procurement and subsidies, are likely to be higher than the gains from additional international competition rules for private restraints of competition. There remains a lot of 'unfinished business' regarding the liberalization of these and other governmental market access barriers and distortions.
2 The *political economy* of GATT negotiations (e.g. reciprocity, package deals, most-favoured-nation and national-treatment requirements, GATT dispute settlement and enforcement procedures) has enabled states to overcome 'free-riding' and to achieve certain reforms (e.g. in the liberalization of services trade and the protection of intellectual property rights) that had never been possible in previous sectoral negotiations outside GATT (e.g. in the World Intellectual Property Organization and in the OECD). The GATT/WTO offer a much more favourable negotiating forum for overcoming protectionist resistance against reforms of trade, competition and intellectual property laws than other worldwide international organizations.[3]

### *The new 'WTO approach': integrated market access guarantees for governmental as well as private market access barriers for goods, services, trade-related intellectual property rights and investments*

The WTO differs from the GATT approach by focusing on broader and integrated market access guarantees. Many WTO provisions also deal with private market access barriers, albeit in an imperfect manner. Some WTO provisions envisage the future negotiation of more comprehensive WTO rules on private anticompetitive practices in goods trade, services trade and intellectual property as a necessary complement to the existing WTO law.

This broader WTO approach corresponds better to the globalization of production and markets by making it easier for internationally active enterprises to choose between alternative 'export strategies', 'foreign investment strategies', or 'licensing strategies' based on intellectual property rights. The reduction of governmental distortions of alternative business, trade, investment and licensing strategies is likely to enhance not only economic productivity, consumer welfare and liberty. It also entails that traditionally domestic policy issues (such as taxation, PPMs, competition laws, labour rights, health, safety and environmental regulations) assume growing international importance due to their increasing impact on transnational trade and investment opportunities.

The broader market access guarantees in WTO law increase the international contestability of markets and, thereby, the relative importance of the remaining private market access barriers. This is reflected in a large number of provisions in WTO law explicitly addressing private anticompetitive practices. For instance:

1 The *Agreement on Technical Barriers to Trade* includes detailed rules designed to ensure that the preparation, adoption and application of technical regulations, standards and conformity asessment procedures by non-governmental bodies are not more trade-restrictive than necessary (e.g. Articles 3,4,8).
2 The *Agreement on Preshipment Inspection* prescribes rules for the activities of private preshipment inspection entities (e.g. Article 2).
3 The *Understanding on the Interpretation of Article XVII of GATT 1994* provides for increased surveillance of state-trading enterprises or enterprises with exclusive or special privileges through strengthened notification and review procedures.
4 The *Agreement on Implementation of Article VI* regulates private injurious dumping and price undertakings in more detail, and refers e.g. to 'trade restrictive practices and competition' as relevant factors in the determination of injury (Article 3.5).
5 The *Agreement on Subsidies* also regulates 'market displacement', 'price undercutting' and 'voluntary undertakings' by exporters in more detail (e.g. Articles 6,18), and requires the examination of 'trade restrictive practices and competition' in determinations of 'injury' (Article 15).
6 The *Agreement on Safeguards* prohibits 'voluntary export restraints, orderly marketing arrangements or any other similar measures on the export or the import side', including 'compulsory import cartels ... which afford protection' (Article 11). Member states are required 'not to encourage or support the adoption or maintenance by public and private enterprises' of equivalent non-governmental measures (Article 11:3).
7 The *General Agreement on Trade in Services (GATS)* includes rules designed to ensure that 'monopolies and exclusive service suppliers' (Article

VIII) do not nullify or impair obligations and commitments under the GATS. It also recognizes that other anticompetitive business practices of service suppliers 'may restrain competition and thereby trade in services' (Article IX). Much of what governments are negotiating in the on-going GATS market access negotiations (e.g. on telecommunications) consists of commitments to control monopolistic abuses of dominant market positions by existing services suppliers (e.g. of telephone, telex, fax, video and other postal services, radio, TV and satellite monopolies). Some of the GATS market access commitments therefore amount to an internationalization of competition policy. These 'specific commitments' (cf. Articles XVI of GATS), and the most-favoured-nation and reciprocity requirements of the GATS, also increase the need for developing more general competition rules.

8 The *Agreement on Trade-Related Intellectual Property Rights* (TRIPS) includes 'unfair trade rules' (e.g. in Article 17 on exceptions for the 'fair use' of trademarks, Articles 22–24 on 'misleading' or 'unfair' uses of geographical indications, Article 39 on protection of undisclosed information 'against unfair commercial use') as well as antitrust rules dealing with restraints of competition so as to ensure 'that measures and procedures to enforce intellectual property rights do not themselves become barriers to legitimate trade' (Preamble). The competition rules reflect the general tension between the protection of intellectual property rights as a pre-condition of market competition (e.g. for the allocation, transfer and further development of industrial property, competition between individual rights) and the potential restraints of competition made possible by over-protection of exclusive intellectual property rights (e.g. in case of monopolistic patent misuse). But the TRIPS provisions on the delimitation of 'legitimate trade' and 'abuse of intellectual property rights' (Article 8:2) – notably in Article 8 on 'practices which unreasonably restrain trade or adversely affect the international transfer of technology', Article 31 on patent uses without authorization of the right holder so as 'to correct anticompetitive practices', and Article 40 on anticompetitive licensing practices – are incomplete in many respects (e.g. Article 6 which deliberately does not 'address the issue of the exhaustion of intellectual property rights'). Not only developing countries with less developed national competition and intellectual property rights laws, but also developed countries will need more systematic rules on the protection of competition among trade-related intellectual property rights and on the prevention of their anticompetitive abuse.

9 The *Agreement on Government Procurement* regulates tendering procedures so as to 'ensure optimum effective international competition' and 'equitable opportunities for suppliers or service providers' (e.g. Article X). It also refers to certain competition problems (such as collusive tendering and 'absence of competition', cf. Article XV) and provides for

'procedures enabling suppliers and service providers to challenge alleged breaches of the Agreement arising in the context of procurements in which they have, or have had, an interest' (Article XX).

In addition to this increasing number of WTO provisions regulating private anticompetitive practices, the WTO Agreement also includes several mandates to examine the competition policy aspects of other trade provisions. For instance:

1 Article 9 of the *Agreement on Trade-Related Investment Measures* requires the WTO Council on Trade in Goods to 'review the operation of this Agreement and ... consider whether it should be complemented with provisions on investment policy and competition policy'. This provision was included at the request of less-developed countries to meet their concern that governmental trade-related investment measures may be necessary in order to counter anticompetitive practices of multinational enterprises.
2 Review provisions are also included in other WTO Agreements regulating private anticompetitive practices (e.g. Article 6 of the *Agreement on Preshipment Inspection*) and may provide a basis for future negotiations on additional competition rules.
3 The accession of Russia, China and other former state-trading countries to the WTO has made it evident that – without more effective competition rules for enterprises with 'exclusive or special privileges' (Article XVII of GATT) – many GATT and GATS commitments are easy to circumvent through governmental toleration of dominant market positions and other private anticompetitive practices.
4 The GATS explicitly recognizes 'that certain business practices of services suppliers ... may restrain competition and thereby restrict trade in services' (Article IX). This may lead to future negotiations on 'specific commitments' on the liberalization of such private anticompetitive practices. The various Annexes to the GATS – such as the Annexes on Financial Services, Telecommunications, Air Transport and Maritime Transport Services – set out framework rules for the progressive liberalization of services trade through future negotiations that are likely to succeed only if they liberalize and restrict the numerous monopolies and private anticompetitive practices in these fields (e.g. bilateral market-sharing agreements for air and maritime transports).
5 The TRIPS Agreement explicitly recognizes that 'appropriate measures ... may be needed to prevent the abuse of intellectual property rights by right holders or the resort to practices which unreasonably restrain trade or adversely affect the international transfer of technology' (Article 8:2). Since the significance and legal scope of the TRIPS Agreement may depend on what competition rules member countries will adopt so as to

ensure 'effective protection against unfair competition' (Article 39) and control of 'anticompetitive practices' (Article 40), the negotiation of agreed minimum standards for such competition rules is bound to become an important subject in the implementation of the TRIPS Agreement.

## II

## Recent proposals for additional international competition rules in the WTO[4]

### *Arguments for further integrating trade and competition rules in the WTO*

There are a number of important economic, political and legal arguments why the WTO should follow the example of the 1948 Havana Charter and include more comprehensive substantive and procedural rules on private market access barriers and market distortions into WTO law. For example:

1 From an economic point of view, competition among divergent national rules (including competition laws) can entail sub-optimal results if, as is the case in many countries, export cartels and other mercantilist abuses of market power are permitted to the detriment of other countries and consumers abroad. Unilateral countermeasures, such as the trade retaliation imposed by the USA in response to alleged private market access barriers in Asian countries, further reduce economic welfare. International harmonization of diverging national competition laws based on agreed minimum standards for trans-border cases, and cooperation among competition authorities (e.g. regarding fact-finding abroad and 'positive comity'), can reduce the costs, distortions and conflicts which diverging domestic competition regimes can create for international business and consumers. In the modern global economy, where about a third of all trade in goods takes place within multinational enterprises and the traditional pattern of manufacture in one country and sale in another has been replaced through globally integrated production, trade and investment strategies, the continuing absence of effective competition laws in most countries is likely to distort international trade and competition. Recent empirical studies confirm that restrictive business practices with anticompetitive effects in several countries continue to be widespread and limit the competitive benefits accruing from GATT/WTO law.[5]

2 From a political perspective, it is noteworthy that less than 60 countries, out of today almost 200 sovereign states, have domestic competition laws. Just as governments find it politically easier to liberalize their own trade barriers in the context of reciprocal agreements rather than unilaterally, reciprocal international competition rules can help governments

to overcome the political opposition from import-competing producers against unilateral market-opening measures. Liberal international trade and competition rules can thus serve 'constitutional functions' by limiting both government failures (such as protectionism and the lack of effective competition laws in many countries, exemptions of shipping and air transport cartels) as well as market failures (such as cartels and other abuses of market power). As liberal international trade rules, liberal international competition rules are politically easier to accept as part of reciprocal, multinational 'package deals' (like the Uruguay Round Agreements) with incentives for joining the multilateral legal disciplines (e.g. reciprocal liberalization with obvious benefits for export industries, technical and financial assistance for trade liberalization and competition laws in less developed countries) and disincentives against 'free-riding' (e.g. stricter application of antidumping laws vis-à-vis exporting countries with protected home markets and without effective competition laws).

3 In GATT/WTO law and practice, the market access rules are construed rather strictly as competition rules designed to protect non-discriminatory conditions of competition. For instance, violations of GATT rules with potentially adverse effects on conditions of competition are presumed to cause 'nullification or impairment' of treaty benefits regardless of whether actual trade flows and investments have already been distorted. In view of the successful liberalization of tariffs and other trade policy border measures, it is economically and legally consequent to progressively extend the scope of GATT/WTO law to internal policy instruments and to private market access barriers.[6] Likewise, the progressive extension of WTO market access guarantees for traded goods to the treatment of foreign investors and intellectual property rights calls for WTO legal disciplines on abuses of such rights of foreign companies and of holders of intellectual property.

4 Both GATT law and the GATS explicitly recognize that the competitive benefits from GATT/WTO rules may be 'nullified or impaired' by private market access barriers. In WTO practice, there is an increasing number of complaints (such as the 1995 US and EC complaints concerning access to the Japanese markets for automobiles, automobile parts and mobile telephony) and of GATT/WTO dispute settlement proceedings against private market access barriers. GATT/WTO rules could be made more effective by a systematic recognition of these interrelationships between governmental and private market access barriers in WTO law (e.g. on the model of Article XVII of GATT and Article IX of GATS). This can be achieved more effectively through conduct-oriented, substantive competition rules and enforcement procedures than merely through general result-oriented trade law obligations that the competitive benefits deriving from GATT/WTO law must not be 'nullified or impaired' through private market access barriers.[7]

5 Over the past decades, it has not been possible to overcome many of the 'protectionist biases' of the world trading system through sectoral negotiations, for example among air transport authorities in the International Civil Aviation Organization, among shipping authorities in the International Maritime Organization, among competition authorities within the OECD, or among intellectual property right bureaucracies within the World Intellectual Property Organization (WIPO). Thus, the widespread cartel arrangements in the international agreements on international air and shipping transports, the lack of competition rules in the various WIPO conventions on protection of intellectual property rights, or the widespread exemptions for export and import cartels in domestic competition laws continue to impede and distort the worldwide division of labour. Nor has it been politically possible to reform many of the protectionist biases and abuses of antidumping laws through negotiations among antidumping bureaucracies within GATT. Only comprehensive, reciprocal 'package deal negotiations', such as future 'WTO Rounds', are likely to attract the political support from heads of governments, and from export industries, which is necessary for overcoming the political pressures for protectionist trade, competition and intellectual property rules. The focus of competition law on consumer welfare and efficiency will assist in limiting the arbitrary 'producer bias' of many trade laws (such as antidumping laws), as well as the protectionist abuses of intellectual property rights (such as monopolistic restrictions of 'parallel imports' by patent holders).

6 The WTO Trade Policy Review Mechanism already covers competition policies and intellectual property rights in member countries. Its more systematic use for examining the manifold interface problems of trade and competition policies could contribute to the better promotion of consumer welfare, private rights and economic liberty.[8]

The setting-up of a WTO Committee on Trade and Competition to examine the interrelationships between WTO rules and competition problems, and future negotiations on additional WTO rules on competition policies and private market access barriers, have been suggested as subjects for the future WTO Work Programme. The experience with the WTO Committee on Trade and Environment suggests that such a systematic examination of the interface problems of trade and competition policies can contribute to clarifying the problems and the interpretation of the WTO rules, and can facilitate future negotiations on additional WTO rules. Concerns at 'overloading the WTO' with complex competition rules and related enforcement procedures are not convincing in view of the economic gains and increased legal consistency of a competition-oriented reform of WTO law, focusing on consumer welfare, individual rights and their legal protection through domestic courts and WTO dispute-settlement proceedings.

### *The 1993 Draft International Antitrust Code (DIAC) as a plurilateral trade agreement in terms of Annex 4 of the WTO agreement: an academic blueprint*

The DIAC was elaborated by a private group of academic experts and practitioners and was submitted to GATT and to the press in July 1993.[9] Its authors shared the belief that, even though political consensus on such detailed antitrust provisions may now seem utopian, an ambitious academic model agreement can assist in stimulating worldwide reflection and debate on the need for international competition rules. The proposal to include the international competition rules as a 'Plurilateral Trade Agreement' into WTO law was motivated by the concern that, even if membership in a DIAC may be limited in the beginning, the agreement must take into account the interrelationships between the competition rules and the WTO rules on trade in goods, services, intellectual property rights, surveillance, dispute settlement and enforcement. The basic principles underlying the DIAC are in part similar to those of GATT law:

1 International minimum standards for transborder cases based on the three pillars underlying most modern competition laws: *per se* prohibitions and rules of reasons with rebuttable presumptions for horizontal and vertical restraints of competition (such as cartels and exclusionary distribution strategies); control of mergers; and control of abuses of market power. The minimum standard principle would allow stricter and divergent national competition laws and experimentation, e.g. in the balancing of the costs and benefits of restraints of competition, or regarding exceptions for 'concentrations'.
2 Incorporation of the international rules into domestic laws and their enforcement primarily through domestic competition authorities and courts.
3 National treatment in the sense that domestic competition laws applicable to national antitrust cases must be applied immediately and unconditionally to all interstate antitrust cases within the scope of the DIAC (e.g. no exemption of export cartels from domestic cartel prohibitions).
4 Supervision of the effective enforcement of domestic competition laws by an independent 'International Antitrust Authority' (IAA) entitled to request domestic competition authorities and courts to initiate antitrust investigations ('principle of international procedural initiative').[10]
5 Intergovernmental dispute-settlement proceedings before an 'International Antitrust Panel' between 'injured' and 'injuring countries', or between the IAA and a member country which violates its obligations under the DIAC, according to the WTO dispute-settlement procedures.
6 Integration of the DIAC into the WTO world trade and legal system as a 'Plurilateral Trade Agreement' in the sense of Annex 4 to the WTO Agreement. This would facilitate the progressive extension of the initially limited membership to other WTO member countries, as well as taking into account the many interface problems of trade and competition rules in

the field of goods trade, services trade, intellectual property rights and foreign investments.[11]

### *The 1995 Expert Group Report on 'Competition Policy in the New Trade Order: Strengthening International Cooperation and Rules': A Pragmatic Proposal*

The Report[12] begins with a number of reasons why worldwide trade liberalization and globalization of business call for a strengthening of domestic competition laws, of its effective enforcement, and of cooperation between competition authorities. For instance:

- The lack of national competition laws, or their ineffective enforcement, in more than 100 countries gives rise to market access barriers, concerns over reciprocity, trade conflicts and retaliatory trade sanctions.
- There are more and more competition problems which transcend national boundaries: international cartels, export cartels, restrictive practices in fields which are international by nature (such as air and sea transports), mergers on a worldwide scale, or the abuse of a dominant position on several major markets (e.g. the 1994 Microsoft case).
- The differences and risks of conflicts among domestic competition rules (e.g. in the case of a merger or concerted practice being authorized in one country and prohibited in another) generate uncertainty and transaction costs.
- The unilateral extra-territorial enforcement of US antitrust laws and trade laws vis-à-vis foreign anticompetitive practices leads to international conflicts (e.g. over jurisdiction, unilateral sanctions and counter-measures) and to practical enforcement problems (e.g. in case of information gathering abroad and foreign 'blocking legislation').
- Developing countries in particular risk being subject to anticompetitive practices (e.g. use of intellectual property rights for limiting domestic competition) and extraterritorial application of other countries' competition laws.

WTO law should therefore deal more systematically with the acknowledged risk that GATT and GATS commitments may be undermined by private anticompetitive practices. The integration of trade and competition rules in EC law, and the acceptance of the EC competition law principles by more than 25 European countries, offer important lessons for overcoming the limits to present international cooperation in the field of competition. These lessons are, in part, similar to those with the integrated trade and competition rules in the regional free trade area agreements between Australia and New Zealand, as well as within the North American Free Trade Area.[13] For instance:

- EC competition rules coexist with national competition rules in all EC member states and are applied through intense cooperation between EC and national competition authorities (e.g. exchange of confidential information, agreed allocation of jurisdiction to initiate and carry out investigations, cooperation within the Advisory Committees on Restrictive Practices, Dominant Positions and Merger Control) and through application of EC competition law by EC and national courts.
- The Agreement on the European Economic Area (EEA) and the EC's cooperation agreements with Central and East European countries, as well as with Russia and the Ukraine, include both substantive competition rules and procedures for cooperation between competition authorities. The EC intends to include similar competition rules and procedures into the 'new generation' of association agreements with Mediterranean countries. These arrangements (e.g. on substantive minimum standards, information exchange and cooperation between competition authorities) could serve as a model for additional cooperation agreements with countries outside Europe.
- The notification, cooperation and coordination requirements, notably regarding 'positive comity' (Article V) and 'negative comity' (Article VI), in the 1991/1995 EC–US Agreement on cooperation in the field of competition policy could serve as a model for similar agreements with other countries outside Europe (cf. the draft agreement EC–Canada). Yet, the number, contents and actual application of bilateral antitrust cooperation agreements and bilateral legal assistance agreements remain limited. For instance, there are no effective procedures for the settlement of disputes over private anticompetitive practices. The 1986 OECD Recommendations on cooperation between member countries on restrictive business practices affecting international trade are widely regarded as inadequate.

The Report makes a number of recommendations for improving international cooperation on, and enforcement of, competition rules through a Plurilateral Agreement on Competition and Trade (PACT):

1 A worldwide competition code, providing also for an international competition authority responsible for its implementation, is no politically realistic short- or medium-term option. Bilateral cooperation remains essential for detecting and limiting restrictive practices with transnational effects, and for preventing or settling conflicts resulting from the extraterritorial enforcement of national competition laws. Both the 'negative comity' and 'positive comity' mechanisms can contribute to a more effective enforcement of competition rules and should be strengthened and extended to other countries (e.g. Japan). Yet, bilateral agreements cannot replace the need for multilateral substantive

minimum competition rules and dispute-settlement procedures so as to contain the risks of commercial frictions and economic distortions resulting from the absence, ineffectiveness or heterogeneity of national competition rules.

2 The proposed PACT should be open to all countries and, in its initial phase, should include at least the OECD countries, the Central and East European countries, as well as major trading countries in Asia. It could have the legal status of a 'plurilateral agreement' in terms of Annex 4 to the WTO Agreement so as to make the trade and competition rules, notably their interpretation and judicial enforcement, mutually supportive. It should be based on three sets of rules:

a) Procedural notification, cooperation, 'negative comity' and 'positive comity' obligations, as recognized e.g. in the EC–USA agreement, which could be multilateralized and possibly extended (e.g. by enabling the exchange of confidential information and by strengthening the positive comity obligations).
b) A limited number of substantive minimum principles for cross-border cases to be incorporated into the national laws of member countries in much the same way as EC Directives (i.e. obligations to achieve a certain result, without need for amending existing legislation if it already contains these principles or is open to similar interpretation). The common principles could include a prohibition of horizontal cartels relating to the fixing of prices, restriction of supply or the sharing of markets, including a prohibition of export cartels. 'Rules of reason' could be provided for other types of cooperation agreements and vertical restraints, on whose pro- and anticompetitive effects opinions may differ depending on the circumstances; one solution might be to prohibit agreements where their restrictive effect on competition is not offset by an advantage for the consumer and/or where they constitute a barrier to market access. As regards abusive behaviour of enterprises in a dominant position, a rule similar to Article 86 of the EC Treaty could be appropriate. In the field of mergers, priority should be given to a harmonization of procedures so as to give competition authorities sufficient time to consult each other. GATT Article XVII on state-trading enterprises should be strengthened by subjecting monopolies and companies with 'exclusive or special privileges' to the same competition rules as other commercial enterprises. In addition, the complementarity of trade and competition policies could be enhanced by inclusion of a provision by which the 'nullification or impairment' – through private practices – of market access commitments under WTO law would be actionable, unless appropriate corrective measures are taken by the country concerned.

c) An international institutional structure should be entrusted with three functions:

- to serve as a forum for analysing, reviewing and in future, possibly, adapting and extending the common principles, covering all aspects of the relationships between competition and trade;
- to establish a 'register of anticompetitive practices' within the contracting parties to the agreement; and
- to provide effective international dispute settlement and enforcement procedures for disputes among member countries over the international procedural obligations, *per-se* prohibitions, rules-of-reason, as well as disputes over 'nullification or impairment' of market access as a result of anticompetitive practices.

### *The 1996 EC initiative for the establishment of a WTO committee on trade and competition*

In June 1996, EC Commissioners Sir Leon Brittan and Karel van Miert submitted a joint communication to the EC Council suggesting an EC initiative for the establishment, by the WTO Ministerial Conference in December 1996, of a 'Working Party to conduct exploratory work, from 1997 onwards, on the development of an international framework of competition rules' for anticompetitive practices with an international dimension, as well as for co-operation among competition authorities (e.g. for obtaining relevant information outside their national jurisdiction).[14] The proposals, which build on the EC Expert Group Report of 1995, were endorsed by the EC Council in July 1996 and were subsequently presented to WTO member countries as a 'non-paper' for the preparation of the Singapore Ministerial Conference.

The 1996 EC Communication mentions four reasons why the adoption of international rules on competition should be considered:

- As part of the EC's strategy on market access, multilateral competition rules would promote more equal conditions of competition world-wide and enable EC firms to tackle anticompetitive practices with an international dimension more effectively.
- A gradual convergence of competition laws could also contribute to avoiding conflicts of law, jurisdiction and remedies in the extraterritorial application of national competition and trade laws to international mergers, strategic alliances, joint ventures, licensing agreements and other anticompetitive practices[15]; this would increase the legal security of firms operating in different jurisdictions, and reduce their costs of compliance with competition laws.
- The effectiveness and coherence of the EC's own competition policy enforcement could be enhanced by overcoming the so-far inward-looking nature of EC competition law, which applies to conduct implemented

within the EC and affecting trade between EC member states, and by enabling the EC to deal also with the external dimensions of its competition policy (such as export cartels).

- Enhanced commitment to competition policy enforcement would also strengthen the trading system by protecting market access opportunities against anticompetitive business practices impeding market access (such as cartels combined with boycotts, exclusionary abuse of a dominant position, exclusionary vertical restraints) or distorting competition (e.g. in case of 'monopolizing dumping' made possible by cartelization in the home market of the exporting country).

Among the four possible fora for negotiating international competition rules (i.e. the OECD, UNCTAD, the WTO or the negotiation of a separate standalone agreement), the EC favours the WTO in view of its quasi-universal membership, its track record of dealing with binding commitments and dispute settlement, and the WTO disciplines on competition-related measures (such as subsidies, public or privileged enterprises, intellectual property, government procurement). An international framework of rules on competition should be built progressively, beginning with:

- The creation of a WTO Working Group open to all interested member countries, without hindering the ongoing work on trade and competition in OECD and UNCTAD.
- Adoption of domestic competition structures: all WTO members should commit themselves to having basic competition rules in domestic laws (covering restrictive agreements of companies, abuse of a dominant position, and mergers); having or creating domestic enforcement structures to guarantee an effective implementation of those competition rules (including proper investigatory instruments and appropriate sanctions); and ensuring access for private parties to the domestic enforcement authorities and courts on equitable, transparent and non-discriminatory terms.
- Identification and progressive adoption, beginning with a limited number of developed and advanced developing countries, of a core of common substantive international principles and rules (e.g. on horizontal restraints such as price or output fixing, market-sharing cartels, bid-rigging, group boycotts, export cartels).
- Development of international procedures on notification, information exchange, national treatment and cooperation between competition authorities, including 'negative comity' obligations (i.e. to take into account the important interests of another country before unilateral action is taken) and 'positive comity' obligations (i.e. to consider requests from another country to investigate, on the basis of the competition laws of the requested country, anticompetitive activities which adversely affect important interests of the requesting country).

- Application of the WTO dispute settlement mechanisms to disputes over the international competition rules and procedures, in addition to guarantees for the private parties affected by anticompetitive practices of access to domestic courts and judicial review.

In the informal preparations of the WTO Ministerial Conference in 1996, most developing countries seemed to support the EC initiative since they would be beneficiaries of enhanced control over anticompetitive practices with an international dimension and of the acceptance by developed countries of most-favoured-nation obligations in the competition field. Some less developed exporting countries however, took issue with the EC view that – following the example of EC law where antidumping actions were excluded only within the EC common market and within the 'European Economic Area', but not in the context of the EC's free trade area and customs union agreements with Eastern and Southern European countries – the development of the new competition policy instruments should only complement, not supplant, the present antidumping instruments. Yet, the EC communication itself admits 'that the incorporation of competition provisions into trade law, and/or more comprehensive and effective enforcement of competition policies through increased international cooperation, would lessen the need to have recourse to instruments of commercial defence.'[16] In view of the many inconsistencies between the 'producer bias' of antidumping laws and the focus on consumer welfare in competition laws, all governments should be interested in using competition policy principles for curtailing the widespread protectionist abuses of antidumping laws.[17]

## III

## Main Policy Conclusion: Linking Negotiations on Competition, Investment, Environmental and Antidumping Rules in the Next WTO Round

The preceding analysis leads to the conclusion that there is a clear need for more systematic and more effective WTO rules on private restraints of competition. Just as multilateral competition rules have been of fundamental importance for promoting undistorted competition in European integration, and have prompted all EC member countries to enact supplementary national competition laws, the time has come for supplementing and reforming WTO law through multilateral competition rules. The emphasis of competition laws on consumer welfare, individual freedom, and protection of private rights through national courts as the main enforcement mechanisms, reflects similar trends in other areas of WTO law (such as the focus of the TRIPS Agreement on private rights and judicial protection); it illustrates the potential systemic gains from introducing competition policy values into other areas of WTO law, such as the need to limit the 'producer bias' of many WTO rules (notably in antidumping law) and to reduce the strain on the intergovernmental WTO dispute-settlement procedures by enabling citizens to defend their private rights before national courts.

Also the existing 'protectionist biases' in competition laws (such as exemptions for export and import cartels) – and the inadequate competition rules in the GATS (e.g. for monopolistic service suppliers), in intellectual property conventions (e.g. for patent misuse) and in the national laws of many less developed countries – are politically and legally easier to overcome by negotiating additional competition rules in the GATT/WTO legal framework than through unilateral reforms. The WTO Ministerial Conference in December 1996 at Singapore should, *inter alia*, establish a WTO Committe on Trade and Competition with the task of identifying interface problems of governmental and private market access barriers and distortions. On the basis of such preparatory work and 'consensus-building', a future 'WTO Round' should include negotiations on supplementing the existing GATT, GATS, TRIPS and TRIMS disciplines by additional competition rules against trade-related private market access barriers and distortions.

As worldwide consensus among WTO member countries on worldwide competition rules will be difficult to achieve, the efforts at negotiating worldwide minimum standards for competition rules should be supplemented by the negotiation of a more limited 'Plurilateral Agreement on Trade and Competition', in terms of Annex 4 to the WTO Agreement, with more ambitious substantive and procedural minimum standards for domestic competition laws and policies regarding trade-related private market access barriers and market distortions. The scope and membership of such a PACT among interested WTO member countries could be progressively extended over time.

The mere continuation of the traditional GATT pragmatism vis-à-vis anticompetitive business practices – such as GATT consultations and WTO dispute-settlement proceedings against government support for private market access barriers (e.g. in the case of the 1996 US complaints against Japanese restraints on the sale of Kodak films), negotiation of specific sectoral competition rules (e.g. as part of the GATS commitments for telecommunication services) or of country-specific competition rules (e.g. in the WTO Protocols of Accession for former state-trading countries), the unilateral extra-territorial application of divergent domestic competition laws, or the conclusion of bilateral or multilateral international agreements on cooperation between competition authorities outside the WTO – appears sub-optimal in view of the apparent inadequacies of the existing GATT/WTO rules and procedures on trade-related competition policy problems and private anticompetitive practices.

The various proposals for additional WTO rules on competition, investment, environmental, social and labour standards are different aspects of a general 'integration problem' which has long been discussed in the context of European integration: To what extent do the regulatory differences among national legal and economic systems reflect 'market failures' or 'government failures'? Are there objective standards for defining and limiting such failures through international rules? Economic theory suggests that 'competition among rules' may lead to sub-optimal results in cases of transnational 'external effects' and 'international public goods'. But these imperfections of 'regulatory competition' must be weighed against the risks of intergovernmental harmonization and of government failures. Notwithstanding the worldwide trend toward liberalization, deregulation and privatization, the views among governments on national and international competition, investment, environmental, social and labour standards continue to differ widely. The existing WTO principles – such as prohibitions of discriminatory or 'unnecessarily trade-restrictive measures', mutual recognition of divergent but equivalent national regulations, consultation and dispute-settlement procedures, or the harmonization of national rules among a limited number of interested countries – offer enough flexibility for the progressive negotiation of international disciplines in the WTO for the more effective protection of international public goods (such as liberal trade and undistorted competition) and the limitation of transnational market failures (such as anticompetitive business practices with an international dimension).

## Notes

1 This contribution builds on a longer article published in the *Journal of World Trade*, June 1996, pp. 5–35.

2 On GATT's border adjustment rules see notably F. Roessler, 'Diverging Domestic Policies and Multilateral Trade Integration', in J.N. Bhagwati and R.E. Hudec (eds), *Fair Trade and Harmonization: Prerequisites for Free Trade?*, Vol. II, 1996, p. 21 ff, who rightly notes that GATT's border adjustment rules leave four options: to exempt e.g. taxes on products exported from country A to B (taxation in the country of destination); to tax exported goods in the country of exportation and exempt them from taxation in the country of importation; double taxation in the countries of exportation and importation; tax exemptions in both the countries of exportation and importation.

3 For an explanation of this argument, and a detailed analysis of the Uruguay Round negotiations from the point of view of 'public choice' and negotiation theories, see E.-U. Petersmann, 'The Transformation of the World Trading System through the 1994 Agreement Establishing the World Trade Organization', in *European Journal of International Law*, 1995, 161–221.

4 For earlier proposals and comparative legal aspects see e.g. H.Hauser and E.-U.Petersmann (eds), 'International Competition Rules in the GATT/WTO System', in Special Issue of the Swiss Review of International Economic Relations (Aussenwirtschaft) 1994, 169–424.

5 Cf. e.g. UNCTAD document TD/RBP/CONF.4/6 of 4 September 1995 on 'Restrictive business practices that have an effect in more than one country'.

6 On the need to introduce a broader concept of market access, embracing trade, investment and competition policy domains, see, *Market Access after the Uruguay Round*, OECD, 1996.

7 Article 46:1 of the 1948 Havana Charter for an International Trade Organization already required that '[e]ach member shall take appropriate measures and shall cooperate with the Organization to prevent, on the part of private or public commercial enterprises, business practices affecting international trade which restrain competition, limit access to markets, or foster monopolistic control, whenever such practices have harmful effects on the expansion of production or trade and interfere with the achievement of any of the other objectives set forth in Article 1.' This general obligation was then illustrated by a list of such restrictive business practices, which left it to both the ITO and individual member states to further specify the contents of the general obligation on a case-by-case basis.

8 On the function of markets to promote individual freedom (including substantive opportunities to choose, decisional autonomy and immunity from encroachments) see e.g. A.Sen, 'Markets and Freedoms: Achievements and Limitations of the Market Mechanism in Promoting Individual Freedoms', in *Oxford Economic Papers*, 1993, 519–41.

9 The private 'International Antitrust Code Working Group' was composed of J.Drexl, W. Fikentscher, E.M. Fox, A. Fuchs, A. Heinemann, U. Immenga, H.P. Kunz-Hallstein, E.-U. Petersmann, W.R. Schluep, A. Shoda, S.J. Soltysinski and L.A. Sullivan. The text, introductory explanation and detailed comments on this Code are published e.g. in, *World Trade Materials*, September 1995, 126–196; *BNA Antitrust and Trade Regulation Report*, Vol. 64 Special Supplement No.1628 of 19 August 1993; Hauser and Petersmann (above note 4), 310–25; W. Fikentscher and U. Immenga (eds), *Draft International Antitrust Code*, 1995.

10 The establishment of such an International Antitrust Authority is one of the major differences between the DIAC and the recommendations of the EC Expert Group Report, which 'does not consider this a realistic short or medium-term option' (p.18). The establishment of an 'International Competition Policy Office' within the WTO, albeit with fewer powers, is also proposed by F.M. Scherer, *Competition Policies for an Integrated World Economy*, Brookings Institute, Washington, DC, 1994.

11 For a critical discussion of the DIAC see e.g. the contributions by Fikentscher, Petersmann and B.J. Philips to Hauser and Petersmann (note 4).

12 Mandated and published by the EC Commission: *Competition Policy in the New Trade Order: Strengthening International Cooperation and Rules, European Commission*, 1995. The Expert Group was composed of three external experts (U. Immenga, F. Jenny, E.-U. Petersmann) and six EC Commission officials acting in a personal capacity (C.D. Ehlermann, J.F. Pons, R. Abbott, F. Lamoureux, J.F. Marchipont, A. Jacquemin). See also E.-U. Petersmann, 'The International Competition Policy of the EC and the Need for an EC Initiative for a "Plurilateral Agreement on Competition and Trade"', in F. Snyder (ed.), *Constitutional Dimensions of European Integration*, 1996, 289–336.

13 For a comparative survey of international agreements containing competition rules see, E.-U. Petersmann, *Competition Elements in International Instruments*, OECD, 1994.

14 'Towards an International Framework of Competition Rules', communication submitted by Sir Leon Brittan and Karel van Miert, EC, 1996, p. 14.

15 For instance, US attempts to enforce US antitrust law outside the US jurisdiction led Canada, France, Germany, the United Kingdom, the Netherlands and Switzerland to adopt 'blocking legislation'. Section 301 of the 1974 US Trade Act also allows trade sanctions to counter the toleration by foreign governments of anticompetitive practices.

16 See above *Competition Policy in the New Trade Order* (note 12), p. 13.

17 Cf. E.-U. Petersmann (note 1), pp. 28–35.

# COMMENTARY ON WOLFF AND PETERSMANN

*Ian Carter*

In this comment I shall look at some of the reasons to be found in the chapters by Petersmann and Wolff for and against economic competition. I shall first analyse these reasons in the abstract and then briefly compare the positions of the two authors on the ethics of competition in a global context.

It seems to me that the various reasons for valuing competition set out in Wolff's chapter (see in particular the seven 'ways of viewing competition' listed near the beginning of his section III) can be usefully categorized in the following way: competition can be valued either *in itself* (that is, intrinsically – e.g. where joggers get pleasure from running in company rather than alone), because it is a *constitutive part* of a certain good (e.g. chess or football), or because it has good *consequences* (that is, instrumentally). The first two types of reason, each of which assigns a particularly strong kind of value to competition, correspond to Wolff's reasons 3 and 4 respectively, and, as Wolff says, are not normally appealed to in arguments for economic competition. The third type of reason (competition's instrumental value) can be separated into four sub-types, which correspond to Wolff's reasons 2, 5, 6 and 7. Recall that in Wolff's terms, 2 means 'weighted lottery', 5 means 'activity enhancement', 6 means 'side-effect of award' and 7 means 'side-effect of activity'. Wolff's reason 1 ('pure lottery') is in my view just a variant on reason 2, where luck, rather than some particular characteristic of the winner, is the relevant criterion for the fair allocation of the 'award'. An analysis of competition's intrinsic and instrumental value is set out in the table below. For simplicity's sake, the table leaves out the case of competition having 'constitutive' value (Wolff's reason 4).

| | *Competition* | *The activity promoted by competition* | *The distribution of resources resulting from competition* |
|---|---|---|---|
| Is a good/bad thing in itself | 3 | 5 | 2 |
| Has beneficial/damaging consequences | 5 2<br>7 6 | 7 | 6 |

For each of Wolff's reasons 2–7, there is a conceivable counterpart reason against competition. (This fact is reflected in the wording on the left-hand side of the table.) However, the reasons put forward against economic competition, like those in favour of it, tend to be of the instrumental kind. I interpret Wolff's own anticompetition argument as appealing to an anti-reason of type 2, since it is Wolff's view that pro-competition reasons of type 7 can under certain circumstances imply an immoral extraction of some good from one person (or group) on the part of another (i.e., a form of exploitation). J.S. Mill's anticompetition argument (cited by Wolff) uses an anti-reason of type 6, since he sees the allocation of the relevant rewards as the cause of 'envy, hatred and all uncharitableness'. An example of an anti-reason of type 5 is the claim that it is wrong to work on the sabbath.[1] And an anti-reason of type 7 is to be found in the objections to global free trade put forward by conservatives like John Gray, to the effect that it will have damaging effects on 'the stability of families and communities', and will bring about an 'impoverishing cultural homogeneity'.[2]

The refutation of such anticompetition arguments is obviously not the aim of Petersmann's chapter. However, we can infer from the nature of his concerns that he considers the above anticompetition reasons as carrying little weight when compared to the pro-competition reasons of type 7 mentioned at various points in his chapter. The values motivating Petersmann's discussion – the ends which he sees the promotion of competition as serving – are, above all, 'economic welfare', which he usually qualifies as meaning *consumer* welfare, and 'economic liberty'. Wolff does not dispute the existence of these benefits. Indeed, he explicitly recognizes the importance of the argument from welfare, and although he suggests that a general appeal to liberty is inconclusive (end of section I), he might at least accept that competition benefits *consumers* in terms of their 'freedom of choice'.

How different are the overall positions of Wolff and Petersmann on the value of competition? On the face of it, they are strongly at odds with one another. Wolff's main concern is with the exploitation of labour, whereas Petersmann concentrates on the 'goods and services' market, and only mentions labour in passing at the end of his chapter; Petersmann champions the consumer, whereas Wolff argues that consumers exploit producers (in particular, that consumers in developed countries exploit those producers who are labourers in developing countries); Petersmann's approach appears to be what John Rawls would call 'teleological',[3] in that it concentrates on maximizing or at least increasing the beneficial consequences of competition for global society as a whole rather than looking at its effects on particular individuals, whereas Wolff's approach incorporates a 'weak equity axiom' which is apparently intended to imply transfers of resources from developed to developing countries even where this does not maximize the overall beneficial effects of competition.

Does Petersmann then advocate what Wolff would call exploitation? In my view, such an account over-states the differences between them. For one thing, the force of Wolff's critique of the pro-competition stance of free marketeers is considerably weakened by his admittal that 'the utilitarian case in favour [of economic competition] is overwhelming' – an admittal which might well imply giving the same weight to the teleological point of view as Petersmann accords it. Furthermore, where Petersmann does mention labour it is in order to give due space to 'proposals for additional WTO rules on ... social and labour standards' (section III). If implemented uniformly at a global level, such labour standards might in theory have the same (weak) egalitarian consequences as those desired by Wolff. It is also worth looking more closely at Wolff's 'weak equity axiom'. The global application of this axiom lets the rich consumer off the hook as far as the accusation of Wolffian exploitation is concerned, since, Wolff says, it shows that that consumer is no longer *indifferent* to the plight of the poor labourer. But does the axiom necessarily prescribe a change in the present trading practices and distribution of resources between developed and developing countries? It does not. The current international trading practices of rich consumers and poor labourers will be compatible with the weak equity axiom as long as the poor labourers do not become even poorer than at present as a result of the continuation of those practices. In this sense, the analogy with competitive games can be misleading: economic competition does not necessarily have 'losers', in the way that games of chess usually do, and one can easily be expoited in Wolff's sense without 'going to the wall'. In practical terms, Wolffian exploitation may turn out to be no more than an attitude problem.

Notice that it is not necessary for liberals to appeal to any of the anticompetition reasons mentioned above in order to resist the teleological defence of competition on which we have seen Petersmann and Wolff converge. For it might be that pro-competition reasons simply get 'trumped' by property rights. At certain points, Petersmann adds 'individual rights' to the list of goods that he sees additional WTO competition rules as promoting. However, unlike strictly rights-based liberals, there are times when he appears to see such individual rights as merely instrumental to the promotion of competition. 'Abuses of market power' (e.g. horizontal and vertical restraints) are to be restricted in the name of competition, and while the 'protection of intellectual property rights' is 'a pre-condition of market competition', the 'over-protection of exclusive intellectual property rights' hampers it, and is therefore to be avoided (section 8 p. 105). Presumably, Wolff would agree that such property rights need to be limited, given the 'overwhelming' utilitarian case for doing so. But it is important to remember that for rights-based liberals in the strict sense, be they Nozickian or redistributionist,[4] respect for property rights is a value to which all social goals, including competition, must be subordinated. The kind of exploitation focused on by Wolff is not the only reason a 'Kantian' might have for opposing the active promotion of competition.

My conclusion is twofold. First, the differences between Wolff and Petersmann on the ethics of international competition are, as they stand, less significant than might at first appear. Second, the egalitarian and the rights-theorist might criticize Wolff and Petersmann respectively for going too far down the utilitarian road. Bringing in more elements from either egalitarianism or rights-theory will imply greater limits on competition than those sanctioned by either of our two authors.

## Notes

1 This is of course not to say that this paternalist reason is the only reason that may be given for outlawing trading on the sabbath.

2 John Gray, *Enlightenment's Wake: Politics and Culture at the Close of the Modern Age*, London: Routledge, 1993, pp. 103 and 181 respectively.

3 John Rawls, *A Theory of Justice*, Cambridge: Harvard University Press, p. 24.

4 Cf. Robert Nozick, *Anarchy, State and Utopia*, New York: Basic Books, 1974. An example of 'redistributionist' rights-based liberalism is to be found in Hillel Steiner's *An Essay on Rights*, Oxford: Blackwell, 1995.

# 9

# TRANSNATIONAL AND INTERNATIONAL EXPLOITATION[1]

*Avner de-Shalit*

Theorists of exploitation have been focusing on exploitation within the state. But in common speech we all talk about the North exploiting the South, the USA exploiting Mexico, Germany exploiting illegal foreign workers, and so on. This question of international exploitation is often raised when free trade is discussed. There is a widespread belief that international exploitation is impossible – even inconceivable – in circumstances of free trade. For example, the Maastricht agreement from 7 February 1992 guarantees free movement of 'persons, services and capital'.[2] Many people believe that if you have the latter – free movement of services (goods) and capital – you have the former – free movement of persons, which is, they claim, the antithesis of exploitation, especially when this is accompanied by agreements which guarantee that every worker is entitled to social rights wherever he or she works. This, they claim, prevents exploitation. Others, however, find it significant that persons are mentioned with and treated like capital. These people argue that until such an attitude is uprooted there will always be exploitation. So in this chapter I wish to apply the current theories of exploitation to the international domain, although prima facie it would appear as if this cannot be done. But first let me review four types of international exploitation.

The first is exploitation between states. In common parlance, this implies that there are cases in which one state benefits from another state's production without a proper return. However, while this cannot be the definition of international exploitation because it may relate to a very good deal which one state makes with the other, it also points to a difficulty with the traditional understanding of exploitation, since this beneficiary's advantage is not always purely economic and does not necessarily derive from enjoying surplus value.

Often this sort of exploitation is related to a state of occupation, which involves two or more nations rather than states. The exploited party's access to land is perhaps not prohibited by law, but is de facto limited, with the effect that the occupied lose their most basic property, namely land. Since it is generally argued that the exercise of exploitation happens when the exploiter takes advantage of the fact that the exploited party has no property, it immediately seems that relations of occupation are relations of exploitation.

However, states can exploit each other without there being occupation. There are cases in which state A finds ways to keep state B poor, so that state B has no purchasing power. The latter then becomes dependent on the former to buy what it produces. It then produces what people in state A are likely to buy, thereby losing its own culture and autonomy. Some people would doubt that this is exploitation at all, so I shall return to this question below.

In all cases of exploitation between states there is either military or economic superiority which allows the exploiting state to explicitly or implicitly threaten to intervene, deprive of benefits, etc. For example, in the USA there are several funds which help finance scientific research in other countries that could have not been conducted without this financial aid. In return the knowledge that is created in these countries becomes common to these countries and the USA. Sometimes this knowledge has to do with security or special industries, and this limits these states' autonomy.

A second sort of exploitation is within one state, but the beneficiaries are mainly people from another state. This type of exploitation is based on an unwritten understanding between capitalists from two or more countries. So when in state A the capitalist is prevented from exploiting the working class for different reasons (it is counterproductive or considered unjust), he or she acquires the fruits of exploitation in other countries. Thus many firms create 'paper-corporations' in other, less affluent, countries to enjoy the fruits of cheap labour or to avoid taxation. Also sometimes natural resources which have been supplied by exploited workers are imported to become raw materials for manufacture. A good example is coffee which is grown and picked mostly by exploited workers in the Third World and is processed in the northern world by firms that are thought to be 'clean' of exploitation.

The third type is the exploitation of illegal foreign workers. These are people who for economic reasons – lack of jobs in their own country or big families who need more income – are forced to emigrate to another country and find a job there. They often do the jobs which the local people are not ready to and can afford not to do (because they will benefit from social security). It is interesting to note that very often it is more convenient for the elites in the countries from which these people emigrate to encourage them to go than to re-distribute power, access to work, or pay unemployment benefit. It is cheaper in both economic and political terms for these regimes to – so to speak – lose these people. So although this exploitation has international aspects, it is often not protested against by the governments of the exploited people.

The fourth type of exploitation happens in similar circumstances, but the exploiting side consists of individuals rather than the state. In addition, these cases include those in which the poorer state does not benefit from its citizens leaving to seek jobs in other places. Since human labour is capital rather than income, when it travels from state A to state B and benefits economy B, the latter is using the capital of A. For example, these people may be skilled workers who have acquired their skills in state A but are now using these skills in B without state B returning anything to A. Of course the demands of free trade would imply that goods and capital (including human beings) can travel freely, but the issue becomes more complicated because the theory of free trade assumes that the interests of free trade are superior to any other interests in this context. In reality, though, selfish interests of the states (in our example state B) override the interests of genuine cooperation. Nationality and national interests do not disappear at the moment free trade is introduced. Thus at least prima facie free trade may lead to this kind of exploitation.

Let us now move on to discuss the main theories of exploitation and how they relate to these cases. In the Marxian school of thought exploitation is related to surplus value, when the workers are at the 'short end of an unequal distribution of means of production'. They are constrained by their lack of property to sell their labour power to capitalists, who own and control the means of production. The capitalist buys labour power, pays the amount needed to make an employee work, but gets the employee's actual work which is worth more. This is the surplus value, which is where the exploitation lies.[3]

As for the liberal theory,[4] exploitation is a bilateral transfer in a situation which involves three or more parties. A exploits B when A and B voluntarily exchange unequally valued goods, due to the fact that C's rights are violated. In other words, when A gets 5X, B gets 3X voluntarily, and yet would rather get 5X as well. B transfers this surplus as a result of the circumstances in which this transfer takes place. A violates the rights of C (by, for example, forcibly preventing C from offering more to B) and thus B has no other option if she still wants to sell her goods but to sell to A for less than she could have received in other circumstances. The reason Steiner claims that C's rights were violated is that A acted as if she possessed the title to C's 5X. So many cases of monopoly or of a violation of free trade would become exploitative. Notice, then, that free trade is the circumstance of exploitation according to the Marxian thesis and the guarantee for lack of exploitation under the liberal one. But as I shall show below, the two theories have more in common than it first seems.

It seems to me, however, that these theories are inadequate to describe international exploitation. Steiner's theory entails the existence of three parties, whereas in many cases of international exploitation there are only two parties. State A occupies nation B and by issuing military threats it forces B to trade with A on the latter's terms. A does not have to violate the rights of a third state in order to prevent B from trading with the other party. It should be noted that institutions which may prevent such exploitation in circumstances within the state – e.g. police and the court – are absent, or lack any real authority in the international domain.[5]

The Marxian theory as it stands now is equally inadequate to describe and explain international exploitation. First, according to this school of thought, the reason surplus labour can be extracted from the worker is his or her lack of access to the means of production.[6] The reason that the worker lacks this access is economic and social: the class structure of society. But in the context of international affairs the reason may be extra-economic coercion, such as military occupation or any other threat. Indeed the extra-economic significance of international exploitation is revealed in another aspect of exploitation. According to the Marxian theory the capitalist hires several workers simultaneously, and capitalizes on the fact that there is no proper communication between the workers. Since the workers negotiate individually with their employer they end up getting less than they could have, had they had proper communication among themselves. But outside a single nation context this has political (not necessarily economic) implications as well, because this kind of multi-contract 'agreement' prevents the development and emergence of communication among the members of the exploited group, which is often a nation or an ethnic group. It thereby reduces the chances of a substantial national deliberation. Preventing the exploited ones from organizing themselves by having monopoly on organizational power, opportunities and means of communication, has far-reaching significance: it may prevent the group from discussing its self-identity and developing its national self-determination. Therefore it seems that the Marxian theory is limited since it is restricted to the *economic* aspects of exploitation.

The terminology of the Marxian theory reveals that what is beyond economics does not count. For example, Roemer writes:

> If S were to withdraw from the society, endowed with its per capita share of society's alienable property (that is, produced and non-produced goods), and with its own labour and skills, then S would be better off (in terms of income and leisure) than it is at the present allocation.[7]

Consider now a possible case of a nation under occupation. Those who work in the occupying state may do well economically speaking. It might be that they could have done better, but comparing their individual material well-being they are all better off than before the occupation. So had they withdrawn from the economy of the occupying party they would not necessarily become better off even if they were endowed with their share of property. And yet, it seems to me that they are exploited. The reason is that we should think of this situation in terms which reach beyond economics. The point is that these people are being exploited because this arrangement has been forced on them. An example can be a case when nation A occupies nation B and offers B a good sum of money (in terms of salaries) to produce what A needs most, which is means of arms to continue the occupation. Now if B's people lack the political institutions and find it difficult to freely communicate, they will fail to organize to prevent this. This may be a case of a Prisoner's Dilemma. Each individual of B will take the job until B stops producing what it wanted to consume and instead produces means of arms for A. This may happen without A controlling or owning B's means of production. Thus B could have been better off in political, rather than economic terms. If they gain independence they may produce what they want to consume rather than what the occupying party wanted to consume. So even though when they gain independence they withdraw – in Roemer's terms – with the most significant share of society's property or means of production, namely soil, the reason they are better off is political rather than economic: they gain autonomy.

In addition to the structural differences between the Marxian theory and international exploitation, there is a difference in the justification or ideology that is involved. In cases of exploitation within the state, to which the Marxian theory relates, there is either denial of exploitation (since we are all equal before the law any sort of exploitation is unlikely) or its justification on the grounds of efficiency. But in international exploitation, especially exploitation between nations, there is a form of natural-superiority justification, which varies from simple paternalism to chauvinism. Indeed, there are cases in which the more powerful state claims a right to intervene in another state's policies and autonomy. Although one state cannot always enforce property rights on another state, it can still claim that while the other state is entitled to its own natural resources it should *not* have autonomy to do whatever it wants with them and to fix its own prices for international trade of these resources. (This argument has been put forward by supporters of the USA in its war against Iraq, when the price of oil was at stake.) This leads us to a new interpretation of exploitation, which relates to autonomy.

It seems to me that although prima facie the theories seem inadequate to explain exploitation in the international arena, if we illuminate another aspect of them, which is usually disregarded, they could do the job quite easily. (Doing this will also reveal the common aspects of the two theories.) Therefore, I want to suggest that exploitation entails A benefiting from an exchange which involves treating B without equal concern in circumstances of bargaining. If so, in order to point to a case of exploitation we need to find the following three conditions:

1 there is an exchange which involves one side treating the other not as equal;
2 the party that treats without equal concern also benefits from the exchange;
3 this is done in circumstances of bargaining.

The third condition is brought in because otherwise every form of lying or mistreatment in the economic context may be interpreted as exploitation. However, this condition should not imply that there is actual bargaining. Rather, the two or more parties are engaged in interaction leading to a deal which will involve them in the near or remote future.[8] Hence killing is also ruled out because it is not done in circumstances of bargaining, which are defined as leading (with the intention that they will lead) to mutual engagement in the future.

The second condition mentions benefiting from not treating as equal. This could be interpreted in three ways. I want now to explain why I prefer one to the others. The one I prefer is that treating not as equals is when one's autonomy and self-esteem are not respected, or in other words, when A fails to see the equal intrinsic value, or the human and the humane in each person. Let me emphasize that I am not talking about not treating as equals – this may be an unintended failure to do so – but rather about treating not as equals. In that sense this treatment is similar to humiliation, which is exactly the opposite of treating as equals. But while humiliation can be done for different purposes, exploitation is humiliation accompanied by a benefit with the intention to benefit by or from this humiliation. At the same time, the fact that the exploiter is aware of his or her actions doesn't imply that the exploited party is aware of them as well: a good example is the worker's false consciousness.

The two other interpretations which I do not follow are the following. First, sometimes it is claimed that when A (the state or a person) relates to B's natural talents as collective or to the fruits of the use of these talents as subject to taxation, A is failing to treat B as an end, hence as equal. I do not follow this interpretation because I disagree with drawing a linkage between one's talents and the idea of self-ownership: I think that talents are indeed either a matter of luck (and therefore their use may be taxed to compensate those who have less luck), or, much more intuitively, they are collective in the communitarian sense, i.e. that in order to develop one's talents one utilizes those of other people as well. Thus B's talents are indeed well-developed, partly due to the fact that B's parents had the free time to be engaged in B's education, due to the fact that they had capital and could employ (without any necessary exploitation) other people to work in their enterprise. Another reason that I do not follow this interpretation is that it is only the liberal – indeed libertarian – reading of benefiting from treating not as equals, whereas I am looking for the reading which is common to both schools of thought.

The second interpretation which I do not follow is that when A uses B's labour power without sharing with B all the economic fruits of this labour power, A benefits from treating not as equals. I do not follow this line firstly because it relates to the stage of distribution only. Such an interpretation could be challenged along the lines that a non-egalitarian distribution in the long run is for the benefit of B as well,[9] or maybe even in the interests of B's descendants, for whom B cares a lot (hence in B's interest as well). But I want to emphasize the stage of production itself. It seems to me that this is where exploitation lies, and that indeed the two schools of thought relate to this stage rather than to the distribution. Secondly, following this interpretation would limit the discussion to the Marxian school of thought (or to a socialist theory), whereas, again, I want to find the reading which is common to both theories.

Now it may be suggested that there is no need to define exploitation as treating not as equals but rather we could use the more traditional, Kantian formula of using only as means rather than as ends. For example, it has been suggested that in exploitation A treats B's vulnerabilities as opportunities to advance A's interests.[10] But this must point to objective criteria with regard to the relations between A and B. It is as if B actually has vulnerabilities. In my suggestion, however, there is no need for vulnerabilities actually to exist, although, of course, they may. The point is that the exploiter treats the other, i.e. regards him subjectively, as not equal. It therefore emphasizes the intention. At the same time, the definition of exploitation cannot relate merely to subjective feelings and to intentions alone. Not every time A wishes to treat B not as equal A succeeds and exploits B, even if this is in circumstances of bargaining. This is why the second condition is brought in: it is necessary that there is a benefit. A benefits (objectively) by treating B not as equal. So if an expected benefit does not materialize the transaction is not exploitative.

Finally, the first condition is brought in because we do not want to claim that every market transaction – all of which involve benefiting from the other, or using the other as means – is exploitative. Indeed in many market transactions A treats B as a means but also respects B and B's right to benefit as well. Therefore A treats B as equal, whereas in an exploitative transaction A does not respect B's right to benefit. While in a non-exploitative transaction both sides enter a deal with the intention of benefiting, they still respect the other's autonomy and chance to benefit even more than they do. In exploitative exchange it is already clear that one side benefits much more than the other. There is no element of 'gambling' ('Let's see if I can make more than you do from this exchange') in this deal.

I now want to claim that indeed this interpretation of exploitation can be found in both the Marxian and the liberal theories of exploitation. The liberal theory refers to a situation of a free market which is abolished by A forcing C not to offer a better deal to B. So A acts as if she possesses the title to C's goods. This is an interference with C's rights, as Steiner claims, but also with her autonomy and self-esteem. C's dignity is violated and her position as a free person who is allowed and authorized to trade with her goods is manipulated. Moreover, with respect to respecting one's autonomy, B is also harmed. By blocking the way of C to trade with B and offering B a better deal, A prevents B from a potential development of B's talents or skills (by enjoying the fruits of his better deal). I therefore think that Steiner's theory already involves benefiting from treating not as equals. Steiner could even present this as part of his rights-based theory of exploitation, arguing that B is mistreated because B's rights to pursue every means of self-development and fulfilment are disregarded or violated.

As for the Marxian theory, it seems that forcing the workers to sell their labour power on other people's terms and to work as others direct them to do is crucial to the theory.[11] (Although one could argue that the workers want to sell their labour power, it is reasonable to answer that they were manipulated to want this by preventing them from having any alternative.) While forcing the workers to do things against their wills the exploiters benefit. This manipulation – first in driving the workers to a position in which they have no other choice but to sell their labour power on such terms, and second in depriving them from doing what they would otherwise want to do – is nothing but treating the workers without equal respect and benefiting from not taking their autonomy seriously, in circumstances of bargaining.

Up to now I have discussed the theories and how they should be revised. I now want to demonstrate how this revision indeed helps us in explaining and analysing exploitation (and the common speech about it) with regard to free trade and the international domain. So first, exploitation between states. At this point it is necessary to say a few words about domination and exploitation and the circular relationship between the two. Domination creates exploitation, which in turn sustains domination by transferring power from the exploited to the exploiter and sustaining the gap in power. This has a visible economic aspect which involves treating as not equals, in particular in cases of occupation or clear superiority in military and economic terms, which is accompanied by hostility and competition. In fact, in the international arena domination happens not only in circumstances of ownership of, or access to, capital, knowledge and means of production, but also in circumstances of using explicit and implicit threats, in particular military ones, in order to sustain the gap between the rich and the poor. I use the term 'poor' rather than 'lacking of property' because in the international case the exploited states are made marketless rather than simply propertyless. They are kept poor or undeveloped so that their people cannot afford to purchase the objects which their economy would have produced. Since usually this state is also incapable of exporting to whoever it wishes, it is forced to produce what the exploiting state would buy. For example, the exploited estate is manipulated to produce cheap vegetables and fruits for the consumption of the exploiters. These fruits cannot travel a long distance without becoming rotten so the producers are forced to sell them to the people who will buy them and have manipulated them to produce them. The trade may appear to be free in the sense that the market sets the prices; but are the actors in the market genuinely free? Although the exploited state seems to decide voluntarily to do so, it is actually forced to give up its own tastes, disregard its own people's demands or needs, sometimes even neglect the local culture and its sustenance. The people of this state are manipulated to do so, while the other side benefits from cheap imports of the good it wishes to purchase.

But as already mentioned, this manipulation consists of cultural aspects as well. The exploited people are gradually but consistently losing their preferences, including national ones, which are part of their culture.[12] Hence traditions are lost. Now it may be argued that there is nothing wrong in such universalization of culture, tastes and norms. Indeed, sometimes the media and education system to which the exploiter has exclusive access backs this phenomena by arguing that the ruling norms are the 'right' ones, and that they represent progress, modernity, etc. It is then claimed that the so-called 'lost' culture is an inferior one anyhow. Terms like 'British heritage' or 'The American way of life' become normative expressions rather than descriptions. This may also apply to political ideologies, such as communism, which are now thought by many in the West to be 'dead', as if capitalism has 'triumphed'. So it is sometimes argued that if Coca-Cola is tasty there is nothing wrong with this process. But it seems to me that not only does it matter because if there is a variety of foods and drinks and of cultures the world is better, but also if these things matter to the people who are losing their cultures and tastes, then turning a blind eye to their agony would imply treating them not as equals.

Next, the theory as it stands now can apply to cases of exploitation within one state from which people in other states benefit as well. A good example is when countries in Africa, especially Liberia and Ivory Coast allow foreigners – either governments or private firms – to bury toxic and radioactive waste in their land. There is nothing in these acts that contradicts free trade. This is exporting land for good money. But certain parts of the population are then exposed to hazardous materials, often without being notified about it. The exploiter is the government of these people. Those who benefit are both these governments, who are paid for this service, and the firms and governments that get rid of their waste. Poor people in many Third World countries are regarded as less human (hence without equal respect): they are likely to be very ill or die for the sake of those who 'produced' the waste being able to continue their mode of life and consumerism.

Thirdly, exploitation of foreign illegal workers by the state or by individuals in the state in which they work. In fact these people are told that they should do whatever they are told to do and work on the terms which they are offered, or else they will be made redundant or even deported. Now since they are not entitled to any welfare service they cannot allow themselves to be made redundant. But they contribute to the state in which they work without sharing any of the prosperity which they produce. Moreover, it is in this case that we can talk of coercion rather than only of forcing the workers to sell their labour power. Coercion implies the presence of an intentional agent, whereas force implies nothing more than the presence of constraints that leave no room for choice.[13] If an illegal foreign worker wishes to stay she may do so as long as the market demands her cheap labour. Then the authorities will ignore her. But if there is unemployment among 'natives', or if the worker tries to become an entrepreneur, thereby competing with the capitalists, she may be deported immediately. Thus there is always this tacit threat to withhold benefits or to execute deportation. So this worker, who is unable to go to court against her employers, and cannot organize, is forced to sell her labour power. But, I have argued, she is also coerced to do so. While it is true that nobody in the state where the worker now works has coerced her to come, indeed she came voluntarily and freely – although she may have been coerced to flee from her own country – it is also arguable that once she starts to work in this new country, the worker is coerced to continue to sell her labour power on these exploitative terms. She is manipulated so that she has no other choice (assuming that returning to her original country is impossible for one reason or another) but to continue working in appalling conditions. Those who coerce her to do so are those who close their eyes and intentionally do nothing to improve her situation. Their attitude towards her is one which they would not allow themselves to have towards their own people. It can be said that they treat her without equal concern, in order to benefit from a better deal in circumstances of bargaining over the terms of her employment.

Finally, I would like to ask a question without necessarily supplying a full answer. Can we overcome international exploitation? Is it feasible? If it is, how will it be related to the institution of free trade? It seems to me that there are two ways of looking at this question. According to the more pessimistic approach, it seems that overcoming international exploitation is a utopian ideal. As long as the world functions according to capitalistic principles, exploitation will exist. Capitalism rests upon the idea of growth: all capitalist economies embrace economic growth and regard it as one of the most important values of our societies. Therefore capitalism always seeks for more. But, as E.F. Schumacher and Lord Keynes have already noticed (separately), this idea is related to greed, which is based on the acknowledgement that ethical considerations are irrelevant to the world of economics. On the contrary, 'foul is useful and fair is not'.[14] Some less pessimistic theorists may maintain that peace agreements are a means of reducing exploitation. But, the pessimist would reply, it may not be so. The Israeli–Palestinian case demonstrates how complicated this issue is. The problem is that exploitation in times of peace is hidden. Incentives to trade with the larger and dominant market are greater; the obstacle of fear is gone; and the chances of making good money are higher. But as I have argued, the essence of exploitation in this case isn't the surplus value which the workers enjoy or do not enjoy; rather it is the benefit from treating them not as equals. And so, as long as the criteria for what to produce remain the taste of the dominant market, these people are exploited. But unlike the case in times of war and occupation when there was enough awareness (for instance due to the occupation) to fuel resentment, in times of peace this exploitation can sometimes be overlooked.

What is left, the pessimist may claim, is free international trade. The more it is institutionalized the more it is practised, and consequently the more there will be economic forces that will make exploitation almost impossible. Perhaps the institutionalizing of free trade will have to be accompanied by a mechanism of international pressures on the party that exploits, e.g. boycotting any trade with it or any import of any good from it. However, the pessimist may remain pessimistic by claiming that even if such measures are taken, the exploiter will find a way to overcome them, since it is powerful enough to survive this or because it has the right connections with other states. In other words, if this state is powerful enough to exploit in the international domain, it may be powerful enough to survive such mechanisms.

On the other hand, there may be a more optimistic way of looking at it. The question of whether it is plausible that there will be an end to international exploitation is related to the degree to which cultural imperialism reaches. Side by side with the elimination of a variety of cultures due to many markets producing according to the tastes, values and preferences of the dominant cultures, there gradually arises an identity which contradicts the dominant culture. This identity is formed around resentment towards the dominant culture. Now when the gap between this identity and the way these people are pictured by the exploiter is big enough, there may be a climax. Such was, for example, the case between Israelis and Palestinians when the Intifada (the uprising) started in 1987, or the case between the Indians and the British authorities in India in the 1940s.

In that case, free trade is not necessarily the solution. On the contrary, a (limited) version of mercantilism may serve to encourage national cultural pride which is necessary to resent the domination of one culture over others. So ironically, it may be the case that the pessimist would stick to free trade and the optimist would not.

## Notes

1 I would like to thank the participants of the workshop for their comments and suggestions. While writing this chapter I benefited from the hospitality and wonderful academic atmosphere of Oxford Centre for Environment, Ethics and Society, and Mansfield College, Oxford.

2 See Article 48 of the agreement.

3 Cohen G.A., *Self-ownership, Freedom and Equality*, Cambridge: Cambridge University Press, 1995, p. 195.

4 I take Hillel Steiner's theory to be the only one. See Steiner H., 'A theory of exploitation', *Ethics*, 94, 1984.

5 Recently the UN has proved to be able to act in very few cases, when there is consensus and when the rival parties are relatively powerless. In other cases the UN lacks the authority and even the legitimacy to act.

6 See Elster J., *Making Sense of Marx*, Cambridge: Cambridge University Press, 1987, p. 170.

7 Roemer J., 'Property relations vs. surplus value in Marxian exploitation', *Philosophy and Public Affairs*, 11, 1982, 281–313.

8 However, I do not mean that the circumstances are exploited, but rather that the person is. On the difference between the two see Wolff, J., *Exploitation*, unpublished MA thesis, University College, London, 1985, pp. 24–41.

9 For example, Rawls's argument about incentives. See Rawls, J., *A Theory of Justice*, Oxford: Oxford University Press, 1973.

10 Wood, A., 'Exploitation', *Social Theory and Practice*, 21 (1995), 150–1.

11 See, for instance, Cohen, op. cit, 167, 195.

12 And so there are talks about 'coca-colization' of the world and of the rule of concerns such as McDonald's and Kentucky Fried Chicken, who compete with rival local small industries and farmers in the Third World by capitalizing on their capability to compete on the long-run until the rival vanishes. They then become monopolies and raise again their prices. This has an economic but also cultural affect in all these countries. For example, following the idea of Swadeshi (emphasizing the indigenous and rejecting multi-national firms), the Indian government closed India's doors to all multi-national firms. However, in the last six years liberalization took place and several firms found their way to the Indian market. This changed ways of life, for example the way farmers raised chickens. The cultural clash brought violent scenes in Bangalore in early 1996.

13 Elster's example is the sentence 'I am forced to live in my native town if I cannot get a job elsewhere, but I am coerced to live there if I would be arrested were I to try to leave'. See Elster, op. cit., p. 212.

14 Schumacher, E.F., *Small is Beautiful*, London: Abacus, 1976, p. 19.

# 10

# DEVELOPMENTS IN THE SERVICES SECTOR

## The GATS

*Michael Johnson*

### Introduction: GATT fundamentals

The justification of principle for trade liberalization is that it maximizes consumer choice, competition and hence efficiency and is therefore good in itself. During nearly fifty years the General Agreement on Tariffs and Trade (GATT), mobilizing the enlightened self-interest of its members, has been the biggest single influence in the liberalization of world trade. GATT pursued this fundamentally liberal principle by developing a complex system of multilaterally agreed rights and obligations. That looks paradoxical, but in practice it was inevitable. While economic theory propounds – or sometimes debates – the intrinsic virtue and efficiency of liberalization, the political reality of trade negotiation is that governments have regarded access to their domestic markets as a threat to their own producers, and therefore as a concession to their trading partners which must be balanced, although not necessarily sector by sector, by benefits received. In 1947 this concept was enshrined in the rubric of Article II of GATT: 'Schedules of Concessions'.

The GATT structure therefore rests on two simple principles: if you want something you have to offer something worthwhile in return; and a measure of liberalization once committed, or 'bound', cannot be withdrawn without offering some equivalent compensating advantage, so that a ratchet effect is built into the liberalization process. The concept of a global reciprocity of concessions contributing to overall liberalization has remained basic to the successive 'Rounds' of multilateral trade negotiations in GATT, up to and including the Uruguay Round.

### Bringing services into the multilateral trading system

The Uruguay Round lasted almost eight years, from September 1986 until the agreements establishing the World Trade Organization (WTO) as a successor to GATT were signed in Marrakesh in April 1994.[1] Several times the negotiations appeared stalled, or even likely to fail, because of irreconcilable differences among the parties. Yet in the end they were concluded, and on terms which on balance were a substantial success. The accumulated negotiating experience of GATT members was overwhelmingly in the established areas of tariffs and trade in goods. Nevertheless the greatest relative advances were made in two of the so-called 'new' GATT subjects: trade in services (the General Agreement on Trade in Services, or GATS), and the protection of intellectual property (IP). An agreement was also concluded on a third new subject, Trade-related Investment Measures. Although this does little more than codify existing practice, it at least brings that topic formally within multilateral disciplines for the first time.

There are several plausible reasons why negotiations in the 'new' areas were relatively so successful. First, the main bargaining was between developed countries who shared similar interests – it was self-evidently to their economic advantage to have multilaterally agreed disciplines on the ways in which governments intervene in the increasingly important services sectors, and to be able to enforce better protection of IP rights. Second, although these topics were 'new' to the GATT forum, they were not new in international negotiation. In the case of IP there were existing international agreements and the work of the World Intellectual Property Organization to build on; while much preparatory work had been done on international trade in services in OECD and elsewhere. Third, the GATT member countries who led the services negotiations were able to do so on the basis of a fairly open-minded approach to the commitments they aimed at. They did not carry a heavy baggage of entrenched sectoral interests and attitudes developed during decades of negotiation, as was the case with tariff negotiations and with the development of the various plurilateral Codes that had emerged from the GATT Tokyo Round (1973–9). Fourth, the countries which had been most reluctant to agree to inclusion of services in the Uruguay Round changed their attitude during the course of negotiation, in some cases because they had embarked on far-reaching economic reforms which included important trade liberalization.

## The politics of services negotiations

The Tokyo Round concentrated on the established GATT area of tariffs, together with the development of voluntary Codes on a number of technical matters, the most important of which covered the conduct of antidumping and countervailing actions, technical barriers to trade, and government procurement. Agreements even on these familiar topics were reached only with difficulty, following a long paralysis in US policy during and after the Watergate affair. Final settlement was stimulated by the fact that the 'fast-track' negotiating authority granted by Congress to the President in the 1974 Trade Act was due to expire in mid-1979. (Under this provision the Congress had agreed that provided it was kept closely associated with the course of the negotiations it would pass the resultant implementing Bill under expedited procedures, effectively giving up its constitutional right of amendment.)

At the end of the Tokyo Round it was already recognized not only that the results fell disappointingly short in the degree of liberalization achieved, but also that developments in the modern world economy required much more comprehensive multilaterally agreed disciplines. Discussion of the need for a new GATT Round began immediately.

International trade in services was among the first subjects canvassed, given the fast-growing importance of services in the economies of the developed countries and their increasing role in international trade. Indeed, pressure for a services agreement had first appeared during the Tokyo Round in the mid-1970s, initiated by the US insurance industry which reacted strongly to expropriation of its interests in India at that time. What followed was a classic American lobbying process: building a coalition of services sectors, centred on the United States Chamber of Commerce, which set out to win over the US Congress and Administration to the concept of an international agreement on services; and then spreading the gospel abroad. Analytical work on international trade in services was started in OECD in the late 1970s, and commitments and objectives relating to services trade were included in the US Trade Act of 1979, which implemented the results of the Tokyo Round. The United Kingdom was among the first countries to support the idea of an international agreement on services, and early in 1981 the then UK Minister for Trade, Cecil Parkinson, made a speech arguing for 'a GATT for services'.

Under the pressure of certain major members, above all the United States, GATT agreed to meet at Ministerial level at the end of 1982 with the intention of launching a new negotiating Round. Many felt this to be specially urgent because of the impact of world recession at the time. Extension of the existing scope of the GATT agreements was however highly controversial. Several major countries were strongly opposed to introducing multilateral rules on the new subjects, in particular services, because this would restrict their freedom to apply their own regulations and controls. In the event the Ministerial meeting could not agree to launch a new Round, but on 29 November 1982 it did issue a declaration setting out a future work programme with a new Round in view.

Against the background of recession this declaration recognized that the world economy was in serious crisis, and that protectionist actions in flagrant disregard of GATT rules were rife. Members declared themselves 'determined to create, through concerted action, a renewed consensus in support of the GATT system'. A series of topics were selected for study, to be completed in some cases by autumn 1983 and in others by 1984. Among the more important were how to ensure that trade measures taken by members were consistent with GATT and not protectionist; better integration of agricultural trade within the GATT system; completion of an agreement to govern the national use of safeguards against disruptive imports (a highly sensitive issue which had been left unfinished in the Tokyo Round); quantitative restrictions and non-tariff barriers; strengthened dispute settlement procedures; and liberalization of trade in textiles and its return to the standard GATT rules. This programme could not however be pursued as a co-ordinated GATT initiative, but only 'individually and jointly' by members.

On services the declaration included the following brief and cautious decision:

1 To recommend to each contracting party with an interest in services of different types to undertake, as far as it is able, national examination of the issues in this sector.
2 To invite contracting parties to exchange information on such matters among themselves, *inter alia* through international organizations such as GATT. The compilation and distribution of such information should be based on as uniform a format as possible.
3 To review the results of these examinations, along with the information and comments provided by relevant international organizations, at their 1984 Session and to consider whether any multilateral action in these matters is appropriate and desirable.

## Launch of the Uruguay Round

Following intensive preparatory work, GATT was finally able to launch a new negotiating Round on 20 September 1986, at Punta del Este in Uruguay. The Punta del Este declaration specified fourteen negotiating areas, broadly encompassing the topics in the 1982 work programme though subject to some extra precision and to differences of emphasis. Additionally there would be a negotiation on services, but only under a separate procedure.

This last point was a characteristic GATT compromise which reflected a long and bitter argument between the proponents and opponents of negotiating on services. It secured a negotiation for those who wanted it, while leaving room for those who did not to reject any eventual result. The motives of the opponents were varied. The most insistent and effective opponents of negotiating on services were Brazil and India, both of which, as developing economies, feared domination of their services sectors by overseas interests, particularly of course from the US and Europe. (For broadly similar reasons India opposed inclusion of intellectual property protection within the new Round.) India and Brazil were followed, mostly tacitly, by a group of other developing countries, many without much by way of a services sector but who were still nervous of agreeing to disciplines in this field.

Within the European Community (EC), France was equally opposed to negotiating on services. At first sight this is surprising, given that by 1986 France was already one of the world's most important services economies. However, then, as throughout the ensuing negotiations, France's prime concern was to minimize any changes to the EC's Common Agricultural Policy (CAP): she did not want to make demands of other GATT partners, particularly developing countries, for which the most likely trade-off demand would be reduction in protection and subsidies under the CAP.

While agreement to the inclusion of services in the Punta del Este declaration represented an important concession on the part of the opponents, the specific negotiating topics included several areas of interest to developing countries, notably liberalization of textiles trade, improved access for tropical products in developed markets, and an undertaking in the tariff negotiation to address the problem of 'tariff escalation', i.e. the tendency for processed products to bear higher tariffs in developed markets than raw materials, thus discouraging industrial development in the producer countries. Therefore these countries too had a real economic interest in the final package which might emerge.

As the Uruguay Round negotiations progressed, those who had opposed the inclusion of services changed their attitude. Following government changes in the late 1980s both India and Brazil, like a number of other developing countries, undertook far-reaching programmes of economic reform in which reduction of state control was accompanied by market-opening and autonomous tariff reductions. The countries concerned recognized their own growing interest in services, both in improving efficiency at home and in securing the right to access abroad. Naturally they continued to demand the biggest possible trade-offs in other negotiating areas; but they dropped opposition to negotiating on services as such.

France meanwhile found that she had more ability than she had perhaps originally realized to obstruct the radical reform of protection and subsidies for agriculture which the US and others demanded. She was therefore able openly to recognize the importance of services to her economy and to move strongly behind the services negotiation as part of a balanced package of EC objectives in GATT. The issue which made conclusion of the Uruguay Round impossible at the scheduled time in December 1990, and which held it up for a further three years, was not services but agriculture.

By April 1994 when the WTO agreements were signed there remained no effective opposition to inclusion of the GATS as an integral part of those agreements. It is subject to the unified dispute settlement system which applies to all the WTO agreements. GATS came into force, together with the rest of the WTO Agreements, in 1995.

## Achievements of the Uruguay Round

Against this background, negotiation of the GATS was a remarkable achievement. Nevertheless the magnitude of the task, the widely differing degrees of interest which the negotiating countries had in trade in services, and the inevitable sectoral interests and pressures on governments, meant that the Agreement is far from comprehensive. In its present form it is still literally work in progress.

This is not the place for a detailed description of the provisions of GATS (in late 1995 the European Commission issued an admirably clear guide to it).[2] Briefly, however, the Agreement defines trade in services 'as the supply of a service:

(a) from the territory of one Member into the territory of any other Member;
(b) in the territory of one Member to the service consumer of any other Member;
(c) by a service supplier of one Member, through commercial presence in the territory of any other Member;
(d) by a service supplier of one Member, through presence of natural persons of a Member in the territory of any other Member.'

GATS establishes a WTO Council for Trade in Services and specifies that GATS is subject to the integrated dispute settlement system of the WTO. It extends to trade in services a number of principles established in the GATT and the predecessor agreements on which GATT was based, namely most-favoured-nation treatment ('MFN', in this case meaning prohibition of discrimination as between services providers based in different partner countries); national treatment (prohibition of discrimination in the home market against service suppliers from other members); and transparency of legislation and regulation. Members are required to provide schedules of specific market access commitments in eleven broad sectors. The commitments made are chosen autonomously, i.e. at the member's own discretion, but once notified are 'bound' and cannot be altered for three years. If after that time a commitment is reduced other GATS members may insist on being offered compensatory adjustment (which may be negotiated in other sectors) in order to maintain the original member's overall level of market access commitment. Under the rubric of 'Progressive Liberalization' it is agreed that 'successive rounds of negotiations' for further liberalization shall begin not later than five years after entry into force of the WTO.

Members are required to provide proper domestic procedures (including tribunals and appeals procedures) for the administration of regulations governing services; to work towards arrangements for recognition of licences, qualifications etc. granted in other member countries; and to assist the increasing participation of developing countries in GATS, inter alia through making market access commitments of particular interest to developing countries, and through technical help. Monopoly and exclusive service suppliers must not breach the home country's MFN and other GATS obligations.

As a specific initial exception, members were permitted to notify sectors in which they would not grant MFN treatment to service providers from other members. Such exemptions apply for up to five years or, subject to review by the WTO Council for Trade in Services, ten years. This temporary provision allows members for a time to continue to negotiate more favourable bilateral agreements for services access with individual partners. Subject to WTO disciplines and control, members may impose restrictions on services trade for the purpose of safeguarding their balance of payments in the event of serious difficulties. Otherwise no restriction may be placed on international current transactions in sectors where a member has made specific commitments.

Member governments are also permitted to join together in so-called 'Economic Integration Agreements' so long as these have 'substantial sectoral coverage', provide for the removal of discrimination between the members, and do not introduce new or more discriminatory measures which affect other members. This provision reflects Article XXIV of GATT (incorporated into the WTO as GATT 1994) which permits the creation of regional free trade areas and customs unions for trade in goods.

There are several general exceptions. Immigration matters are not covered, except that members are encouraged to negotiate specific commitments relating to the movement of natural persons supplying services. Members are not required to disclose confidential information contrary to the needs of law enforcement or to the public interest. In a standard international formulation employed in GATT and elsewhere it is also agreed that GATS obligations do not prevent members from introducing restrictive measures to protect public health, order, morals or security, provided that such measures are non-discriminatory.

Certain areas where international disciplines are needed, but where the difficulties are such that negotiations need more time, are recognized. Thus members are encouraged to consult with a view to eliminating restrictive business practices. Negotiations have to be opened (time unspecified) on action against national subsidies which distort another member's market. Negotiations are required on emergency safeguard measures which may be taken in the event of serious disruption of a member's market, the results to enter into effect not later than three years from implementation of the WTO. Although government procurement in services is excluded from GATS, negotiations on this issue have to be opened within two years of the coming into effect of the WTO.

Specific provisions relating to air and maritime transport, financial services and telecommunications are set out in Annexes. It was agreed that negotiations should continue for a further period in some of these sectors where comprehensive agreement could not be reached in time for the formal conclusion of the Uruguay Round.

## Problems of the GATS

GATS aims, with only limited exceptions, to cover all commercially traded services. Conceptually it sets out within a single framework disciplines capable of protecting the trading position of a single hairdresser who moves from country A to country B to work, and at the other extreme of those who provide financial services through electronic means. However the framework is still incomplete. The signatories, whether acting individually, in their bilateral relations, or jointly in the Council for Trade in Services, have much to clarify in the working of the existing Agreement, and many complex issues to tackle before there are comprehensive multilateral disciplines in services.

The first and fundamental difficulty with GATS is that despite the willingness of the main participants to negotiate in a relatively open-minded way, as described above, the new structure of agreed standards and disciplines for the way in which governments regulate services is grafted onto the traditional bargaining processes of GATT tariff negotiations, in which 'concessions' are exchanged in a way that permits – indeed requires – some calculation of their value. GATT negotiations and disputes about the observance of GATT obligations had hitherto related to more or less quantifiable matters such as tariffs, tax rates, margins of dumping, the impact on trade of industrial standards and marking requirements, and equal treatment under quantitative restrictions. Even where a dispute about trade in goods does not require quantification of damage, but only demonstration that an obligation has been breached, the complainant has a fair idea of the damage done to its commercial interests.

GATS however is based on commitments of market access and equal treatment, reflecting legal and economic principles. And while in the case of merchandise trade a tariff, a tax, a quota or a discriminatory standard may raise very much the same issues regardless of the nature of the goods involved, the same is not true in services where the range of fundamentally different activities is very wide. Market prices and cost structures may be much harder to identify than in the production and distribution of goods. In some sectors technology is developing very fast, and transactions may no longer conform to any traditional concept of 'trade'.

Admittedly GATS does not use the word 'concessions'. It is drafted in terms of commitments and of 'promoting the interests of all participants on a mutually advantageous basis and ... securing an overall balance of rights and obligations'. However while it may be fairly easy to establish as a question of fact whether two partner countries allow equivalent access rights to each other's service providers in a particular sector, whether there is genuine national treatment for foreign-owned firms, or whether natural persons are admitted to a country to provide services, this form of reciprocity of commitments does not permit the economic value of the commitment to either partner to be quantified. GATS does not require quantification of injury in the event of a dispute, but the concept of a 'mutually satisfactory adjustment' between the parties may in some cases imply a need to quantify the damage done, which may be harder in the case of a service provider than in the case of physical goods which have been excluded from a market.

Basic requirements for non-discrimination are a necessary and obvious starting-point for the GATS. In practice the government actions which may give rise to accusations of discrimination will often occur in specialized areas of domestic law such as local planning controls, immigration, recognition of professional qualifications or prudential regulation, where international trade considerations have not regularly featured and may not be well understood. The administration of such laws by governments is often subject to domestic political controversy. Injecting into it principles of non-discrimination which are derived from GATT is not easy.

Initially therefore GATS members have undertaken liberalization commitments which they believe to be right in principle and to their own economic advantage, but which they can neither quantify nor balance against quantified concessions offered to them by others. The result, inevitably, is caution: limited initial market access commitments (even if the regime actually applied is more liberal), lists of exemptions from MFN treatment, postponement of negotiations on certain topics as listed above, and failure both before and after the GATS came into force to achieve comprehensive agreements on financial services, air and sea transport and telecommunications.

Compromises on some basic points were also necessary in the provisions which GATS does include. Inevitably these weaken the Agreement. The autonomous nature of the binding market access commitments made by members in their schedules leads to partial and uneven coverage (for example, US dissatisfaction with the commitments of some other members in the financial services sector led to the special provision for financial services negotiations to continue after the GATS was formally agreed at Marrakesh, and to the US then refusing to join the partial agreement on financial services which was made in July 1995). Members were permitted to notify sectors to be exempted for a time from MFN treatment. GATS does not yet cover government procurement of services, and while the separate Agreement on Government Procurement (effective as from 1 January 1996) does cover services, it does not form part of the WTO and anyway has been signed by a relatively small number of mainly developed countries.

Equally, GATS members may encounter problems in the practical administration of regulations which in principle comply with GATS. For example, a domestically owned and a foreign-based bank should be subject to the same prudential regulation; but it may not be equally easy for the regulatory authority in the host country to be satisfied in each case as to the ownership, capital and liquidity of the bank.

On the other hand the overlapping of certain provisions within GATS may be helpful. As noted above GATS does not yet contain provisions related to subsidies beyond a recognition that they can distort trade in services, a requirement to exchange information about subsidies and to consult where problems arise, and an open-ended commitment to negotiate. However if a member provided a subsidy to a domestic firm which distorted trade in a sector where there was a market access commitment this would probably be actionable under the national treatment provision.

## Specific problems in future negotiations

Apart from financial services, the members of GATS also held open further negotiations in certain sectors such as air and sea transport and telecommunications. This paper does not discuss the problems subsequently encountered in bringing those sectors within GATS, though the experience clearly demonstrates the difficulty, even between advanced modern service economies, of agreeing mutually on liberalization objectives, and the continuing power of sectoral lobbies. It is however worth considering the prospects in the four areas where, as specified in GATS itself, future negotiations are envisaged. It has been noted above (p. 142) that these are restrictive business practices, subsidies, safeguards and government procurement.

As regards *restrictive business practices* (RBPs) some degree of commitment to action under GATS is implicit in the recognition that RBPs can restrict trade, but there is no specific undertaking to negotiate. This is because so far the subject of RBPs in general has been seen as too difficult to tackle on the multilateral level. The 1948 Havana Charter on international trade covered RBPs, but it was never implemented. So far international action has taken the form of extraterritorial enforcement of the national competition laws of some countries, in particular the US – a matter of much controversy – and of increasing cooperation and exchange of information about competition law and practice under the auspices of OECD. It is increasingly clear that the globalization of the world economy and speed of communications require agreement on which RBPs in international trade are damaging, and on action which governments can take jointly and severally to counteract them.

This issue is now high on the list for the future work programme of the WTO. Since the WTO will effectively be starting from scratch in devising new multilateral obligations in this area it would make most sense to negotiate provisions covering both goods and services. This should be feasible, since the competition laws of individual WTO and GATS members already do not distinguish between trade in goods and services, but are based on definitions of trading practice which are common to both. However the wide range of industries and trading practices to be encompassed, the differences between national competition laws (which persist despite, for example, experience of cooperation within OECD) and the conflicting interests of developed and developing countries mean that negotiation will be a long business.

There is an open-ended commitment to negotiate disciplines on *subsidies*. Understanding of state subsidies and the distortions they can cause in merchandise trade has been highly developed in GATT, first in the relevant Tokyo Round Code and now in the WTO Agreement on Subsidies and Countervailing Measures. GATT definitions and provisions have been incorporated in the countervailing law of many countries. GATS recognizes that state subsidies can also distort trade in services, and it calls for 'negotiations with a view to developing the necessary multilateral disciplines to avoid such trade-distortive effects'. Cautiously, it requires such negotiations also to 'address the appropriateness of countervailing procedures', i.e. there is no presupposition that such procedures must be introduced for services. Further than this GATS does not go.

The definition of what constitutes an unacceptable subsidy in services will be particularly difficult. If (say) a government subsidised rents for one of its national banks to establish branches or subsidiaries in another member country, would that be unfair competition for the banks in the host country, or a welcome addition to competition and efficiency? If a government subsidizes (as many do) overseas tours by orchestras or theatre companies, is that unfair competition for local orchestras or theatres, or is it a welcome extension of cultural experience and international understanding? Governments commonly subsidize travel expenses for delegations of exporters travelling overseas to seek new markets, and their participation in trade fairs overseas. Would that be regarded as distortive in the case of service providers?

GATS sets a date of not later than three years from the entry into force of the WTO for implementation of provisions governing *emergency safeguard measures* (as a temporary measure, existing market access commitments can be modified or withdrawn after one year, provided that the member can demonstrate urgency to the Services Council). Here too the issue is whether it is feasible to transfer into services the established GATT principle that temporary safeguards may be applied against a surge of imports damaging to domestic producers. In services, a proliferation of foreign-based banks or insurers in a market could well reduce the operations of local undertakings. But it could equally well enhance them by improving the overall efficiency of the market and increasing its attractiveness as an international centre. If action were taken, would it be in the form of some sort of financial penalty? Or by restricting the establishment of new units? Or would it also restrict the activities of those already present in the market? Whatever way was chosen, there could be effects on inward investment prospects. Even if action was temporary, its effect on investment could be much longer term. How could safeguard actions taken among the OECD countries in services sectors, even if legalized under the WTO, be made compatible with their existing OECD obligations as regards national treatment and the liberalization of capital and invisible transactions?

On one level the case of *government procurement* looks easier, since the GATS members felt able to set a deadline of two years for opening negotiations. The new Agreement on Government Procurement (GPA) contains provisions relating to services. However at the time of writing it had been signed only by OECD countries, Israel and Korea. If GATS sought to incorporate the services provisions of the GPA, the unitary nature of WTO obligations means that those provisions would have to be accepted by WTO members as a whole. But would it make economic or legal sense for the WTO to adopt only the services provisions, even if that were technically feasible, and not the GPA provisions relating to goods? Perhaps the only reasonable course would be for the GPA as a whole to be accepted as part of the WTO, but the negotiating history is not encouraging in this direction. Even so, protectionist policies are rife in government procurement, including procurement of services, and effective international measures are essential if that position is to be in any way countered.

## Conclusion

This chapter does not attempt an appraisal of the GATS, which is far from being in full operation and in any case has to be seen at its present stage as work in progress. Rather, it has set out to analyse the influences which led to the GATS taking the form which it does; the difficulties of operation which are inherent within the current structure and coverage of GATS; and some of the issues which must be solved if the GATS is to develop into a truly comprehensive multilateral agreement.

Some influential writers and thinkers question the need to have brought services within the GATT/WTO structure at all. They argue that in the modern world economy access for services can be left to market pressures. Evidence all round the world shows, on the contrary, that that is no more true of services now than it was for goods when GATT began its work fifty years ago. Despite all its imperfections and gaps, agreement on the GATS was a remarkable international achievement which went much further than many (including the writer) believed possible when the Uruguay Round was launched. The trading world as a whole has come to recognize the huge and growing importance of services in international trade. In everyone's interest – governments, service providers, and above all consumers – there needs to be agreement on limits to the ways in which government regulation and intervention affect and limit services trade. No doubt many of the difficulties in operating the existing GATS will be ironed out as the Agreement gets into its stride, agreed interpretations and understandings are developed, and jurisprudence begins to build up under the WTO disputes procedures. Equally, where deadlines have been set for continuing negotiations they will doubtless be missed, and there will be many more late-night crises. But it has been accepted that there are common criteria for regulation and market access which in principle can apply across the full range of services, and a framework has been set for progressive development of multilateral disciplines in this area.

## Notes

1 *The Results of the Uruguay Round of Multilateral Trade Negotiations*, World Trade Organization, Geneva, 1994.

2 *GATS: The General Agreement on Trade in Services – A Guide for Business*, Office for Official Publications of the European Communities, L-2985 Luxembourg, 1995.

# COMMENTARY ON DE-SHALIT AND JOHNSON

*David Milman*

Avner de-Shalit outlines a new theory of exploitation specifically designed to illuminate discourse in the international arena. Existing Marxian and liberal theories of exploitation, argues de-Shalit, are inapppproriate tools to employ in this context. I propose to undertake a preliminary critique of de-Shalit's chapter from the perspective of a lawyer.

In the first place I feel obliged to take issue with de-Shalit on a semantic point. From a lawyer's perspective the word 'exploitation' does not necessarily convey a pejorative meaning; in the legal community we talk of the exploitation of one's rights and mean by this phrase the full utilization of entitlements. Clearly de-Shalit uses exploitation in the negative sense to mean the abusive exercise of economic power.

There is one other general point on which I would challenge de-Shalit. His chapter may appear to some to be written on the assumption that exploitation in the field of international trade is exclusively an aspect of the capitalist world order. No one would deny that international exploitation and capitalism go hand in hand, but it is important to recognize that the abusive use of political/ economic power can be a feature of trade arrangements in a socialist world order. One need only refer to the one-sided trade 'agreements' between the Soviet Union and the former Eastern European Bloc countries in the years after 1945 for proof of that particular assertion.

Turning to de-Shalit's definition of international exploitation there are a number of features in the three conditions which a lawyer would seize upon as requiring clarification. These are not criticisms, merely points deserving of further exploration. Does the requirement of 'benefit' relate solely to economic benefits or would it encompass other benefits, such as reinforcing a feeling of moral superiority on the part of a developed nation by entering into an apparently disdvantageous trade deal with a developing country? Must the benefit actually materialize? In other words, is an abusive trade agreement that fails to produce the intended dividend because of *force majeure* any less exploitative than one that goes smoothly? Does the theory apply equally to negotiations involving trade blocs (rather than individual states) and does it therefore need to be adapted to cope with increasingly important multilateral bargaining?

The chapter by Michael Johnson focusing upon GATS is less contentious from my perspective. It seeks to trace the evolution of the latest world accord on the provision of services across national barriers: an accord embodied in GATS.

Services represent a growing proportion of the world economy and it is entirely appropriate that some regulation be established. In view of the early opposition to the regulation of international trade in services one might wonder why a successful conclusion was reached on this occasion. Johnson puts forward some convincing arguments and I am happy to lend my support to these. Permit me to supplement these with two ideas of my own. Could it not be said that there are fewer species within the genus of 'services' (as compared to goods), and therefore there is less scope for special pleading to prolong negotiations? Secondly, the lack of quantifiability that Johnson refers to clearly aided the final agreement because it was much more difficult for parties to assess whether they would be net winners or losers under the new regime. Any lawyer will concede that it is much easier to secure agreement on a vague document because all parties are left with sufficient room for manouevre. Of course, if ambiguity has facilitated agreement it may well return to haunt the signatories once the protocol is applied in practice.

The question of exploitation does indeed connect these two chapters, one of which is concerned with constructing a viable theory, the other with practical *realpolitik*. An understanding of the former must surely inform the practice of negotiation. The fundamental question is whether exploitation is facilitated by the establishment of a new world order in trade or whether it is controlled.[1] It is relevant to this debate that much of[2] the early opposition to a new global accord on services came from developing countries, such as India and Brazil, who feared that regulation in this area might result in domination from the developed countries. This is understandable as the ability to export *services* is often seen as a second stage of economic development which follows the initial ability to trade in *goods*; developing countries are therefore unlikely to benefit from accords in this area in the short term.[3] The preamble to GATS by implication acknowledges this particular difficulty with developing countries. Expertise in many of the service areas is often supported by restrictive and sophisticated professional regulatory structures which hamper penetration by service providers from developing countries. To be set against these concerns is the fact that, as much of the pressure for agreements in the services area comes from the developed nations, that gives the developing countries important political leverage in negotiations in other trade areas (such as goods). Ironically, therefore, the GATS negotiations may have contributed to the developing countries getting a fairer deal in world trade overall. However, as far as the new structures on services set up by the World Trade

Organization are concerned we must reserve judgement upon that particular issue. The new GATS regime has a long way to go before its impact on equity and exploitation in the modern world trade order can be objectively assessed.

## Notes

1 A Marxian perspective on this might suggest that any form of legally enforced regulation could only work in the interests of the capitalist world order on the one-dimensional reasoning of Marxists that law is a tool of capitalism.

2 The developing countries were joined by France which had its own political reasons for caution in this area – see Johnson.

3 This is particularly true as cross-border provision of the most basic service of labour is often severely curtailed by immigration laws and other entry/work permit controls ostensibly designed to protect public health and order. Such controls are often preserved by international accords – see for example Article XIV of GATS and paragraph 4 of the GATS Annex on Movement of Natural Persons.

11

# ENVIRONMENTAL REGULATION AND ECONOMIC DEREGULATION

## Is there a conflict?

*Bhaskar Vira*

### Introduction

A century and a half after the repeal of the Corn Laws, there continues to be debate about the merit of participating in a global market-place for goods, services, capital, labour and ideas. Proponents of globalization suggest that the route to general prosperity lies in a recognition of the interconnections between national economic systems, and that their integration provides opportunities for a more efficient pattern of resource exploitation and use. Those who disagree argue that such generalized propositions on welfare may conceal the disproportional impact of deregulated commerce upon particular nations and groups, and reject an uncritical acceptance of the virtues of globalization. Furthermore, they suggest that the process of economic deregulation increases the impact of human society on the natural environment, and undermines efforts towards achieving the goal of ecological integrity.

This chapter explores the substantive conflict between economic deregulation and environmental regulation. In doing so, it refers to the contemporary debate on international trade and the global trading system, but avoids discussion of the institutional specifics of this system, particularly the recently concluded General Agreement on Tariffs and Trade (GATT). It presents the major arguments in favour of economic deregulation, and suggests that these arguments do not establish the expansion of economic freedom as an overriding moral consideration. The chapter proceeds to discuss circumstances where the implementation of environmental policy may be incompatible with economic deregulation. In such cases, it is argued that the conflict between competing values must be resolved by reasoned debate, and that it is inappropriate to assume the inherent superiority of either of these objectives.

### The case for economic deregulation

The deregulation of economic activity consists of the removal of state-imposed controls on the operation of agents within the market. If such controls affect exchange and transfer activities across national boundaries, they pertain to the international trade regime of the country. The doctrine of specialization and exchange in the market suggests that such a process is beneficial to all parties. It is possible to identify two sets of arguments which establish the case for deregulating international trade as a primary objective for economic decision-makers:

1 trade according to comparative advantage benefits all countries and promotes global efficiency in resource use; and,
2 the expansion of economic freedom which follows from trade deregulation is to be valued as an end in itself.

Further, it is suggested that deregulated trade may be environmentally beneficial, and two supporting arguments are commonly put forward:

1 deregulated trade promotes growth, which generates both the resources and the desire for a cleaner environment; and,
2 opening up markets increases domestic producers' access to less environmentally damaging technology.

These arguments need to be scrutinized more carefully, particularly in terms of their implications for situations where deregulation conflicts with other aims of social and economic policy. The discussion which follows qualifies these arguments and suggests that economic deregulation cannot be supported as an overriding objective of public policy – it must be weighed against competing claims, especially those which follow from the need for environmental regulation.

### *Comparative advantage and global efficiency in resource use*

The theory of comparative advantage is based on the principle of specialization and production for exchange in the market. In an international context, comparative advantage refers to the relative efficiency of different countries in the production of goods. Traditional theory suggests that the determinants of comparative advantage include resource endowments, technology and the relative skill of the labour force. It is international differences in these factors which form the basis for trade between countries. Specialization and trade minimizes costs and results in a higher level of total output compared to that under autarky – this is potentially available to the trading partners to increase welfare in each country.

Economists are aware that the principle of comparative advantage applies only under a set of well-defined conditions, and recognize that comparative advantage may fail to work out in practice.[1] Extensions to and qualifications of the simple textbook model highlight four sets of assumptions which are critical: no externalities; stable prices which are competitively determined; no changes in *dynamic* comparative advantage; and the immobility of factors of production.

In reality, these assumptions are frequently violated.[2] Externalities exist, particularly when dealing with the valuation of natural capital, which is often under-priced as an input into the production process. In the presence of such externalities, production and specialization according to market prices are distortionary and inefficient, and corrective policy measures are required.[3] If prices fail to reflect true scarcity, the gains from deregulated trade may be over-stated. Clearly, the first-best solution is to ensure that market prices fully reflect the social and environmental costs of production, so that externalities can be internalized. However, most countries have not taken any substantial steps towards implementing such a framework for environmental accounting – market signals are inadequate for the optimal allocation of resources. In a 'second-best' world, environmental quality can be improved by correcting for external effects using various types of regulation, and these may involve restrictions on the behaviour of agents in the market either by changing the terms of trade (with taxes, and price and incentive-based regulation), or by direct controls (such as quantity restrictions).

Second, comparative advantage calculations based on fixed and stable prices may be inaccurate. If firms have significant market power, prices may not be competitively determined, and there may be need to regulate their activities. Furthermore, if prices are unstable, production costs may vary and alter comparative advantage. If terms of trade change significantly over time, comparative advantage may vary in a dynamic sense, leading to instability if production processes are inflexible. Specialization may carry additional risks since it undermines the ability of economic and ecological systems to cope with changing circumstances,[4] and increases vulnerability due to the dependence of specialized producers on trade.[5] A diversified production base allows economies to cope with changing conditions in world markets, and allows them to exercise the freedom *not* to trade when prices are not favourable. Specialized economies may be forced to participate in the trading system even when price movements are adverse, if they are not self-sufficient in the production of essential goods, such as food. Despite facing declining terms of trade, export revenues may be necessary to finance these imports, and to service previously accumulated international debt.

Dynamic comparative advantage is partly determined by the impact of specialized production on the rest of the economy.[6] Specialization may generate positive externalities in production, technology, and human resource development, but such an impact would vary across products and sectors. In particular, a focus on the export of unprocessed primary products may be associated with fewer widespread benefits than the linkages related to specialization in manufactures.[7] In such circumstances, there is a case for specialization in the activity which may be expected to yield the greatest benefits over time, although this may not necessarily be that in which a country has static comparative advantage. The state plays a key role in choosing sectors which are likely to be more dynamic in the long run, since current prices may not be indicative of long-term comparative advantage. Instead of suggesting the complete deregulation of trade, such considerations would emphasize the role of the state in targeting specific industrial policy measures for investment in sectors which have greater spill-over effects on the rest of the economy.[8]

Finally, factors of production are internationally mobile, and move to the location where they earn greatest returns. Specialization according to comparative advantage is a sensible strategy if capital is not free to move to other countries. If resources freely cross national boundaries in pursuit of absolute advantage, trade may no longer be beneficial for all countries.[9] International arbitrage, deflation and wage and exchange rate flexibility may ameliorate these effects and restore the competitiveness of countries which have an absolute disadvantage, but it cannot be assumed that there are universal gains to be had from specialization according to absolute advantage.[10]

### *The expansion of economic freedom*

While the theory of comparative advantage presents an efficiency-related argument to support deregulation, the expansion of economic freedom may be promoted as an end in itself. The logic follows from the principle of allowing free agents the liberty to make choices in the economic sphere without 'artificial' restrictions imposed by the state. In the liberal conception, freedom is a property of the individual and consists in the absence of constraint or interference by others. The state exists to guarantee this freedom, but also threatens it by the imposition of restrictive laws and regulations. This suggests the need clearly to delineate the division between the private and the public spheres of decision making. Further, the economy is conceived as a collection of free individuals who voluntarily engage in exchange based on prices and their values and preferences – any regulation of this process is seen as an interference with the individual's right to freedom.[11]

There are two logical steps which are required to embrace such an argument. The first is to acknowledge that there are spheres of private activity which should be free from coercion by others, and the second is to accept that freedom of the individual to trade in the market is one such activity. While there is little dispute with the proposition that there are areas of non-interference with individual liberty, where precisely this frontier lies has been the subject of historical and political debate. As Berlin has stressed, interdependence is pervasive in human affairs, and no person's activity is so completely private as never to obstruct the lives of others in any way.[12] In a pluralist conception, the frontier between private and public decision making cannot be considered universal or immutable, but must be recognized as contextualized by society. If, in practice, interdependence exists and individual actions have implications for the well-being of others, there is a need to exercise restraint based on some socially accepted framework of regulation. At a minimum, such a framework includes mechanisms for the enforcement and policing of contracts; beyond this, society and the state may also choose to regulate private activity for a number of other reasons, social, cultural and political.

Although a key component of libertarian economic thinking, there is reason to question the argument that regulation of private individuals' economic activity in the market is unwarranted. Economic theory acknowledges that markets fail in their allocative role for the provision of public goods, or where there are externalities, or if the market is non-competitive. In these circumstances, there is a role for state intervention to correct for market failure. The state also supplements the market by coordinating economic activity, reducing transaction costs and providing signals for productive activity.[13] Furthermore, the market as an institution depends on the state to define and enforce the fundamental rules that govern exchange.[14] State intervention may also be justified by paternalist moral arguments, such as the provision of 'merit' goods, and the prevention of market-type transactions for certain activity (such as the donation of body parts).[15]

The rhetorical use of terms such as freedom and regulation in the debate on international trade suggests a pre-existing, 'natural' state of the economic system which is disturbed by artificially imposed regulations. This assumes that the unregulated market is able to satisfy social needs, and that individuals exercise their economic freedom without affecting the claims and entitlements of others. However, this misrepresents the nature of exchange in most market-like situations, where there are usually well-defined legal and institutional boundaries as well as social norms which define what is permissible. The suggestion of a natural state, pre-regulation, which has been distorted due to the presence of government is both historically inaccurate and descriptively false. An institutionally sensitive understanding of the market does not support the promotion of economic freedom as an *absolute* value which always trumps other social and economic considerations. Free trade and economic deregulation must be justified with reference to some wider conception of social well-being.

### *The environmentally beneficial impact of growth*

Setting aside the objections raised during the earlier discussion of comparative advantage, let us assume that the deregulation of the international trading regime does lead to an increase in aggregate growth, and that this growth dividend is shared by the trading partners. Some studies have found a statistical relationship between per capita income and environmental quality, with the evidence suggesting that increasing income is associated with increased environmental degradation up to a point, beyond which environmental quality improves – such a relationship has been described as an inverted U.[16] Extrapolating from an empirical relationship which holds for a selected set of pollutants in certain circumstances, it has been suggested that environmental quality may generally be expected to improve with higher per capita income.[17] The argument suggests that higher incomes are associated both with the desire for, and the ability to pay for, an improvement in environmental quality, so a policy which promotes economic growth is likely to be environmentally beneficial in the long run.

However, the inverted-U relation is not sufficient to ensure that the wealth generated by the growth process is actually spent on environmental improvements. The statistical results need to be interpreted carefully, particularly since much of the empirical work is based on cross-sectional studies.[18] Further, there is a distinction between notional and effective demand for environmental quality, where the latter is supported both by the ability of citizens to pay for public goods and by the capacity of the state (or other collective organizations) to supply the desired improvements.[19] An increase in wealth may lead to the desire for improved environmental standards, but this may not be effective without specific changes in supporting environmental legislation and the institutional framework for the implementation of environmental policy. It cannot be assumed that such changes would automatically be forthcoming once countries achieve a higher level of per capita income.[20]

Furthermore, some processes of environmental degradation are irreversible.[21] Here, the ability to pay because of increased wealth would be insufficient to ensure ecological restoration. A lack of perfect substitutability between man-made and natural capital would suggest the need for defining critical minimum standards for environmental quality, below which the natural ecosystem loses its ability to recover. A case can then be made to limit the growth process if it threatens to lower standards below this critical minimum. In this context, it has been emphasized that the Earth's resource base is incapable of supporting indefinite growth, and that the increased through-put of environmental resources associated with growth may strain global carrying capacities, leading to an inherent contradiction between growth and environmental sustainability.[22]

These qualifications would suggest that results which indicate a positive long-term relationship between growth in per capita income and environmental quality need to be interpreted with caution. The beneficial links between deregulated trade and the environment are based on a two-part argument – first that deregulated trade leads to growth in per capita incomes, and second that such growth leads to improvements in environmental quality. However, the present discussion has suggested that both these arguments may be conceptually flawed and empirically inaccurate. There are circumstances in which the process of economic deregulation needs to be controlled because of its potentially adverse impact on environmental quality.

### *Trade-related access to 'cleaner' technology*

A supplementary argument relating deregulated trade with positive environmental effects rests on the suggestion that less environmentally damaging technologies which are developed in countries with stricter environmental regulations can be diffused more rapidly through deregulated trade.[23] While access to a greater range of technological options may be desirable, it is important to recognize the oligopolistic nature of the supply side of technology.[24] Direct foreign investment by multinationals is a dominant form of technology transfer, with overseas producers retaining ownership and control over technological developments and exercising substantial market influence.[25] Firms which have invested in the development of new, clean technologies have a competitive advantage, and are unlikely to disseminate these without adequate compensation.[26]

In such a market, it is necessary to recognize the unequal bargaining position of buyers and sellers of environmental technology. While it is true that expanding the menu of choices available to buyers increases their bargaining power, technologically less-developed countries may need to adopt supplementary policies which regulate the form and terms of technology transfer. At the same time, the multilateral system must work out alternative means to compensate those who have invested in the creation of new technology. The deregulation of trade by itself is insufficient to ensure that cleaner technologies are diffused rapidly and on equitable terms.

## Environmental regulation: implications for deregulated trade

There is a developing scientific consensus that the present scale of human activity is exacting an environmental cost which is not sustainable. The concept of environmentally sustainable development has become widely accepted, and the United Nations Conference on Environment and Development in Rio de Janeiro in 1992 provided the most public affirmation of this concern. More recently, a small group of ecologists and economists met in Sweden to explore the common ground between these disciplines, and released a consensus statement which stresses that:

> If human activities are to be sustainable, we need to ensure that the ecological systems on which our economies depend are resilient. The problem involved in devising environmental policies is to ensure that resilience is maintained, even though the limits on the nature and scale of economic activities thus required are necessarily uncertain.

And, further:

> We conclude that economic liberalization and other policies that promote gross national product growth are not substitutes for environmental policy. On the contrary, it may well be desirable that they are accompanied by stricter policy reforms.[27]

Such statements are representative of a widespread recognition that environmental problems necessitate the adoption of specific regulatory policy, and support the earlier proposition that economic growth by itself is insufficient to mitigate the environmental impact of human activity. Environmental policy measures include controls on the harvest of resources, both renewable and non-renewable, regulations on the use of polluting substances, and controls on production processes due to their impact on resource stocks or pollution.

All environmental policies operate by altering the terms on which commodities are exchanged in the market, either through the use of price instruments (taxes and subsidies or marketable permits) or by quantitative restrictions and prohibitions. Environmental policies, then, cannot be neutral to the markets of products or to production processes, and will usually have an impact on trading opportunities. From such a perspective, the increased role of the state in regulating the environment would appear to be fundamentally incompatible with the reduced scope for government activity under a regime of economic deregulation. However, the motivation for a number of environmental policies is the failure of the market mechanism to account adequately for the environmental cost of production and consumption decisions. Environmental taxes and subsidies work through adjustments to the price mechanism and correct for such distortions. Clearly, such policies are not incompatible with the objective of economic deregulation, and 'full cost internalization' is an objective which is shared by environmentalists and by advocates of free trade.[28]

The potential for conflict between trade deregulation and environmental regulation is greatest where such 'first-best' environmental policies are not available. In such circumstances, regulation takes the form of direct quantitative controls on resource extraction, or physical limits on the use of polluting products and technologies. What is relevant to the present discussion is the specific impact of environmental regulations on the international trade regime; in particular, circumstances where environmental policy objectives directly affect the volume or composition of international trade, and environmental regulations which discriminate in their treatment of domestic and foreign producers.

Direct controls on the extraction of potentially exhaustible resources through quantity restrictions are based on estimates of the desirable rate of harvest, and are usually determined by policy makers on both ecological and economic grounds.[29] Quantity controls include prescriptions for the maximum permitted harvest in a local area, complete prohibition on resource extraction in a local area, or a nation-wide moratorium on exploitation. Such controls have a direct impact on the quantity of goods available for trade. If the country is a net importer, the volume of international trade will be affected as domestic consumers purchase their surplus requirements from overseas, while regulations in countries which are net exporters would alter the amount of the product available on the international market. With substitution possibilities, there may also be an impact on the volume of trade in other related products.

If such quantity restrictions are non-discriminatory in their treatment of domestic and foreign purchasers, advocates of deregulated international trade should have little cause for concern, since the price for the product would adjust to the altered supply available in the market. The quantity restriction should be viewed no differently to any other physical impediment to the supply of a particular product.

Quantity restrictions are sometimes imposed on products used as intermediate inputs, such as chemical fertilizers, or on the flow of pollutants from production processes. The effectiveness of such regulation relies on the existence of mechanisms to monitor and punish those who violate established standards. Standards regulating the use of polluting substances are determined by the capacity of the environment to absorb the by-products of human activity, and on the impact of pollutants on public health and safety. Local physical conditions, such as prevailing wind patterns and the flow of rivers, are important determinants of the assimilative capacity of the environment. Apart from scientific estimates of acceptable levels of environmental concentration for pollutants, standards are also a function of public attitudes towards risk. There are likely to be significant differences in the relative ability of the local environment to absorb pollutants, as well as in social and cultural attitudes towards public health and safety. Such differences are reflected in inter-regional and international variations in environmental standards.

It is this diversity in international environmental standards which is held responsible for disruptions to free trade, and it is alleged that differences in environmental compliance cost affect competitiveness.[30] Producers operating in jurisdictions with stricter regulation claim that such differences lead to 'unfair' competitive pressures, and may result in reduced market access. Countries which impose lower standards are accused of environmental 'dumping', and there is a demand for states to take retaliatory trade policy measures to neutralize this implicit subsidy, or to subsidize domestic producers for the additional environmental compliance costs.[31] Furthermore, domestic producers exert political pressure on regimes to avoid introducing stricter standards, arguing that this will result in a further loss in competitiveness. Contrary to these claims, however, some empirical evidence suggests that environmental regulations have not been significant determinants of industrial competitiveness, measured in terms of net exports, overall trade flows, and plant-location decisions.[32] More radically, it has been suggested that stringent environmental regulations may not be a disadvantage but may actually enhance the competitive position of domestic industry in world markets.[33]

Some economists argue that since regulatory standards are based on local preferences and endowments, international variations reflect 'natural' differences in comparative advantage between countries, and they should be treated in the same way as variations in the abundance of other factors of production, such as land, capital and labour.[34] Environmentalists react by arguing that trade based on differences in environmental standards exaggerates the externalization of costs of production, and increases the impact of such processes on the environment.[35] However, international differences in regulations which are overtly environmental are not necessarily indicative of the relative 'price' associated with the use of the environment in different countries.[36] The nature of the legal system, the extent of public investment in infrastructure, land use controls and zoning requirements are factors which are only partly environmental, and are determined by the wider political economy of different societies. These factors are important determinants of the net impact of human activity on the environment, and a failure to recognize these broader dimensions represents an incomplete analysis of the relative environmental costs of production in different countries. International differences in regulatory standards may be a poor explanatory variable for the extent of internalization of these environmental costs.

Greater global harmonization of environmental standards would eliminate problems which arise due to the diversity of regulatory regimes; however, there is considerable resistance to such proposals from those who believe that harmonization compromises national sovereignty. Production processes are controlled by countries based on their domestic standards for public health and safety, and the imposition of universal standards is difficult to defend as a liberal principle. Countries may differ in their social attitudes to risk, and may have varying standards. Where there are genuine differences in the assimilative capacity of the environment, a process of harmonization may not be efficient from an environmental perspective. Further, the presence of significant scientific uncertainty makes it more difficult to coordinate international policy to reach agreement on the permissible level of pollutants, and on appropriate standards for production processes. Finally, developing countries argue that higher Western standards are too expensive to implement, and demand financial and technological transfers to accompany the harmonization process.[37] These observations suggest that moves towards harmonization are likely to be slow and politically difficult to negotiate, and it appears likely that there will continue to be some element of diversity in global regulatory regimes.

While individual states have the sovereign right to set their own domestic environmental standards, it is inappropriate for them unilaterally to impose these standards on other countries. The use of trade restrictions to prevent market access to producers who are subject to less stringent regulatory regimes may well be old-fashioned protectionism operating under the guise of environmental concern. Assuming the product itself is physically indistinguishable from one produced under stricter environmental standards, the target is the processing and production methods employed overseas. If the environmental repercussions of these methods are experienced entirely within a foreign jurisdiction, it is difficult to defend an import restriction. The threat of refusing access may work if the buyer is a large player in the world market, but this must be recognized as coercion to impose the preferences of one country upon another, and is effective only because of the asymmetric economic power of the trading partners. Equity demands that if such restrictions are to be used as a tool of trade policy, they must be equally accessible to all countries regardless of size.

If divergent environmental regulations have implications beyond the borders of the producing country, there is legitimate cause for concern. Countries have the right to set their own domestic environmental standards, but also have a responsibility to the world community when such actions have transboundary impacts. An immediate consideration relates to defining which processes have such transboundary effects. In some cases, such as the emission of ozone-depleting gases, or the use of fossil fuels, the global implications may be relatively easy to demonstrate, and quite widely accepted. Other cases are more contentious, such as competing claims over tropical forests which perform a local function by providing subsistence and other products, but also have a global impact because of their critical role in the carbon cycle. The appropriate forum to resolve such issues must necessarily be multilateral negotiation among all concerned nations, rather than the unilateral imposition of preferences by one nation or regional group. In some circumstances, however, there may be considerable disagreement due to scientific uncertainty, and it may be difficult to achieve consensus through the multilateral forum.

The interests of equity suggest that multilateral environmental treaties should recognize the historic contribution of countries to global pollution and resource depletion, and be based around a notion of environmental entitlements.[38] The difficulty with such negotiation is that while some countries fail to accept their liability for previous environmental damage, others do not have the ability to introduce more stringent standards without substantial financial and technological support, and the bargaining process often ends in deadlock.[39] However, negotiation does work in many cases, and a number of multilateral environmental agreements have been concluded successfully. An important enforcement mechanism for multilateral environmental agreements involves the use of trade sanctions, both as an incentive for non-parties to comply with established standards (as in the Montreal Protocol on Substances that Deplete the Ozone Layer), and as a sanction against violations.[40] Clearly, in such circumstances, there is incompatibility between the objectives of environmental regulation and those of deregulated trade. Further, the restriction of trade is an explicit objective of some environmental agreements, such as the Convention on International Trade in Endangered Species of Wild Fauna and Flora (CITES), and the Basel Convention on the Control of Transboundary Movements of Hazardous Wastes and Their Disposal.

The conflict between trade objectives and environmental regulation may be most difficult to resolve where there are 'psychological spillovers' associated with the use of particular production techniques in other countries. In such circumstances, it is not necessary to demonstrate the existence of a physical impact beyond the producing country's borders. Psychological factors and moral standards are specific to particular societies, and measures taken to protect such principles must not be dismissed as reflecting 'cultural imperialism'. There is, however, some reason to discuss the circumstances under which these measures would include the unilateral imposition of trade sanctions against a foreign producer. A trade restriction may be an expression of moral disapproval, whereby a country chooses to boycott the import of goods produced under conditions which it believes are unacceptable. If such actions are genuinely motivated by the desire to preserve a country's cultural and moral integrity, they may be defensible. However, there is a danger of such restrictions being used to disguise what is purely protectionist policy, and the potential misuse of such unilateral policy must be weighed against the extent to which cultural and moral sensibilities are disturbed by the presence of the offending product.

If countries use trade restrictions more aggressively, in order to alter foreign production practices, their effectiveness would depend on the relative economic power of the enforcing country. Countries which are large relative to the size of the market would be able to force changes in techniques by threatening to restrict imports. Such coercion, however, is an option which would be available only to the richer and more economically powerful countries. To accept unconditionally that countries have such a right would bias the international system against poorer nations. Finally, trade sanctions in support of a moral agenda may not be targeted at specific products, but more generally applied to punish countries which are believed to be in violation of international law. Where there is widespread acceptance of moral standards, such as the international condemnation of South Africa's apartheid regime, imposing trade restrictions may be justified as an aggressive measure. Environmental considerations may trigger such a reaction, but the forum for such decisions is necessarily through multilateral negotiation at the level of international politics, and it is difficult to justify unilateral trade sanctions in this context.

## Concluding remarks: principles for conflict resolution

This chapter has discussed some of the substantive areas of overlap between trade policies and environmental policies. In particular, it has suggested reasons to question the promotion of deregulated trade as an over-riding policy objective, and has identified particular environmental policy objectives which may require the restriction of trade. While it is recognized that there are circumstances where trade restrictions are not first best in achieving environmental goals, the first-best policy choice may not always be attainable. In cases where trade restrictions are necessary to promote environmental objectives, it has been suggested that the weight given to the relative trade distorting impact of environmental regulations should be inversely proportional to the seriousness of the environmental harm being addressed, and to the degree to which it is directly felt by the affected country. As a general principle, it seems eminently reasonable to reject the unequivocal promotion of any single objective and to suggest a procedure which weighs the relative desirability of conflicting goals. In actual practice, decision makers are frequently faced with the problem of determining such trade-offs without any common metric for comparison, and the relative importance accorded to the objectives of free trade and environmental protection is likely to provoke considerable discussion.

Given that production and consumption decisions are associated with externalities, the 'polluter pays' principle is one general way in which agents can be made more responsible and take full account of their actions. Furthermore, it is necessary to recognize that there are ecological limits to human expansion, and that ecosystems may be irreversibly damaged if this threshold is exceeded. It is argued that there is inconclusive scientific evidence to support the contention that we are close to these limits; however, if scientific uncertainty is combined with the possibility of potentially irreversible and catastrophic damage, sensible decision making would suggest minimizing the risk of such an eventuality, by adopting the 'precautionary principle'.

The present discussion has established that deregulation of trade and environmental regulation are not always compatible. The resolution of disputes will need to recognize the rights of national sovereignty enjoyed by countries in international law, but also their obligations to each other as members of a global community of nations. The multilateral process is the most appropriate forum for such discussion, with a clear recognition that economic deregulation is not necessarily an objective to be pursued at the expense of other legitimate policy goals.

## Notes

1 P. Ekins, C. Folke and R. Costanza, 'Trade, Environment and Development: the Issues in Perspective', *Ecological Economics*, 1994, volume 9, pp. 1–12; H. Daly and R. E. Goodland, 'An Ecological-Economic Assessment of Deregulation of International Commerce under GATT', *Ecological Economics*, 1994, volume 9, pp. 73–92; H. Daly, 'Against Free Trade and Economic Orthodoxy', *The Oxford International Review*, 1995, Summer, pp. 28–34.

2 Clearly, the significance of these effects must be investigated empirically when specific policies are being planned. Here, it is necessary to point out the implications of these assumptions, and to suggest that the comparative advantage argument must not be accepted uncritically.

3 In an environmental context, this is perhaps most evident in the case of transportation using fossil fuels. The failure to account for the environmental costs of fossil fuel use results in the underpricing of transportation costs, and a greater volume of trade using transport than may be otherwise expected.

4 N. Johnstone, 'Trade Liberalization, Economic Specialization and the Environment', *Ecological Economics*, 1995, volume 14, pp. 165–74.

5 Ekins, *et al.*, op. cit. p. 4.

6 Ibid.

7 I. Ropke, 'Trade, Development and Sustainability: a Critical Assessment of the "Free Trade Dogma" ', *Ecological Economics*, 1994, volume 9, pp. 13–22.

8 For a study of the manner in which the Korean state promoted the development of its export sector, see H.-J. Chang, *The Political Economy of Industrial Policy*, London, Macmillan, 1994.

9 R. Prasch, 'Reassessing Comparative Advantage: the Impact of Capital Flows on the Argument for Laissez-faire', *Journal of Economic Issues*, 1995, volume 29, pp. 427–34.

10 While it is an empirical reality that capital is increasingly mobile across national boundaries, Daly questions the desirability of this trend. He suggests that transnational capital is difficult to control because it transcends allegiance to national communities. Daly, op. cit., p. 29. One reflection of this is the volatility of short-term speculative flows of capital – if the volume of such flows is significant, capital flight can result in significant macroeconomic disturbances, as recently experienced by Mexico.

11 M. Friedman, *Capitalism and Freedom*, Chicago and London, University of Chicago Press, 1962; F. Hayek, *The Road to Serfdom*, London, Routledge and Kegan Paul, 1972.

12 I. Berlin, 'Two Concepts of Liberty', in I. Berlin, *Four Essays on Liberty*, Oxford, Oxford University Press, 1969.

13 Refer also to the discussion of dynamic comparative advantage in the previous section.

14 T. Eggertson, *Economic Behaviour and Institutions*, Cambridge, Cambridge University Press, 1990.

15 A review of such theories of state intervention may be found in Chang, op. cit., chapter 1.

16 M. Radetski, 'Economic Growth and the Environment' in P. Low (ed.), *International Trade and the Environment*, Washington, DC, The World Bank, 1992, World Bank Discussion Paper No. 159. The inverted-U relationship is sometimes referred to as an environmental Kuznets curve, drawing a parallel with Simon Kuznets' pathbreaking work on the relationship between income inequality and the level of economic development.

17 W. Beckerman, 'Economic Growth and the Environment: Whose Growth, Whose Environment?', *World Development*, 1992, volume 20, pp. 481–96.

18 Johnstone, op. cit., p. 167.

19 Ibid.

20 Work on theories of institutions and institutional change suggests that a demand for institutional change is inadequate to ensure that this is forthcoming. The ability of the state to respond to such demands is a function of specific political and economic factors – on this, see D. North, *Institutions, Institutional Change and Economic History*, Cambridge, Cambridge University Press, 1990; and D. W. Bromley, 'Reconstituting Economic Systems: Institutions in National Economic Development', *Development Policy Review*, 1993, volume 11, pp. 131–51.

21 C. Folke, M. Hammer, R. Costanza and A.-M. Jansson, 'Investing in Natural Capital – Why, What, How?' in A.-M. Jansson, M. Hammer, C. Folke and R. Costanza (eds), *Investing in Natural Capital: the Ecological Economics Approach to Sustainability*, Washington, DC, Island Press, 1994.

22 K. Arrow, B. Bolin, R. Costanza, P. Dasgupta, C. Folke, C.S. Holling, B.-O. Jansson, S. Levin, K.-G. Mäler, C. Perrings and D. Pimentel, 'Economic Growth, Carrying Capacity and the Environment', *Ecological Economics*, 1995, volume 15, pp. 91–7.

23 Ropke, op. cit., p. 15.

24 S. Lall, *Learning to Industrialise*, London, Macmillan, 1987.

25 F. Stewart, 'Technology Transfer for Development' in F. Stewart, *North–South and South–South*, London, Macmillan, 1992.

26 The justification for the creation of temporary monopolies under the patent system is to provide incentives for private-sector research and development. Information has the non-

rival characteristics of a public good, and investment in research and development could either be financed through public subsidy, or by encouraging private-sector involvement by promising 'rewards'. The patent system is one such ex post reward mechanism, where the inventor receives exclusive rights over the commercial use of the product for a defined period of time.

27 Arrow, *et al*,, op. cit., p. 93.

28 D. Esty, *Greening the GATT: Trade, Environment and the Future*, Washington, DC, Institute for International Economics, 1994.

29 The term exhaustible is used here since it encompasses the common economic distinction between renewable and non-renewable resources, where the latter are resources which are found in finite quantities, such as minerals. Renewable resources have a regenerative capacity, but may be depleted if the rate of extraction exceeds the rate of regeneration. Viewed in this manner, both renewable and non-renewable resources are *potentially* exhaustible.

30 Esty, op. cit.

31 Daly, op. cit.

32 A.B. Jaffe, S.R. Peterson, P.R. Portney and R.N. Stavins, 'Environmental Regulation and the Competitiveness of US Manufacturing: What Does the Evidence Tell Us?', *Journal of Economic Literature*, 1995, volume 33, pp. 132–63. United States data quoted by Low reveals that the weighted average share of pollution abatement operating costs in total output for all industry was 0.54 per cent, with the highest proportionate costs being recorded by the hydraulic cement industry at 3.17 per cent. These are relatively small fractions of the total operating costs of industry, and are unlikely to be the most significant factors affecting international competitiveness. P. Low, 'Trade Measures and Environmental Quality: the Implications for Mexico's Exports' in P. Low (ed.), *International Trade and the Environment* World Bank, Washington, DC, 1992.

33 M. Porter and C. Vanderlinde, 'Toward a New Conception of the Environment-Competitiveness Relationship', *Journal of Economic Perspectives*, 1995, volume 9, pp. 97–118. The 'Porter Hypothesis' relies on the ability of firms to seek out new technologies as a means of compliance. If there is such a tendency, firms are likely to gain significant market power and would resist moves towards the transfer of clean technologies, as suggested above on p. 157. A critical theoretical examination of the Porter Hypothesis is found in K. Palmer, W. Oates and P. Portney, 'Tightening Environmental Standards: the Benefit-cost or the No-cost Paradigm', *Journal of Economic Perspectives*, 1995, volume 9, pp. 119–32.

34 J. Bhagwati, 'The Case for Free Trade', *Scientific American*, 1993, November, pp. 18–23.

35 Daly and Goodland, op. cit.

36 Johnstone, op. cit, p. 168.

37 A. Agarwal and S. Narain, *Towards a Green World*, New Delhi, Centre for Science and Environment, 1992; P. Ekins, *Harnessing Trade to Sustainable Development*, Oxford, Green College Centre for Environmental Policy and Understanding, 1995.

38 Agarwal and Narain, op. cit.

39 R. Blackhurst and A. Subramaniam, 'Promoting Multilateral Cooperation on the Environment', in K. Anderson and R. Blackhurst (eds), *The Greening of World Trade Issues*, New York, Harvester Wheatsheaf, 1992.

40 Esty, op. cit., lists twenty multilateral environmental agreements which include trade provisions.

41 A number of my thoughts on this issue have been clarified and sharpened due to a series of discussions with Antonia Layard, for which I am grateful.

42 Individual consumers in a particular country may, nevertheless, legitimately demand information about production methods, particularly in terms of their environmental impact. This alternative is called 'ecolabelling', and may be preferable to an import ban in some circumstances. If there are different processes to produce goods which are physically indistinguishable, such labelling enables buyers to make more informed choices about products, and preserves the individual sensibilities of the consumer. However, it is necessary to ensure that the certification and labelling process is equitable and transparent, and does not bias consumer choice.

43 Ekins, op. cit.

44 One application of this principle is to recommend the prohibition of trade in toxic products. The ability to externalize clean-up costs reduces incentives to deal with such pollution on-site, particularly given the high risks involved in the transportation and handling of such products.

45 T. O'Riordan and J. Cameron (eds), *Interpreting the Precautionary Principle*, London, Earthscan Publications, 1994.

# 12

# 'WHAT NOW?' TRADE AND ENVIRONMENT

## An overview of the current debate*

*James Cameron*[1]

> If the GATT fails to promptly address legitimate environment concerns, the cause of free trade, particularly in the United States, risks an assault by environmentalists and, troubling, protectionists in green garb.[2]

### Introduction

Dan Esty wrote those words in 1994. There has been some progress since then but the risks he identifies remain. Recent political developments mainly in the US but also in Europe highlight those risks. This chapter aims to outline the most recent developments in the international trade and environment debate. The chapter will look at the history of the interplay between these two ostensibly conflicting interests – trade liberalization and environmental protection and it will examine the progress that has been made in establishing common ground between the two, illustrating to what extent they are in fact mutually supportive aims. Themes of both separation and integration will emerge. I will focus on a recent panel decision now before the Appellate Body, the *Gasoline case*[3] and the agenda of the Committee on Trade and Environment (CTE). Finally, some suggestions will be made as to what steps might be taken to further improve the interaction between these two vital policy objectives at the first Ministerial Conference of the World Trade Organization (WTO) in Singapore in December, 1996.

### 'Only connect'

The 1992 Earth Summit in Rio displayed a political consensus that many of the problems of the environment were bound up with issues surrounding international trade law and its regulatory structure. Environmentalists within and without government alike accepted that the two were connected. The point had come where any further attempts to tackle environmental problems at a global level required some integration with the governing world trade regime.

There was an acknowledgement by the most industrialized Western nations that, apart from the moral responsibility to be more eco-friendly, there were ever more apparent economic incentives to clean up their industrial practices. The realization dawned that the cycle of wealth generation at the cost of spiralling pollution was limited, and that the longer environmental damage continued unchecked, the greater the ultimate expense of cleaning up. This is most obvious in the examples of 'systems failure' – like contaminated land, global warming or habitat loss. Sustainable development as a concept offered the twin goals of continuing development alongside respect for and protection of the valuable, not to say invaluable, resources that our environment represents. The two camps, crudely put – traders and environmentalists, whatever aspirations they might have shared, had not previously considered their compatibility in terms of means and ends. As a result the process of welding the concerns of the environmentalists to those of the trading libertarians has proved difficult, as neither are traditionally predisposed to placing the needs and concerns of the other on their agenda.

Their incompatibility can be illustrated by the distrust of each other's methods: the secretive nature of the debate surrounding the negotiation and application of trade policy, which contrasts to the more transparent and accountable decision-making processes advocated by environmentalists of nearly all shades. But just as environmentalists are right to demand more open decision-making processes, so too traders are right to question the ideas held by some environmentalists, that trade and its priorities are inherently damaging to a sustainable society. This view is in need of equivalent levels of reassessment.

This debate can seem very abstract but it is in fact, and in law, connected to the everyday. Barriers to markets created by environmental regulations include pesticide residues in foods, BST in milk, Chernobyl-originating radiation in agricultural products, recyclable boxes for the sale of cut flowers, regulations aimed at the way fish are caught, animals trapped or simply the trade in endangered species, trade in ozone-depleting substances or hazardous waste, the labelling of products to give consumers information on environmental performance, the energy content of goods, trade in intellectual property rights based on genetic materials; all this in addition to the environmental effects of the increased volume of international trade which could be measured and internalized to account for transportation costs. This is a live, 'food in the shops' debate that also brings in some fundamental concerns about international governance. How do we make policy in a globalized world economy? Much of this debate is unresolved. Many of the problems are speculative. Uncertainty and complexity abound. Eric Hobsbawm observed in a radio interview before he died that the 'defining characteristic' of the end of the twentieth century was the trend towards globalization and the inability of individuals or their public institutions to cope with this trend. There is a sense of that in the trade and environment debate.

## A little history: GATT (General Agreement on Tariffs and Trade)

Until 1995 when the World Trade Organization officially took over from the GATT regime, there had been little appreciation of environmental economics let alone environmental policy and law within the regime. The priority of the GATT was ensuring good conditions for global trade:

> GATT's competence is limited to trade policies which may result in significant trade effects for GATT contracting parties. In respect neither of its vocation nor of its competence is the GATT equipped to become involved in the tasks of reviewing national environmental priorities, setting environmental standards or developing global policies on the environment.[4]

The GATT was successful in large part because it was focused and committed. It did not hinder itself with UN-style rhetorical debates. It does get on with progressively reducing barriers to trade. But there were always exemptions. Had the ITO been created in 1947 these would have been fully developed. Practice may well have helped resolve many of the current conflicts. Instead we have Article XX and some parsimonious panel decisions. The GATT's treaty exceptions article is the place on which much of the legal debate on the trade and environment relationship is now focused.

### *Article XX: general exceptions*

> Subject to the requirement that such measures are not applied in a manner which would constitute a means of arbitrary or unjustifiable discrimination between countries where the same conditions prevail, or a disguised restriction on international trade, nothing in this Agreement shall be construed to prevent the adoption or enforcement by any contracting party of measures:
>
> ... (b) necessary to protect human, animal or plant life or health; (or)
>
> ... (g) relating to the conservation of exhaustible resources if such measures are made effective in conjunction with restrictions on domestic production or consumption.

Whilst Article XX doesn't refer to the environment it clearly encompasses environmental issues. The WTO/GATT has not used Article XX to exploit its full potential for integrating environmental protection with free trade. The experience so far is that the Article has been construed very narrowly in GATT panels, and in trade policy discourse. For example, the Tuna/Dolphin case (which shall be discussed later) took too restrictive a view of the necessity test when judging the efforts of The Marine Mammal Protection Act to address the problem of dolphin netting. Notwithstanding this, the argument that the mechanism and rules for governing world trade do not have an impact on shaping environmental policy is untenable. There is a realization by prudent environmentalists that this is an organization which *must* have reference to the environmental agenda, as global economic policy is such a powerful factor influencing directly or indirectly many forms of environmental degradation and the policies designed to address that degradation.

## World Trade Organization

The WTO[5] is a profoundly important global institution. In due course it will surpass in influence the existing Bretton Woods institutions. 1995 saw the rolling GATT agreement evolve into the WTO and a range of changes to its institutions were established in the Uruguay Round of the GATT negotiations. The settlement procedure in trade disputes has become more sophisticated. Panel adoption is now automatic and only consensus can block its decisions – which contrasts with GATT where a consensus was needed to move the procedure forward. This, along with the newly created Appellate Body ought to assist the role of law to develop, and to maintain the claims of the weak against those of the strongest trading nations.

The WTO fulfils the need today for a multilateral body designed to create new trading opportunities even for the biggest world traders. In these days of global marketplace the WTO is the obvious institution to oversee trade issues and as a result it also has a unique ability and obligation to tackle environmental concerns which arise within a trade context.

Some environmentally conscious advances were made on the old GATT in its transition to the new WTO which now identifies non-actionable subsidies related to environmental retro-fitting, recognizes the Environmental Services Sector, and includes sustainable development goals in its preamble.

The final round also saw the creation of WTO Committee on Trade and the Environment which over the first two years will address: the use of trade measures for environmental protection purposes (especially within multilateral environmental agreements – MEAs); ecolabelling and eco-packaging; domestically prohibited goods; market access; dispute-settlement procedures and other issues. This demonstrates an appreciation by the WTO that it ought to take environmental issues into account, but it does not go far enough in establishing those issues on the trade agenda, nor does it make environmental policy an integral consideration when deciding on the application of trade. The Committee is to report to the Ministerial Conference in Singapore in December 1996.

In integrating the needs of the environment with those of international trade, disputes will emerge, and if we can confidently predict this, then the position regarding the relationship between trade and environment policy would be best clarified in advance, and the dispute settlement system reformed so that it can cope with these sorts of dispute.

## Conflicting interests: two cases

### Mexico *v.* United States *Tuna/Dolphin Dispute*[6]

Here, trading and environmental interests clashed and involved the GATT in a very heated public squabble between neighbours with apparently different environmental and economic agendas. The infamous disputes between Mexico and the United States erupted over a ban imposed by the United States on the import of yellowfin tuna caught with 'purse seine' nets which were responsible for the incidental killing or harming of dolphins in excess of standards set by the United States in the Marine Mammal Protection Act.[7] The GATT dispute panel concluded that this ban was impermissible under the GATT agreement and could not invoke the exemption of Article XX primarily because:

1 The ban constituted a trade measure which was aimed at preserving resources outside the jurisdiction of the United States.
2 The United States failed to demonstrate that the measure was aimed primarily at conservation.
3 The panel felt that the ban was discriminatory to a production method of the goods as opposed to a characteristic of the good itself, and so became a quantitative restriction which is excluded by GATT Article XI.

There are three lingering concerns about the reasoning in the Tuna/Dolphin dispute. First, how does a state deal with preserving resources, perhaps migratory, outside its jurisdiction short of multilateral agreement? How does the reality of somebody else's methods, perhaps even enterprises taking advantage of lower standards, get addressed in a way that survives tests of national treatment? Ideally, one would like to encourage states to deal with global commons issues in a non-discriminatory way, but how is the trade regime helping them?

Second, how did the 'primarily aimed at' test get to (a) exist and (b) be so restrictively applied? 'Primarily aimed at' is not in the Agreement, it is not a Treaty test. But if it is to be applied to Article XX(g) cases by practice, the overall purpose of Article XX – to allow public policy exceptions to free movement of goods – is at least as important as the trade disciplines set out in Articles I, III and XI. Despite the reality of industry capture and unholy alliances (such is ordinary political life) the idea that the Marine Mammal Protection Act was really a front for protecting the US tuna industry came as a surprise to the conservationists who fought for it for many years.

Third, and it is a matter I deal with later, the issue of production and process methods (PPMs) and Article XI (the 'like product' debate) remains unresolved. Of course, environmentalists don't have a thing against tuna itself, they are concerned with method. They are, more than that, concerned about fishing method and fisheries collapse, at least as much as whales, dolphins, turtles and sea birds. Frankly, these are vital economic arguments, missing from the very formulaic reasoning of the panel.

In a subsequent dispute initiated by the EU and The Netherlands, a second panel was asked to look again at the GATT considerations involved in the US Marine Mammal Protection Act, which was designed to address the problem of tuna import via third parties, thereby affecting European importers of Mexican tuna. The panel decision reflected the stance taken in the primary dispute but the reasoning altered – the problems in this instance being that measures designed to force a policy change in third parties were not justifiable as exceptions under Article XX(b) or (g).

The tuna/dolphin issues embroiled the GATT dispute resolution panel in a trading dispute which had at its centre the interests of species protection and protection for the domestic market. The language of protection has become a battle ground in itself (see 'The New Protectionism' by Hines and Lang). In the United States the outcome of this dispute has, for the environmentalist lobby, undermined the credibility of GATT/WTO as a forum capable of rationally adjudicating between the dual interests of environment and trade. Although some blame should be shouldered by the US government for a poorly framed, if not ill-conceived piece of legislation which left itself vulnerable to ambiguous interpretations regarding its intent. More of this later. Even the most fervent environmentalist must acknowledge the basic unfairness of a regime that calculated the key dolphin kill ratio at the end of year so that the Mexican fishermen had no idea whether they could comply until the end of the season, and in the meantime were cut out of their most important market.

### Venezuela/Brazil *v* United States *(the Gasoline case): (1996)*[8]

This latest dispute offers a second illustration that the needs of trade and environment can often conflict directly. The case centred around a challenge made by Brazil and Venezuela to US regulations, on fuels and fuel additives concerning standards for reformulated and conventional gasoline, devised by the Environmental Protection Agency (EPA). The dispute was examined by the Dispute Settlement Body (DSB) under Article XXII of the GATT. The substance of the issue was whether the extremely technical specifications issued by the US EPA for gasoline being sold in US territory and which applied to US refiners, blenders and importers, were discriminatory. These rules were established in an effort to tackle the ozone and pollution damage experienced by cities in the US as a result, principally, of car exhaust fumes. While the aim may have been laudable the manner in which the US sought to achieve it was viewed as protectionist by its petrol producing neighbours. This was despite the fact that the US authorities went to considerable lengths to make the new standards palatable to those affected, by introducing a complex range of both specific and flexible criteria, to attempt to ensure equanimity of application.

The EPA issued a regulation on reformulated and conventional gasoline providing certain baseline emissions standards. The regulation established two different sets of baselines. Domestic refiners that were in operation for at least half of 1990 were required to compute an *individual baseline* based upon its 1990 emissions. Three methods were available for determining this individual baseline, depending on the types of data available to the companies. (Method number one required the most exacting data, method number three, the least.) Additionally, importers that were also foreign refiners were required to calculate an individual baseline if 75 per cent or more of the volume produced at their refinery was imported into the US (the 75 per cent rule).

Refiners that did not operate for at least six months during 1990 were required to comply with standards regulated under a *statutory baseline*, a weighted average of total emissions that was often stricter than the requirements mandated by the individual baselines. In addition, foreign importers and blenders that could not establish an individual baseline by using method number one, were ordered to comply with the statutory baseline. As a result, foreign importers and blenders that were not refiners importing at least 75 per cent of their total volume to the US were precluded from establishing an individual baseline under two of the three methods available to US and select foreign refiners. (This was because the US believed that data used to establish an individual baseline under the second and third methods would be unreliable coming from foreign refiners.)

Despite the efforts of the US authorities, however, the rules were attacked as being discriminatory in favour of American multinationals, as it allowed them access to the market with domestically established 'baseline' fuel content whereas imports of foreign gasoline had to comply with more stringent statutory baselines, so domestic importers would demand gasoline at lower prices as an incentive for taking it. The net effect was to leave foreign producers at a competitive disadvantage contrary to Articles I and III.

The US resisted the challenge and sought to have the rules brought within the Article XX exemptions, (b), (d) and (g). The panel noted that the US would have to establish three elements to successfully shelter its regulations under Article XX(b):

1 that the *policy* in respect of the measures for which the provision was invoked fell within the range of policies designed to protect human, animal or plant life or health;
2 that the inconsistent measures for which the exception was being invoked were *necessary* to fulfil the policy objective; and
3 that the measures were applied in conformity with the requirements of the *introductory clause* of Article XX.

The panel found that the first requirement was satisfied. However, the second test (necessity) failed. The panel determined that the test does not consider the necessity of the policy goal, but instead determines whether or not it was necessary that imported gas be effectively prevented from benefiting from as favourable sales conditions as were afforded by an individual baseline tied to the producer of a product. Citing section 337 and the 1990 Thai Cigarette case, the panel declared that the regulations cannot be 'necessary' if either consistent or less inconsistent measures were available to the US that could be reasonably expected to achieve similar results. The panel declared that less inconsistent or fully consistent measures could be effectively applied in this case. As a result, Article XX(b) was not applicable.

The panel further ruled that the US had to demonstrate three elements to shelter its regulations under Article XX(d):

1 that the measures for which the exception were being invoked – that is, the particular trade measures inconsistent with the General Agreement – *secure compliance* with laws or regulations themselves not inconsistent with the General Agreement;
2 that the inconsistent measures for which the exception was being invoked were *necessary* to secure compliance with those laws or regulations; and
3 that the measures were applied in conformity with the requirements of the *introductory clause* of Article XX.

The panel held that, even assuming that the system of baselines constituted a law or regulation not inconsistent with the General Agreement, the discrimination between foreign and domestic gasoline which violated Article III:4 did not 'secure compliance' with the baseline system. Therefore, the US failed the first step. The panel determined that the baseline system was not an enforcement mechanism. Instead, they were simply rules for determining the individual baselines. As such, they were not the types of measures with which Article XX(d) was concerned.

The GATT panel concluded that the US had to establish four elements to shelter its regulations under Article XX(g):

1 that the *policy* in respect of the measures for which the provision was invoked fell within the range of policies related to the conservation of exhaustible natural resources;
2 that the measures for which the exception was being invoked – that is the particular trade measures inconsistent with the General Agreement – were *related to* the conservation of exhaustible natural resources;
3 that the measures for which the exception was being invoked were made effective *in conjunction* with restrictions on domestic production or consumption; and

4 that the measures were applied in conformity with the requirements of the *introductory clause* of Article XX.

The panel found that clean air can be an exhaustible resource, and thus, the first step was satisfied. However, it determined that the US regulations were not 'related to' the conservation of natural resources within the meaning of Article XX(g).

It would seem that the DSB again opted for trade as the priority and decided, again with legitimate reason, that the rules constituted a barrier to trade for foreign producers. The case reiterated the lesson of *Tuna/Dolphin*, that when the two issues clash within the context of the WTO any merits contained in the environmental regulation fall foul of the legitimate demands for even-handed (non-discriminatory) trade policies. This case had what is known amongst advocates as 'bad facts'. An EPA official had admitted in giving evidence at an earlier inquiry that there had been some protectionist intent in the design of the rule. But at least the environmental motivation of the role was accepted by the Panel as legitimate. The US has declared its intention to appeal this – it will be very interesting to see what the Appellate Body makes of this their first case. In particular, whether the Appellate Body challenges the reasoning the Panel uses to interpret Article XX.

## GATT 1994 and UNCED 1992: Common-but-differentiated responsibility

Despite the fact that many parties to the UNCED agreements are also members of the WTO, the change of hats involved in the shift from one forum to the other has raised a number of questions concerning the priorities of trade versus the environment and the connection of both to development. At the outset, however, I should say that the North/South dichotomy does not easily display itself in the trade and environment debate. What follows is too simplistic an analysis. It can be used only for illustration. Ambassador Lang from Austria, a highly respected international lawyer and negotiator, is fond of saying there are always four camps – environmentalists and traders, North and South, and ultimately they meet and divide on issues not political geography – in the WTO (CTE).

Both at UNCED in 1992, and within the context of the GATT negotiations, developing countries objected to the focus on upward harmonization of environmental standards whilst little attention was being paid to how the resulting discrimination towards their products might be resolved if genuinely international standards could not be reached. They (the developing/'South') argued the onus should not be on raising abatement standards but on lowering Western waste and consumption. They felt that the North had somewhat obscured the focus of the debate and received a social and environmental subsidy from developing countries in that they created and benefited from the problems which they now expect everyone to pay for. In the Rio agreements this broad debate focused on the application of the principle of common-but-differentiated responsibility. Later, as the North pushed for upping standards without filling the financing gap experienced in Rio, concern grew that 'greening GATT' would only benefit the North. In fact, environmental issues were marginalized in the closing stages of the Uruguay Round as the negotiating focus shifted to interaction between the US and Europe on agricultural subsidies. Fears that least developed nations would, in addition, not benefit from the Uruguay Round have proved to be well founded, with 70 per cent of projected trading benefits from the WTO being reaped by Europe and North America ($320 billion per annum, according to a November 1993 study by the GATT Secretariat).

The concerns of many underdeveloped countries – namely that higher environmental standards would extenuate the disparity between North and South and introduce a barrier to industrial and economic development – explains the antipathy which the emerging economies display towards environmental arguments in the WTO; they are reluctant to cooperate without exchange of technology and finance being offered in tandem with the demand for higher environmental standards.

While this problem subdues the impetus for improvement from individual countries, the whole process of development through liberalized trade is ultimately impeded by the inability of the WTO to recognize or endorse a broader set of interests based on principles of distributive justice. This is very hard for the existing WTO (staff and delegates) to contemplate. The priority of the International Trade Policy is barrier reduction; environmental issues are viewed as just another obstacle and development concerns are covered mostly through the assumption that liberalized trade will lead to greater wealth (the Generalized System of Preferences is an exception). Although there is increasing acknowledgement of the view that environmental protection should be reclassified as an internal production cost, the GATT/WTO lacks a true environmental or social agenda and while it only has trade negotiation objectives it ignores both its capacity and responsibility to take action in the global public interest. In sum, I do not think it is possible for the WTO to carry on as if it were the GATT. Single-minded trade barrier reduction in long rounds is not the future of the WTO. Integrated trade policy in the global public interest is.

The only acknowledgement of environmental protection within GATT/WTO has been the unsatisfactory Article XX. This clause allows environmental protection to fit into the GATT framework subject to the requirement that restrictions do not 'constitute a means of arbitrary or unjustifiable restriction on international trade'. This ought to be a hurdle about which no legislator should feel concerned. Adhering to these disciplines ought to be transparently a good thing. But the interpretation of the 'necessity test', the 'least restrictive requirements' and the 'primarily aimed at' tests have made the task of the domestic legislator extremely difficult. How does the US accept the burden of common-but-differentiated responsibility for global warming, buy off a strong domestic energy lobby and avoid discrimination? There is bound to be a less trade-restrictive route available but in an open democratic system how do you make perfect legislation? Trade protectionism, especially when allied to nationalism is ugly. No one should discriminate by choice. But implementing UNCED commitments is hard for governments to do. If common-but-differentiated responsibility for global environmental problems is to mean anything the technology transfer and finance to developing countries must come with some understanding that perfect legislatures in the countries who must take the lead in emission reduction do not exist.

Another major problem is the form that any dispute resolution process has taken. The WTO has improved upon GATT in many ways. The dispute resolution panel may now have the benefit of expertise[9] in the area under dispute, but it is another area which could benefit from clarification, and ultimately reform, within the four-year review period for the DSU. How does the DSU relate to other dispute settlement mechanisms in MEAs? Who characterizes the dispute? Is it just a question of consent between states or a case-by-case basis?

It is worth remembering that while there is considerable scope for improvement on the past interpretation of Article XX of the WTO, it would be naïve to attach too much responsibility for environmental improvement on trade measures alone, which when operating without cohesive political support and planning can be ineffective at addressing environmental problems. Economists and trade policy analysts rightly criticize examples of unilateral ineffectiveness. Tropical deforestation will not be solved by simply banning trade in timber products from the Amazon. Perhaps trade measures may play a small part – say in respect of a particular species like mahogany – but that can be dealt with multilaterally through CITES. We know that unilateralism is only available to the strong – the big markets – and that environmental policy is a good cover for protectionism. Nonetheless, the WTO should have the confidence to amend Article XX, insert 'the environment' and 'measures taken pursuant to MEAs' and trust in an active and credible dispute settlement procedure to 'out' the discriminatory protectionists.

## Production and Process Methods (PPMs)

The question of PPMs is a pertinent example of where the interests of trade and the environment most obviously diverge. Whilst environmental protection requires that production processes be tackled, the traders cannot confidently allow this matter to enter the debate. Trade policy makers argue that discrimination against products would be expanded to a potentially devastating level for trade liberalization enterprise. Compromise offers a huge challenge to all concerned as the interests of both the environmentalists and traders seem at times irreconcilable. The concerns regarding PPMs cross geographical divides – traders dislike them everywhere – North, South, East or West.

Again, it's a question of priorities. At least, that is the first step. Then we need to deal with complexity. The destruction of habitat and the pollution involved in creating some apparently harmless products is often a bigger source of concern than finished products. However, once traders begin to look at the production processes it becomes a frighteningly complicated issue knowing where and how to set standards. Who selects standards and with what agenda in mind? There is a disparity of focus between the environmental community and the traders, regarding the inclusion of PPMs as issues at all. The protection of non-domestic interests by unilateral action which was the source of the *Tuna/Dolphin* case, has proved to be a rightly contentious issue, but no solutions are appearing from within the WTO. The answer at the moment is 'no flexibility' on PPMs: 'we don't do that here'.

Ecolabelling provides a good example of how an ostensibly legitimate attempt to regulate production through a commitment to the life cycle approach and consumer information, when attempted unilaterally, creates an impediment to free trade. Ecolabelling schemes can discriminate against imports when they reflect exclusively the environmental concerns of the importing country, consequently they can include criteria that can be inappropriate to the conditions experienced by the country of supply. While few would argue about the validity of informing and improving standards, the manner in which it is done has yet to be resolved satisfactorily within the trade regime. All this hinders the development of the labels.

The discomfort within the GATT of the Austrian policy of labelling tropical timber demonstrates the difficulties involved with unilateral action in addressing extrajurisdictional matters of international concern. The Netherlands is proposing a labelling scheme of its own which will provide a further test. The OECD continues the search for solutions and has to date recommended transparent programmes, consultation and appropriate time periods for ecolabelling schemes. We await with interest the result of the CTE's work.

## Multilateral Environmental Treaties (MEAs)

MEAs offer the possibility of securing prior world-wide consent and establishing comprehensive environmental standards to protect the global commons. MEAs like the Montreal Protocol, the Basel Convention and the CITES encourage commitment through a carrot and stick approach, by restricting trade in the relevant area and extending those restrictions to non-parties, and by providing financing to meet the objectives of the MEA.

The carrot and stick approach functions, alongside a shared concern in the resolution of a global problem, because a nation considering whether or not to join will simply balance the benefits of compliance with the costs of trade restrictions, a balance which tilts against free riding as more and more nations join, and trade restrictions encourage membership. The successful MEAs seem to limit their use of trade measures to those which are effective and use them only sparingly. Each of these MEAs is a package. Trade and environmental measures come with finance, and compliance is regularly reviewed through the conference of the parties.

It is clear to me that trade restrictions have proven to be one of the most useful methods of making MEAs effective. While no nation has yet challenged trade restrictions contained in MEAs this does not mean that the threat of future challenges should be easily dismissed, since it is unlikely that every WTO member will be party to every MEA there remains for WTO members not bound by an MEA the incentive to challenge its trade restrictions, as well as the risk that a party to both will challenge the consistency of an MEA with the GATT, upon dissatisfaction with its obligations.

The WTO needs to familiarize itself with these other international treaties, to connect them to its work and to maintain its own relevance to their debates. Where there exists a match of states that are parties to both a specific MEA and the WTO there should be a presumption of compatibility, as is already the case de facto. But non-parties who have not derogated their WTO rights maintain the opportunity for redress within that system, this presents an opportunity for the WTO to offer support to multilateralism by making it extremely difficult for a state to challenge an MEA within the WTO.

From a trade perspective the problem of 'measures taken pursuant to' the objectives of an MEA which involve the use of Trade Related Environmental Measures (TREMs), or have an effect on trade, is the most worrying. There exists a concern that the use of these could offer international endorsement to unilateral trade measures. But as is referred to above, what if it solves a problem of global concern? Is not that what common-but-differentiated responsibility is all about? Why should not developing countries favour one country taking the lead? OECD studies have suggested that in the context of climate change, the domain in law of the Climate Change Convention, the most efficient type of international abatement agreement would combine simultaneous abatement commitments by all major emitting countries, economic incentives (global carbon taxes or tradable permit systems) used to achieve abatement objectives and the reduction of subsidies for existing energy sources (excluding renewable). But an instrument such as the proposed carbon dioxide/energy tax put forward by the EEC could face opposition over its ability to comply with GATT Article III or even Article I. In particular it would be subjected to close scrutiny regarding export subsidies and remission of taxes for exports.

The WTO must be concerned about the possible abuse of any trade measures, however, this should not obstruct environmental policy making and unduly restrict the choices states have to solve global environmental problems – especially when there may be compensating mechanisms available in the trade regime. Indeed, border tax adjustments may be seen as the point at which trade and environmental policies converge.

David Wirth,[10] in a paper delivered at the recent GETS conference in New York, ably demonstrated the exaggerated fear of the trade measures in the

Basel Convention. He did this by focusing on the legal analysis of the apparently competing obligations between signatories of both Basel and the WTO. He argued simply for a derogation of rights to the MEA from WTO members, leaving only the non-party concern. Thereafter, problems do remain because the US is a non-party and because of a lack of clarity surrounding trade in recyclable waste and lack of attention to South/South trade. However, problems of scope, emphasis and drafting are inherent in such documents and should not prevent the WTO from accommodating the concept of an MEA using trade to achieve its objective.

In principle, in the WTO, member states have the flexibility to implement their chosen policies, especially those which have been inspired by multilateral environmental management processes. Incorporating MEAs into the WTO would mark a significant culture change but it would recognize the comparable value of MEAs to international society. MEA and WTO concerns would be placed on an equal footing in the eyes of dispute settlement panels. Amending Article XX would encourage the environmental community to become more supportive of trade liberalization, avoiding a situation such as that in the US where environmentalists have begun again to espouse protectionism.

The European Community has gone some way in demonstrating how we can hope to balance trade and environment interests through integration. The EC Treaty revised at Maastricht sees a number of references to social and environmental concerns incorporated into what was essentially a trading treaty.[11]

In Articles 2 and 3 we see references to the objectives of improving living and working conditions as well as raising the standard of living. Express environmental objectives were introduced by the Single European Act into Articles 130 R, S and T of the EC Treaty. These articles have succeeded in securing for environmental protection a legitimate place on the community agenda, thus obviating the need to demonstrate on a case-by-case basis the link between environmental protection and common market goals. Placing the environment firmly on the trading agenda was also pursued by NAFTA. Through an environmental side agreement progress was possible in linking trade and environment issues with broader economic proposals. A sum of $2 billion has been committed to the Border Environmental Cooperation Commission for technological transfer, capacity building, information exchange and other activities. There are different approaches displaying the essential differences between the European *Union* and the free trade area of NAFTA.

The European Community has taken steps towards integrating trade and environmental policy though law and the dynamics within its institutional structure. It is hard to imagine them being accepted at the international level. Nonetheless, the WTO can observe and learn.

Given the status quo, the biggest challenge for environmental law makers is to legislate in a manner which can survive the challenge of GATT/WTO. The Brazil/Venezuela – US Gasoline dispute illustrates this well. Flexibility of interpretation in order to smooth the acceptance of higher standards by the business community, provided loopholes for the domestic market which Venezuela and Brazil rightly saw as unfair. Unfortunately, legislators for environmental protection seem to consistently face the choice between downward harmonization of standards, to ensure acceptance by all, or raising standards to see them rendered unenforceable through external challenge.

## The First Ministerial Conference of the WTO in Singapore, December 1996

The CTE has a 'process' problem. It does not have all the players involved who can assist in the search for balance between trade and environmental policy. The Committee is not making much progress towards clear recommendations for Ministers in December but there is time yet – the pressure of negotiations can often deliver unexpected results.

Let us have no doubts, there must be a demonstrable 'success' on trade and environment in Singapore. No recommendation by the CTE and a simple report of two and a half years' work is unacceptable on any view. The frustration is that there is little to fear in change provided that the dialogue, the process of integration and the inevitable disputes continue. How can anyone be so positive about disputes? The answer is that conflicts are needed to test the principles and boost authority and credibility. Whilst it is politically important for all the agenda items in the CTE to remain there for the current negotiations – MEAs, ecolabelling, market access, domestically prohibited goods (DPGs), transparency and even dispute settlement – towards the end a minimum list of concrete recommendations leading to a change in the status quo must follow.

1. A recommendation on MEAs – dealing with amendments. Perhaps an understanding setting clear criteria for compatibility.
2. A recommendation on multilaterally inspired domestic action or measures taken pursuant to MEAs. Setting out the circumstances where they are compatible with GATT/WTO. This can form part of the amendment of Article XX.
3. A recommendation, recognizing that these amendments would remain challengeable exemptions under Article XX, that the Dispute Settlement Understanding would undergo review to accommodate environmental interests. This would mean continuing the application of existing rules on expert involvement and adding means of access to dispute settlement procedures for non-state actors.
4. A recommendation defining the basic principles for trade in goods with ecolabels.
5. A recommendation for negotiation of an understanding on PPMs.
6. A recommendation for the continuation of the CTE with new rules of participation (including NGOs and other IGOs, subject to rules of procedure).

7 A recommendation for the creation of a regular dialogue with IGOs, Secretariat of MEAs, experts and NGOs.

## Conclusions

The Winnipeg Principles on Trade and Sustainable Development, developed under the auspices of the Canadian International Institute for Sustainable Development with the participation of an expert group provide a useful reference point for progress in this trade and environment debate. Consider this list of principles:

1. **Efficiency and cost internalization**
   Efficiency is a common interest for environment, development and trade policies.
2. **Equity**
   Equity relates to the distribution both within and between generations of physical and natural capital, as well as knowledge and technology.
3. **Environmental integrity**
   This requires respect for limits to the regenerative capacity of ecosystems, actions to avoid irreversible harm to plant and animal populations and species, and protection for valued areas.
4. **Subsidiarity**
   Subsidiarity recognizes that action will occur at different political levels, depending on the nature of issues. It assigns priority to the lowest jurisdictional level consistent with effectiveness.
5. **International cooperation**
   Sustainable development requires strengthening international systems of cooperation at all levels, encompassing environment, development and trade policies.
6. **Science and precaution**
   The interrelated nature of trade, environment and development can give rise to conflicts in short-run objectives, and policies designed to address these should be shaped by objective criteria.
7. **Openness**
   Greater openness will significantly improve environmental, trade and development policies.

These principles are supported by others (see for example *Environmental Priorities for the World Trading System*, FIELD/NRDC, January 1995) and are widely discussed in policy-making communities. How well are we doing in implementing these principles? There is loose talk that nothing will happen in Singapore, nothing more than a report of discussions with no recommendations. This could happen. Ultimately, there will be recommendations, maybe limited to one or two agenda items. But to deal with the trade and environment mandate in this way would be tantamount to a missed opportunity for the WTO CTE to send a signal to the world that it has considered the aspirations of international trade and environmental protection and concluded that compatibility, or to use the Agenda 21 phrase, 'mutual supportiveness' is possible.

## Notes

* This piece was written before the 1996 Ministerial Conference. At the Singapore event the CTE Report was adopted but contained few recommendations, and none that really altered the status quo. The CTE's mandate has been renewed. It is now considering focusing its discussions on particular sectors such as timber, textiles and electricity. This should be more productive. Meanwhile trade and environmental conflicts are finding their way into the DSU.

1 The author would like to acknowledge the research assistance of Beatrice Chaytor, Conor McCaughan and James Meschewski.

2 Professor Dan Esty, Director, Yale Centre for Environmental Law and Policy.

3 The case has since been decided by the Appellate Body. The Appellate Body reached the following conclusions:

(a) the Panel erred in law in its conclusions that the baseline establishment rules contained in Part 80 of Title 40 of the Code of Federal Regulations did not fall within the terms of Article XX(g) of the General Agreement;

(b) the Panel accordingly also erred in law in failing to decide whether the baseline establishment rules contained in Part 80 of Title 40 of the Code of Federal Regulations fell within the chapeau of Article XX of the General Agreement;

(c) the baseline establishment rules contained in Part 80 of Title 40 of the Code of Federal Regulations fail to meet the requirements of the chapeau of Article XX of the General Agreement, and accordingly are not justified under Article XX of the General Agreement.

4 Chairman of GATT Council, GATT Focus 1992.

5 Throughout this chapter I use the WTO as a shorthand expression for the WTO and its Members, i.e. the Secretariat and its masters – the States.

6 33 ILM 842 (1994).

7 30 ILM 1594 (1991).

*8 International Trade Law Reports* (*ITLR*), Vol.1 8–85, including commentary. The Appellate Body has now ruled on the reformulated Gasoline case. It found in favour of Brazil and Venezuela but the reasoning is significantly different. See the commentary in ITLR.

9 It is interesting to note that the Panel in the Gasoline case did not call upon independent experts.

10 Associate Professor of Law, Washington and Lee University. The paper was delivered 19 January 1996, for the Global Environment and Trade Study, at a conference held at New York University Law School.

11 The Amsterdam Treaty of 1997 has continued this trend towards integration. See new Objective of Treaty and Art. 3d, amended 100AG and Commission Declaration on Environmental Assessment of Policy.

# 13

# TRIT – A NEW WTO CODE OF CONDUCT ON TRADE-RELATED ASPECTS OF INTERNATIONAL TAXATION?

*Asif H. Qureshi*[1]

## Introduction

Whilst the GATT, i.e., the General Agreement To Talk and Talk, may well have been extinguished, thank heavens for the continued international consensus to talk and talk! Without it such acronyms as TRIPS, TRIMS, and TREMS would not have found a place in the international trade dictionary. Why not a TRIT (i.e trade related aspects of international taxation)?[2]

Of late, there has been little comprehensive academic or political consideration of TRIT.[3] The power of taxation is central to the functioning of the sovereign State, and thus there is no clear political lobby for its international regulation. It is also a technical area in which the chief participants in the international trade forum, i.e. trade officials, may be said to have a limited and particular view of the subject – mainly with respect to indirect taxes on products. Yet the linkage between taxation and international trade will need to be addressed sooner or later in a more concerted manner.

The increment in the general level of the abolition of non tax barriers raises the potency of taxation as a distorting feature of international trade; [4] and conversely the susceptibility of international trade to it. Further, this linkage needs to be understood not just at the political and economic levels. This is because where a benefit accruing to a Member of the World Trade Organization (WTO) is being nullified or impaired, a cause for action under the WTO dispute settlement procedures can exist not only in cases involving a violation of a particular provision of the WTO code[5] of conduct, but also where any domestic taxation nullifies or impairs a benefit under the WTO code, or impedes the attainment of any of its objectives, whether or not the tax conflicts with the code.[6]

Integrating TRIT into the international trading system involves an understanding *inter alia* of the nature of the State activity of tax collection, the limits of State fiscal sovereignty, and the existing WTO framework.

## Nature of tax-collecting activity

There are in fact three standpoints from which this State activity may be perceived. First, it is axiomatic that taxation facilitates revenue collection. Second, taxation may be characterized as a normative exercise. In the context of international trade, it is an instrument of trade regulation – a trade policy instrument. Finally, and more controversially, taxation may be stated to partake of, and/or is akin to a 'State trading activity'. In other words, the very nature of the exercise is such that it renders the State a participant in the milieu of the international trading activity. Thus, the act involved by the State in purchasing boots for the army, or the business of the provision of nuclear energy, arguably bears some similarity to the collection of taxes for the rendering of public benefits. Such characterization of State fiscal activity and its consequential subjugation to a normative framework has parallels in other spheres of International Law, namely the restrictive doctrine of State Immunity. Under this doctrine certain activities of a State conducted in another State are not immune from the jurisdiction of that other State, because they are no longer considered as sovereign acts but rather as private commercial acts.

In fact, State fiscal activity partakes of all these three characteristics. However, the amenability of a State to have its fiscal jurisdiction constrained by international norms is dependent on how it perceives the fiscal activity. Thus, the caricature of taxation as a State trading activity is considered problematic – as indeed are any limits on revenue collection. On the other hand, the propriety of the claim of the international trading order in the field of taxation is also dependent on how State fiscal activity is characterized. Thus, to the extent that it is a trade policy instrument it is subject to international constraints, where it is distortive of international trade. To the extent that taxation partakes of a State trading activity, might it not be legitimately the concern of the international trading order also?

## Fiscal sovereignty and liberal trade

Many years ago, Chretien[7] took the view that a State's legislative fiscal jurisdiction is unlimited or at worst minimal. This view is echoed by other international lawyers in their analysis of the limits of a State's legislative fiscal jurisdiction under General International Law.[8] The view of minimal (or unlimited) fiscal jurisdiction has not gone unchallenged however. It has been asserted that a State's legislative fiscal jurisdiction is in fact limited.[9] It is limited under General International Law by the requirement that a State can only exercise legislative jurisdiction if there is a reasonable link/connection between the State and the taxpayer – through for example, nationality, domicile, residence or the source of earnings. The view that a State's fiscal jurisdiction is limited is grounded mainly on the premise that a State's jurisdiction is an aspect of sovereignty, and thus given that State sovereignty is not absolute, but limited, it follows that a State's fiscal jurisdiction is limited.

The debate amongst fiscal jurists as to the parameters of a State's fiscal jurisdiction is one that is not resolved. It is of course critical in evaluating competing fiscal claims by taxing authorities. It does however raise a fundamental question in the context of this conference, namely the significance of the question of the limits of a State's fiscal legislative jurisdiction to liberal trade.

From the perspective of liberal trade, the question of the limits of a State's fiscal legislative jurisdiction (and *a fortiori* State fiscal sovereignty) raises the following issues:

### *Whether under International Law the rules on the allocation of fiscal jurisdiction are such that they promote or at any rate do not hinder liberal trade*

The international rules on the allocation of fiscal jurisdiction between States are uncertain, incomplete and not necessarily coherent. Under General International Law the reasonable link theory of fiscal legislative jurisdiction is not necessarily founded on, or consonant with, the dictates of equity (individual equity and inter-nation equity) and efficiency (capital import and export neutrality) which are relevant considerations in evaluating international tax practices from the view point of free trade. The reasonable link is a formalistic view of legislative fiscal jurisdiction. It is concerned with the validity of jurisdictional exercises in terms of formal connections with a State. It is not concerned, at least directly, with the allocation of legislative fiscal jurisdiction amongst States, from the standpoint of both equity and efficiency.

The treaty practice, on the other hand, is mainly bilateral, and not necessarily uniform or complete. It is influenced by the OECD Model Tax Convention, and therefore is orientated in favour of the resident State's fiscal jurisdiction. There is some regional practice, although in the context of regional integration.

### *Does liberal trade undermine fiscal sovereignty? (Does it thereby inhibit trade liberalization?)*

This is a question in part that is dependent upon how State fiscal activity is characterized, i.e., as revenue collecting, regulatory, or partaking of a State trading nature. It is also an enquiry which calls for a cost–benefit analysis. There is in fact no straightforward answer. Certainly where liberal trade is 'the offensive weapon of the strong' that Chris Brown refered to in his paper at the conference on free trade, Manchester 1996, the preservation of the advantage by the strong, must imply in the end greater government revenues from the fruits of international trade. But taxation is not merely about raising revenue.

It is also a regulatory instrument. As such, liberal trade must imply an undermining of the capacity of States to use fiscal policy as an economic/social regulator.

For developing countries, liberal trade can impact on revenue collection. Some developing States rely significantly on the taxes involved in protectionism.

### *Does liberal trade necessitate greater fiscal sovereignty?*

Increased liberalization of trade threatens the capacity of States to protect their tax base. This is however more a question that relates to fiscal enforcement jurisdiction. As such it can be dealt with, and need not hinder progression to liberal trade.

## The WTO framework[10]

The relationship between taxation and trade has been considered in the framework of the General Agreement on Tariffs and Trade (GATT).[11] In 1968 a Working Party[12] concluded that determining the impact of taxation on international trade (i.e commodity prices) 'was full of difficulty and of a very complex nature'.[13] This is of course not surprising particularly given that the issue of fiscal sovereignty is critical to the existence of the nation state. Thus, apart from tariff concessions negotiated, the WTO code significantly does not limit the prerogative of the State to raise revenue. It only regulates this sphere in a minimalist fashion. Indeed, a GATT panel has specifically ruled that the Members enjoy a broad freedom in relation to their internal tax policy as well as their internal taxation of goods.[14] This includes the freedom to decide the objectives, level, principles and methods of the system of internal taxation of goods.[15]

In fact, the WTO perspective is limited to the trade-related aspects of international taxation. Even in this context, it is not systematic or coherent. Generally, the provisions on TRIT in the code are scattered, the treatment of goods and services is not uniform, and direct and indirect taxes are treated differently. Further, the WTO remit is confined mainly to three prohibitions, i.e. non-discriminatory taxation; protective taxation; and the edict against fiscal subsidies. In addition, the code is also orientated towards indirect taxes – at any rate in so far as express provisions are concerned. This is not only because such taxes directly affect product prices in an obvious fashion but also because it is necessary to regulate them in order to preserve the integrity of tariff concessions negotiated between Members.[16]

The provisions of the WTO code as they pertain to international tax issues are varied. Here only some of the principal aspects are focused upon, mainly to provide a sense of TRIT, and to demonstrate the absence of a systematic regime in this field.

### *Non-discriminatory taxation as between Member States*

In so far as taxes pertaining to goods are concerned, all such taxes in connection with importation or exportation are to be applied on a most-favoured-nation (MFN) basis, i.e. they must not discriminate according to the origins or the destination of the products.[17] Thus, the MFN standard appears to be confined to indirect taxes, even though direct taxes can operate as fiscal barriers to trade. Further, the standard is undermined by certain exceptions.[18] In relation to services, the MFN principle applies to all taxes[19] (direct and indirect). Again, deviation from this standard is possible in certain circumstances, if the tax is specifically exempted in the Member's Annex on Article II Exemptions; [20] or in relation to certain exchanges of services to and from adjacent countries.[21]

It should be noted that whereas there is an express exception to the application of the MFN standard in the General Agreement on Trade in Services (GATS) in relation to bilateral double taxation agreements, [22] no such express exception has been stated in relation to goods under GATT 1994. Therefore suggestions of the conflict between Article I of GATT 1994 (i.e the MFN standard) and bilateral double taxation agreements may still be proffered.[23] Indeed, that the opportunity was not used to clarify Article I of GATT 1994 in this respect may reinforce arguments as to the existence of the conflict.

### *National treatment and protective taxation*

Internal taxation on products is not to be applied in a manner so as to afford protection to domestic production; [24] or in a manner inconsistent with the national standard.[25] The reference to internal taxation is in contra-distinction to duties or charges. This distinction is not based on the policy underlying the charge, but rather on whether it is due when imported or at the time or point of importation, or whether the charge is collected internally.[26] The objective of this standard is to ensure a level playing field (i.e through non-discriminatory and non-protective internal taxation) once the goods have been cleared through customs, and in order to protect the benefits arising from the tariff concessions given by the Member.[27] The standard does not apply to direct taxation. Thus, the tax in question must be a tax or charge on an imported good.[28]

The application of the national standard involves equivalence in the tax borne by a 'like' domestic product and the imported product.[29] Of note however is the fact that equivalence need not entail a reduction of internal taxation. The discriminatory and protective element can also be eliminated by raising the tax on the domestic product.[30]

In the current practice of GATT the determination of conformity of a fiscal measure with Article III [2][31] is arrived at by first considering whether the product is a like product and second whether the fiscal measure is discriminatory or protective[32] (a two-tiered test). The application of this test can give rise to difficulties. Indeed, the test itself, so formulated, has been challenged.[33]

In evaluating the discrimination under Article III [2] of GATT 1994, account must be taken not only of the rate of tax but also of the taxation methods (including types of taxes, the taxation on the finished product (direct tax), the taxation on the raw materials used in the various stages of production (indirect tax)) and of the system of collecting the tax.[34] In particular, the manner of the computation of the base value upon which the charge to tax is levied must not be less favourable for imported goods.[35]

The prohibition is on the discriminatory burden on imported products.[36] It is not subject to a *de minimis* standard.[37] Further, it does not allow for subsidies through tax credits or tax reductions of indirect taxes to domestic producers.[38]

However, the prohibition on discrimination does not require a particular method or system of taxation. These can be different with respect to domestic and imported products,[39] as long as they do not have a discriminatory or protective effect against imported products.[40] Nor does the provision proscribe the application of different methods for the calculation of the price of a product.[41] Further, the prohibition is not contingent upon a 'trade effects' test, and may be deviated from by way of direct payments of subsidies to domestic producers.[42] Thus, the national standard is in fact minimalist, even to the extent of its coverage.

In relation to goods an internal tax is not to be applied in such manner as to afford protection to a directly competitive or substitutable domestic product.[43] This prohibition on protective taxation is subject to a *de minimis* rule. Thus, there is a level below which a tax difference will cease to have a protective effect under Article III [2] of GATT.[44]

The requirement not to afford protection is distinct from the prohibition on discrimination. For the prohibition of non-discrimination the tax on an imported product and the like domestic product has to be equal in effect.[45] The tax however may still be protectionist, even if the internal tax is not discriminatory.[46]

In relation to services, the national standard applies only to services and service suppliers in sectors specified in the Member's schedule of concessions in services, and subject to any qualifications stated therein by the Member.[47] Further, the national standard may be deviated from as long as it is aimed at ensuring the equitable or effective imposition or collection of direct taxes in respect of services or service suppliers.[48]

### *The calculation of the tax base*

In so far as goods are concerned, for the purposes of the application of customs duties, the calculation of the tax base is governed by Article VII of GATT 1994, and the Agreement On Implementation of Article VII of GATT 1994 (the

Agreement). The basic principle is that the customs value is the 'transaction value'.[49] The transaction value is broadly defined as the price actually paid or payable at the time of sale for export to the country of importation.[50]

The process of calculating the prices of goods in order to determine tax liability (other than customs duties) between related exporting enterprises and foreign buyers ought to be based on the arm's length principle[51] in determining the existence (or otherwise) of a subsidy.[52] The GATT Council concluded in 1981 that Article XVI:4 of GATT 1947 required that the arm's length pricing be observed, i.e., prices for goods in transactions between exporting enterprises and foreign buyers under their, or the same control, should for tax purposes be the prices which would be charged between independent enterprises acting at arm's length.[53] This GATT Council ruling is reflected in a recent Panel Report involving subsidies.[54]

It should be noted however, in so far as goods are concerned, that the requirements of the arm's length principle in the context of subsidies, and the transaction value in the determination of customs value, do not necessarily imply that there is a general requirement to apply this principle in the WTO code in relation to goods for the purposes of determining fiscal liability. There is some ambiguity in this respect, despite the OECD emphasis on the arm's length principle.

In the case of services there are as yet no detailed disciplines for the determination of the value of services. However, a Member may impose regulations, provided these are not arbitrary or unjustifiably discriminatory in order to ensure the equitable or effective imposition or collection of direct taxes.[55] In particular, a Member may apply regulations (even if inconsistent with the national standard) in order to prevent the avoidance or evasion of taxes, so as to safeguard its tax base.[56] Thus, the problem of transfer pricing is in some measure recognized under GATS, and Member States are free to determine how they deal with the phenomenon.

However, as the criteria for such regulation is geared to safeguarding a Member's tax base, and preventing avoidance or evasion of its taxes, there is no compulsory method prescribed for the determination of the value of services for the purposes of either direct or indirect taxes. Indeed, GATS Article XIV does not even require that the value of services reflect the market price of the service; or that only that share of the supplier's profits be taxed which may be 'legitimately' allocated to any specific fiscal jurisdiction. This lacuna is compounded by the fact that the GATS does not have a subsidies code. Thus, flexible administration of the arm's length pricing rule in the field of services could serve to shift profits to low tax jurisdictions.[57]

### *Disguised taxes*

The problem of taxes taking other regulatory forms, for example being expressed as penalties or fees or charges, appears to be recognized in the WTO code. Thus, in relation to goods all fees and charges (other than tariffs and other taxes conforming with the national standard) levied on importation or exportation are to be limited to the approximate cost of services rendered, and must not constitute taxation for fiscal purposes.[58] There is no equivalent provision in relation to services. A Member has the general obligation, however, to accord to services and service suppliers of any other Member treatment no less favourable than that provided for under the terms specified in its schedule.[59]

The difficulty of determining disguised taxes was highlighted[60] by the EC, when it claimed that a certain US penalty for passenger automobiles which fell below a specified average fuel economy level, was in fact a disguised tax. The EC contended that, given that the penalty payment was based on a precise count of cars manufactured or imported in the United States the penalty was in fact a measure equivalent to a tax. Further, it claimed that if such measures were not considered to be a tax on products, contracting parties would be able to avoid the application of the national treatment principle in Article III by converting product taxes as year-end penalty payments. The Panel considering the matter observed, however, that the fact that the particular US measure has some of the economic effects of a tax did not imply that the penalty was a tax. The Panel took a formalistic view, emphasizing the importance of the language used in the national legislation under challenge.

### *Tax subsidies*

Taxation can operate to subsidize international trade in a variety of manners, for example, at the levels of the tax rate and the tax base, in the form of taxes foregone, and disguised remissions.

In the field of services, other than the requirement to consult, the general MFN and national standards, and the requirement to honour the commitments given in the Member's schedules, there are as yet no specific disciplines on subsidies.[61]

However, in relation to trade as it affects goods, there are well developed provisions.[62] A tax subsidy is defined as a government revenue that is otherwise due but is forgone or not collected, for example, fiscal incentives such as tax credits.[63] Thus, the prohibition on subsidies impinges on direct taxation through a proscription of a direct tax levy that is lower than that borne through domestic earnings.[64]

Three types of subsidies are distinguished, i.e., prohibited subsidies, actionable subsidies, and non-actionable subsidies. A tax subsidy contingent upon export performance, or upon the use of domestic over imported goods, is prohibited.[65] A tax subsidy that has an adverse effect on the interests of other Members is an actionable subsidy, and a Member may have either to remove the adverse effects of the subsidy, or to withdraw the subsidy.[66] In the sphere of taxation, an export subsidy is specifically defined in relation to both direct taxes[67] and indirect taxes.[68]

In accordance with the definition of a direct tax subsidy, where the direct tax allows a part of the process of the export activity, which originated within the territory of the taxing State to escape tax, this constitutes a partial exemption of taxation, and as such a subsidy.[69] However, the GATT as it affects trade in goods offers no criteria as to what constitutes the 'export process'.[70] This is as much a lacuna in the GATT jurisprudence, as it is symptomatic of the general underlying problem of defining the 'source' of earnings in the field of international taxation.[71] The two questions: what is the 'source' of earnings and what constitutes the 'export/import process', are in a sense one and the same inquiry. The difficulty is not merely inherent in the concept of 'source' at one level but arguably is also dependent on the economic standpoint from which it is viewed. Thus, as has been rightly pointed out, the OECD Model Tax Convention and the UN Model Double Taxation Convention contain diverging definitions in this respect.[72]

In so far as services are concerned, it seems that in the GATS some definition of the 'supply of services' in the international context has been provided.[73] This must be because of the obvious need to provide guidance concerning services, as it is more difficult to delineate the export process in the context of services than in relation to goods.[74]

### *Border tax adjustment*

Border tax adjustment is a process pertaining not so much to the 'border' but rather simply to the adjustment of taxation applied to goods entering into international trade.[75] Border tax adjustments have been defined, as they are applied in OECD countries, as comprising fiscal measures which give effect to the destination principle.[76] The destination principle involves the relieving of exported products from tax charged in the exporting State in relation to like domestic products sold in the home market, and the charging of a tax on imported products equivalent to that levied in the importing State on similar domestic products.[77]

The following points are to be noted in so far as the destination principle is concerned. First, it is applied both to imports and to exports.[78] Second, the principle provides a guide to the maximum adjustments on imports and exports, it does not require the maximum to be the adjustment.[79] Third, the destination principle applies to indirect taxes, i.e., specific excise duties, sales taxes, cascade taxes and the value-added tax.[80] On the other hand direct taxes (e.g social security charges and income taxes) are not eligible for tax adjustment at the border[81] and are subject to the origin principle. Fourth, the distinction for the purposes of the application of the destination principle is whether the taxes are direct or indirect, not the different policy considerations underlying the taxes.[82] Fifth, stamp duties, property taxes and registration duties in the practice of States have not generally been eligible for adjustment.[83]

### *Double taxation*

The focus on double taxation in the WTO code is mainly tangential. This is despite the fact that double taxation is a central problem of international taxation, and impinges in important respects on the flow of international trade. There are no specific provisions enjoining Members to relieve double taxation. Members are not forbidden to tax profits earned outside their territory.[84] A proposal was made some time ago for the inclusion of an Article in the GATT dealing with double taxation, but no action resulted from it.[85]

There does, however appear to be a general appreciation of the problem, and an approach is generally adopted which reinforces the efforts of Members in relieving double taxation through the network of bilateral double taxation agreements. Thus, a consequence of the adoption of the destination principle for border tax adjustment is that double taxation is avoided.[86] Similarly, Members are not prevented from adopting measures to relieve double taxation.[87] Further, Members are free, without prejudice to their rights under the WTO Agreements, to resolve transfer pricing problems through bilateral double taxation agreements.[88] In the case of services Members are expressly authorized, despite their MFN obligation, to resolve double taxation issues through bilateral tax agreements.[89]

### *Fiscal harmonization in regional economic integration programmes*

Fiscal harmonization in regional economic integration may take place under the disciplines set out in the WTO code.[90] Significantly, if this is not the case, then the WTO dispute settlement framework may be invoked by an affected Member.[91] Unfortunately, however, many of the disciplines suffer from lack of clarity and poor enforcement. This however is a general problem not specific to taxation.

Essentially, the disciplines involved are as follows. First, both in the case of services and goods, the duties and other measures are not to be higher than their general incidence prior to the process of regional integration.[92] In terms of tax this may relate to, for example, rates of taxes, the tax base, the cost of compliance, and double taxation. Second, the integration must involve, both with respect to trade in goods and services, substantial sectoral coverage of the trade as between the parties to the integration process.[93] In the case of goods, the regulation, as it affects third countries, must be substantially the same.[94] Thus, the harmonization process must affect third economies equally. In the case of services, the process of integration must involve absence or elimination of substantially all discrimination in the sectors covered as between the parties to the integration process.[95] This is an injunction *inter alia* for the national treatment standard in the field of taxation within an economic 'union'.

The effects of fiscal harmonization on trade relations with third States are difficult to gauge given the difficulties in differentiating between tax and non-tax distortions.[96] There are a number of positive effects, for example, the ability of individual Member States in the integration process to use the tax structure in a protectionist manner in relation to third States is reduced;[97] in the long run harmonization leads to improvements in the economic community (particularly allocative efficiency, and external competitiveness), thus facilitating more trade liberalization;[98] and finally there is an increase in transparency, in particular for third States.[99]

However, the harmonization process may also have negative consequences for any specific 'union', and the economies of third States.[100] Some of these have been catered for. Thus, in relation to services, in accordance with the GATS Article V [6], where there is a service supplier of a third State in the economic region, and the supplier is a juridical person under the laws of one of the members of the economic union, that entity must receive the same benefits as are enshrined under the framework of the integration process. This would include, for example, double taxation relief. However, to prevent the abuse of shopping into the benefits of harmonization processes (by entities from third States), there is a requirement that the juridical entity[101] in question should be engaged in substantial business operations in the economic region. Another form of discrimination that may be caught under GATS Article V [6] is where, according to third State entities based in the economic union, the harmonization process does not involve the same benefits for cross-country mergers or acquisitions within the union.[102] However, no such provision applies in relation to suppliers of goods.

## TRIT – a new WTO code?

This somewhat emotive area touching on national fiscal sovereignty need not necessarily evoke national political concern, provided the remit of the more focused attention is confined to the trade distortive effects of taxation, and does not unduly limit the freedom of a State in the amount of tax collected. There is, it is suggested, a case for a clearer code of conduct for tax legislators and tax administrators, from the perspective of the trade-related aspects of international taxation. The code would draw from the existing strands of the WTO code, and clarify, sharpen and augment them. This proposal for a code on TRIT is a modest one, and is not to be confused with the somewhat different proposal made amongst international taxation experts for a comprehensive multilateral agreement on international taxation (e.g a General Agreement On Taxes).[103]

The code must affirm the principles of equity and neutrality in international taxation. In particular the following points require attention:

1 A definition of taxation that focuses on economic effects of a governmental measure.
2 Broadening the scope of the MFN and national standards (including the prohibition on protective taxes) so as to include direct taxes.
3 Extending the scope of the arm's length principle.
4 Dealing in the service sector with taxation issues, e.g. disguised taxation; arm's length pricing; tax subsidies.
5 Requirement of according double taxation relief. Ensuring that the methods of double taxation relief are not trade distortive.
6 Taxation and developing countries:
ensuring that developing country tax incentives are not undermined; ensuring that the international tax order is orientated towards the source country fiscal jurisdiction. Improving the capacity of developing countries to enforce direct taxes so as to reduce reliance on revenue from tariffs.
7 More focused surveillance of TRIT through the Trade Policy Review Mechanism of the WTO.
More focused consideration of the impact of regional tax harmonization on third countries.

## Notes

1 This work draws in part from an earlier publication in the *Journal of World Trade* (*JWT*), vol.30 no.2, 1996. The author is grateful to the Institute of Fiscal Studies for funding this research, and would also like to thank Petros C. Mavroidis, from the Legal Department of the World Trade Organization, for his comments on an earlier draft.The errors and views remain the author's own.

2 The reference to TRIT is a reference mainly to taxation that is discriminatory, protectionist, and distortive of international trade.

3 See GATT Working Party on Tax Adjustments, BISD 18S/100; Justus Fischer-Zernin, 'GATT versus Tax Treaties? The Basic Conflicts between International Taxation Methods and the Rules and Concepts of GATT', *JWT* 1987; A.H. Qureshi, Chapter 5, *The Public International Law Of Taxation-Text, Cases and Materials*, Kluwer Law International, Netherlands, 1994.

4 For example see G. Kopits (ed.), *Tax Harmonization in the EC-Policy Issues and Analysis*, IMF, Washington DC., 1992, p. 4; A. Razin and J. Slimrod (eds), *Taxation in the Global Economy*, University of Chicago Press, Chicago, 1992, p. 1; and D.Puchala (ed.), *Fiscal Harmonization in the EC*, 1984, at p. 20.

5 In other words the Agreements and Understandings arrived at under the Uruguay Round of Multilateral Trade Negotiations.

6 See GATT 1994 Article XXIII [1][b]; also Article XXIII [1][c] for a situation complaint. See also, for example, A.H. Qureshi, 'The New International Trade Dispute Settlement

Framework under the Uruguay Round of Trade Negotiations', *International Company and Commercial Law Review*, vol. 5, Issue 6, (1994) p. 201.

7 'Un Etat ne peut vivre librement que s'il peut imposer librement', p. 63 in M. Chretien, *A La Recherche Du Droit International Fiscal Commune*, Paris, 1955.

8 See, for example, K. Knechtle, *Basic Problems in International Fiscal Law*, HFL, London, 1979 p. 37 and 41.

9 See, for example, F. Mann, 'The Doctrine of Jurisdiction in International Law' Hague Recueil, vol.1, (1964–1) pp.109–19; R.S.J. Martha, *The Jurisdiction to Tax in International Law: Theory and Practice of Legislative Fiscal Jurisdiction*, Kluwer, 1989; and *US Restatement of the Law: The Foreign Relations of the US*, para 411.

10 For general works on the WTO see, for example, A.H. Qureshi, *The World Trade Organization: Implementing International Trade Norms*, Manchester University Press, 1996; M.J. Trebilcock and R. Howse, *The Regulation of International Trade*, Routledge, 1995; E.McGovern, *International Trade Regulation*, Globefield Press, Exeter, UK, 1995.

11 See GATT *Analytical Index*, GATT, Geneva, 1994 at p 816; (hereinafter, the title, GATT *Analytical Index*, will refer to this text). See also *BISD* 3S/242, and Working Party Report on Border Tax Adjustment L/3464 in *BISD* 18S/97.

12 BISD, 18S/97.

13 Ibid., para. 22.

14 See 1987 GATT Panel Report: *Japan – Customs Duties, Taxes And Labelling Practices On Imported Wines And Alcoholic Beverages*, BISD, 34th Supplement.

15 Ibid.

16 A member may impose tariffs on goods only to the extent of those set out in its schedule of concessions. See GATT 1994, Article II; Understanding on the Interpretation of Article II:[b] of GATT 1994; and GATS Article XVI.

17 GATT 1994 Article I.

18 See, for example, GATT 1994 Article 1.

19 GATS Article II.

20 Ibid., Article II [2].

21 Ibid., Article II [3].

22 GATS Article XIV [e]; also, for discussion on the MFN standard in GATT 1994 and double taxation agreements, see Justus Fisher-Zernin, 'GATT Versus Tax Treaties? The Basic Conflicts Between International Taxation Methods and the rules and concepts of GATT' *JWT*, 1987.

23 Ibid.

24 'The contracting parties recognize that internal taxes and other internal charges ... should not be applied to imported or domestic products so as to afford protection to domestic production'; GATT 1994 Article III [1].

25 'The products of the territory of any contracting party imported into the territory of any other contracting party shall not be subject, directly or indirectly, to internal taxes or other internal charges of any kind in excess of those applied, directly or indirectly, to like domestic products. Moreover, no contracting party shall otherwise apply internal taxes or other internal charges to imported or domestic products in a manner contrary to the principles set forth in paragraph 1', GATT 1994 Article III [2].

26 See 1952 Panel Report: *Belgian Family Allowance*, BISD, 1st Supplement; 1978 Panel Report: *EEC – Measures on Animal Feed Proteins BISD* 25S/49; 1985 Panel Report: *Canada – Measures Affecting the Sale of Gold Coins*, L/5863, 1985 (unadopted); 1988 Panel Report: *Canada – Import, Distribution and Sale of Alcoholic Drinks by Canadian Provincial*

*Marketing Agencies*, BISD 35S/88; 1990 Panel Report:*EEC – Regulation on Imports of Parts and Components*, BISD 37S/132. See also GATT, *Analytical Index*, pp.182–4.

27 See GATT *Analytical Index* , p. 143, and 1987 Panel Report: *United States – Taxes On Petroleum and Certain Imported Substances*, BISD 34S/83.

28 1952 Panel Report: *Special Import Taxes Instituted by Greece* BISD 1S/48, 49–50, paras, 5, 7, 8.

29 See GATT, *Analytical Index*, 1994, p. 137; also 1987 Panel Report: *United States – Taxes on Petroleum and Certain Imported Substances* GATT 34S/163; 1990 Panel Report: *EEC – Regulation on Imports of Parts and Components, BISD* 37S/132.

30 Ibid.

31 Prohibition on discriminatory and protective measures.

32 See *Japan – Customs Duties, Taxes and Labelling Practices on Imported Wines and Alcoholic Beverages*, adopted on 11 November 1987, BISD 34S/83.

33 See *United States – Taxes On Automobiles*, GATT DS31/R.11 October 1994; (not yet adopted).

34 See *supra*, note 32, and GATT *Analytical Index*, p. 140.

35 1992 Panel Report: *Canada – Import, Distribution and Sale of Certain Alcoholic Drinks by Provincial Marketing Agencies* BISD 39S/27, 83, paras 5.24–5.26; and GATT *Analytical Index*, p. 140.

36 See *supra*, note 34.

37 GATT Panel Report: *United States – Measures Affecting Alcoholic and Malt Beverages*, BISD 39S/206, 270–1, para. 5.6; also GATT *Analytical Index* p. 121.

38 See *supra*, note 37.

39 See *supra*, note 34.

40 Ibid.

41 Ibid.

42 GATT, 1994, Article III 8 [b].

43 See Article III [1] and [2] and Ad Article III paragraph 2 of GATT 1994; see, for example, 1987, *Panel Report on Japan – Customs Duties, Taxes and Labelling Practices on Imported Wines and Alcoholic Beverages, BISD* 34S/83; 1992 Panel Report: *United States – Measures Affecting Alcoholic and Malt Beverages, BISD* 39S/206; 1987 Panel Report: *EEC – Measures on Animal Feed Proteins*, BISD 25S/49 and GATT, *Analytical Index*, 1994, p. 146.

44 See *supra*, note 32.

45 Ibid.

46 See GATT *Analytical Index*, p. 145.

47 GATS Article XVII [I].

48 GATS Article XIV [d].

49 Article 1 of the Agreement On Implementation of Article VII of GATT 1994.

50 Ibid.

51 Agreement On Subsidies And Countervailing Measures, note 59 to para. [e] of Annex I.

52 Further guidance in relation to the determination of the tax base of direct taxes is provided through characterizing as prohibited subsidies certain deductions. See Agreement On Subsidies and Countervailing Measures, para. [f].

53 The GATT Council adopted the Panel Reports on *United States Tax Legislation (DISC)* and on *Income tax practices in France, Belgium and the Netherlands* on this understanding. See GATT L/5271 and GATT *Analytical Index* , p. 426.

54 *United States – Imposition of Countervailing Duties On Certain Hot-Rolled And Bismuth Carbon Steel Products Originating in France, Germany And the United Kingdom*, GATT

SCM/185, 11 November 1994 (*not yet adopted*). Essentially, the question in this case was whether a subsidy existed in circumstances where an entity, the beneficiary of a subsidiary had passed on the benefit upon a transfer to another entity of the assets, where the transfer was at arm's length.

55 GATS Article XIV.

56 Ibid., footnote 6.

57 However, the transfer pricing practices of a monopoly supplier which undermines the member's commitments in its schedule of concessions are to be regulated (see GATS Articles VIII and XVI).

58 GATT 1994 Article VIII. See also Panel Report: *United States – Customs User Fee*, BISD 35S/245.

59 GATS Article XVI.

60 *United States – Taxes On Automobiles* GATT DS31/R (11 October 1994) (not yet adopted).

61 GATS Article XV.

62 See GATT, 1994, Article XVI, and the Agreement On Subsidies And Countervailing Measures.Subsidies in the field of agriculture are dealt with in the Agreement On Agriculture – see particularly Articles 3, 6, 8, 9 and 10.

63 Article 1 of the Agreement On Subsidies And Countervailing *Measures*.

64 See Justus Fischer-Zernin, *supra*, note 22.

65 Agreement On Subsidies And Countervailing Measures, Article 3.

66 Ibid., Article 7.

67 Ibid., Annex I, Illustrative List Of Export Subsidies para. [g].

68 Ibid.

69 1976 Panel Reports:*Income Tax Practices Maintained by France*, BISD 23S/114; *Income Tax Practices Maintained by Belgium*, BISD 23S/127; *Income Tax Practices Maintained by the Netherlands*, BISD 23S/137; also GATT *Analytical Index* 1994.

70 Ibid. See also Justus Fisher-Zernin, *supra*, note 22.

71 See for example K. Vogel, 'Worldwide vs.Source Taxation of Income – A Review and Re-evaluation of Arguments', *Intertax*, 1988/8–9.

72 See *supra*, Justus Fisher-Zernin, note 22.

73 GATS Article 1 [2] 'For the purposes of this Agreement, trade in services is defined as the supply of a service: [a] from the territory of one Member into the territory of any other Member; [b] in the territory of one Member to the service consumer of any other Member; [c]by a service supplier of one Member, through commercial presence in the territory of any other Member; [d] by a service supplier of one Member, through presence of natural persons of a Member in the territory of any other Member'; see also Article XXVIII [b] and [d].

74 See *inter-alia* Justus Fisher-Zernin, *supra*, note 22.

75 GATT L/3464 *BISD*, 18th Supplement, Working Party Report para. 5.

76 See *The Working Party on Border Tax Adjustment*, BISD 18S/97. See also GATT *Analytical Index*, p. 134.

77 Note the exemption of an exported product from taxation borne by the like product when destined for domestic consumption, or the remission of such taxation in amounts not in excess of those which have accrued, are deemed not to be a subsidy. See Agreement On Subsidies And Countervailing Measures, footnote 1.

78 Ibid. *supra*, note 77.

79 Ibid.

80 Ibid.

81 Ibid. See also 1987 Panel Report: *United States – Taxes on Petroleum and Certain Imported Substances*, 34S/163.

82 Ibid.

83 Ibid.

84 GATT, Council Meeting, 7–8 December, 1981, GATT l/271, BISD, 26th Supplement.

85 BISD 3S/242.

86 See P. Demaret and R. Stewardson, 'Border Tax Adjustments Under GATT and EC Law and General Implications for Environmental Taxes', 28 *JWT* 4, August 1994, p. 6.

87 Para. [e] footnote 59 of Annex I of the Agreement On Subsidies and Countervailing Measures.

88 Note 59 Ibid.

89 GATS Article XIV.

90 See GATT 1994 Article XXIV, and the Understanding on the Interpretation of Article XXIV of the GATT 1994 and GATS Article V.

91 See para. 12 of the Understanding on the Interpretation of Article XXIV of the GATT 1994.

92 GATT 1994 Article XXIV, and GATS Article V.

93 Ibid.

94 GATT 1994 Article XXIV.

95 GATS Article V [1].

96 G.Kopits (ed.), *Tax Harmonization in the European Community*, IMF, Washington DC, 1992, p. 51.

97 Ibid., p. 51.

98 Ibid.

99 Ibid.

100 Ibid., p. 3.

101 Juridical person is defined under GATS XXVIII [L] as:'any legal entity duly constituted or otherwise organized under applicable law, whether for profit or otherwise, and whether privately-owned or governmentally-owned, including any corporation, trust, partnership, joint venture, sole proprietorship or association'.

102 See E. Gardner in Kopits (ed.), *Tax Harmonization In The European Community* at p. 53. He states 'Such discrimination can arise from two sources. First, international mergers incur a higher tax burden than domestic mergers if the capital gains attributable to the contributing or acquired company are taxed at the time of the merger rather than upon realization, as in the practice for domestic mergers. The second tax obstacle results from different degrees of personal and corporate tax integration. Specially, the acquiring company may force a higher cost of capital if the tax advantages of dividend distributions are not extended to foreign-source income, and the after-tax value of dividend distribution of the acquired company may decline if the imputation system is not extended to foreign shareholders.'

103 See, for example, J. Owens, 'Globalization: The Implications for Tax Policies', *Fiscal Studies*, vol.14 no.3, 1993, pp. 21–44.

# COMMENTARY ON QURESHI

*Anthony Carty*

I have considered Qureshi's chapter in the context of Brown's[1] contribution. Brown engaged, *inter alia*, in a study of the slipperiness of political and economic rhetoric about sovereignty, free trade, the relationship between the free market and types of political structures. He concluded with a discussion of differing British and German perspectives on what was implied by intensifying free trade in Europe. Does it have to mean federal political union? The British tradition, going back to Adam Smith, would be more inclined to try to separate the political from the economic. The German tradition, since Kant, felt that economic freedom and liberal, democratic government had to go together. Economic union implies political union.

Qureshi's contribution is a highly technical discussion of state practice with respect to the exercise of the sovereign right of states to tax. However, his practical knowledge provides answers to the contradictions which Brown highlights. He points out how the GATT and the WTO do not regulate the final, basic economic power of the state, the power of direct taxation. International economic law focuses on protectionist uses of indirect taxation and has no coherent position on taxation power itself. At the same time Qureshi points out how fiscal harmonization can be in furtherance of regional economic integration. It is indeed critical to trade liberalization, but it needs a special political mandate. For example, taxes premised on a social policy, such as maintaining standards for labour, must have trade implications and, at the same time, involve the taking of political decisions, with respect to which there should be, ideally, a regional consensus. Otherwise, one country will have an unfair or unequal trade competitive advantage over another.

I would draw out of Qureshi's analysis that there is no happy resting point between trade liberalization and economic integration. The indirect effects of the social use of fiscal powers will impinge on trade. This is a chief structural cause for tension between keeping an association of states at the stage of a free trade area and going for economic integration. Such is the context in which to explore again the rhetoric which Brown presented. In the British tradition of economic liberalism, internationalism, and with it peace and progress, mean simply the removal of government interference. To what extent is this perspective realistic? At the same time one sees a German conviction that economic internationalism has to mean political integration. Free trade and competition take place under the umbrella of a common liberal, democratic (republican) constitution. Perpetual peace is not assured through removal of trade barriers but through, effectively, political union.

In conclusion I would say that discourse analysis of national traditions of political and economic rhetoric needs to be and can usefully be brought together with close legal analysis of the implications of different types of economic institutions, national and international, to solve very serious problems of international relations.

## Note

1 Paper presented at the conference but not published here.

# 14

# TRADING WITH THE ENEMY

*Hillel Steiner*

Do we have moral duties not to trade with 'the enemy'? And, if so, is it morally permissible to enforce our fulfillment of them?

I presume that, before answering these questions, cautious persons would want to know such things as what sort of enemy we're talking about here, exactly whose enemy it is, and what kinds of trade are under consideration. Moreover, and even if the answers to these latter questions are sufficient to imply a moral duty not to trade, they may nevertheless not suffice to imply the moral permissibility of enforcing that duty. That is, they may not justify legal trade restrictions. For the fact that no decent person would engage in such trade does not, in itself, supply an answer to the question of whether decent persons would scruple at forcing other, less decent persons to forbear from engaging in it. Why is this so?

Basically, because only *some* moral and political theories license the direct inference from D's being a duty to D's being permissibly enforcible. Such inferences are most easily accomplished by single-valued moral codes, e.g. utilitarianism, which offer no competing consideration that might morally override the value-maximizing promise of D. So if force turns out to be the most efficient (or the only) way of securing D's performance, there can be no moral scruple about deploying it.

Equally, some pluralistic codes can also license such inferences. For such codes, though they entertain a plurality of values which *can* generate mutually competitive considerations, need not include personal liberty among those values. Accordingly, the impermissibility of enforcing D would follow only if D's moral worth were less than E's, where D and E are both valuable but jointly unperformable acts. But under such a code and in these circumstances, the *impermissibility* of D's enforcement would simply be an implication of the *permissibility* of E's enforcement.

So if there are moral codes that *do* sustain the impermissibility of enforcing a value-maximizing act like D or E, they must be pluralistic ones that endorse personal liberty as one of their values. Elsewhere I have argued that there are good conceptual reasons for (i) construing *rights* as essentially prescriptive allocations of personal liberty, and for (ii) understanding any consistent such set of allocations as being (or being reducible to) a set of *property* rights. I have further argued that (iii) a set of moral rights is one derived from exercises of persons' foundational rights to equal liberty, and that (iv) duties to respect that set of rights must lexically override – 'trump' – the demands of other moral values.[1] Codes containing such a set of rights embody the view that there are several kinds of intrinsically bad act and that the worst of them are ones which violate those rights. It follows that any forcible encroachment on those rights is morally impermissible. Let's call a world in which such encroachments are absent a 'just world'.

Now as we know from Honore's classic essay on the subject, ownership signifies a complex rather than a simple connection between an owner and the thing owned: it typically consists of a bundle of different Hohfeldian jural relations which include various claims, liberties, powers and immunities.[2] These several 'incidents' of ownership, whose mutual differentiability varies with the nature of the thing owned, need not all be located in one single person or corporate agent and can be dispersed amongst several such parties. Indeed, Honore is quite insistent that there is no one incident that constitutes the core, the *sine qua non*, of ownership – a view which, in at least one sense, appears to have been embraced by the European Court of Human Rights.

The case in question was an appeal by a Mrs Liselotte Hauer, against a legislative prohibition on one use of her agricultural land, on the grounds that this measure violated the right to property enshrined in the European Convention for the Protection of Human Rights and Fundamental Freedoms.

> The interesting issue for the Court was whether the prohibition on new planting of vines should be classified as an expropriation or merely as a restriction of the right of property. The Court did not find the question difficult to answer. The individuals affected by the prohibition were not being deprived of their property. They remained free to keep them for themselves or to transfer them to others. The content of the right was being reduced only to the extent that temporarily one particular form of enjoyment was being precluded.[3]

Whether, in fact, the Court's reasoning supports Honore's 'no core incident' claim or rebuts it – is the Court implying that legal restrictions on powers of transfer *would* constitute expropriation? – need not detain us here. What is important analytically is not which subset of incidents we should attach the 'ownership' label to, but rather the fact that one party's lack of an incident implies its possession by another. Each of these parties can be described as having legal property rights in the thing in question. Thus both Mrs Hauer and the state hold property rights in 'her' agricultural land. And therefore, reverting to the standard mentioned above, whether this distribution of legal property rights is morally permissible depends upon whether it derives from exercises of just rights.

In the modern world, one of the more significant types of incident involved in the ownership of a thing consists in powers to dispose of entitlements to any or all of its incidents (including those powers themselves). Trade is a major form of the exercise of such powers. And legislated restrictions on trade represent an assumption, by the state, of some of those powers. When the state prohibits my selling (entitlements to) machine parts to the government of Iraq, it reduces my powers with respect to those machine parts. When it prohibits my purchase of foreign-grown wheat, or levies a surcharge on my so doing, it reduces my powers with respect to my money. In both cases, the effect of the law is to transfer property rights from me to the state which exercises them in a manner different from that which I might have done. And the question we have to answer is whether it is possible to justify such transfers – redistributions – as just ones.

One general line of justification which is unsatisfactory (because incomplete) casts the state in the role of each person's agent: an agent duly authorized by each of its principals to possess those rights, with that authorization being constitutive of principals' enforcible duties to comply with the agent's decisions. Leaving aside the familiar problems that beset consent-based accounts of states' powers, this argument is unsatisfactory because it is simply too sweeping. Taken by itself, it fails to discriminate between different kinds of right, and thereby offers no resistance to claims that *any* or *all* individual rights – and not just trade-related ones – are subject to this state-empowering principal–agent construal. This argument may well help us to understand *how* states can be empowered in a manner consistent with the requirements of justice. But what it obviously lacks is any account of *why* persons would transfer some of their own powers, including trading powers, to the state.

How much justificatory mileage can be got, then, from the claim that certain kinds of trade restriction would be so authorized because they protect us from our enemies? Since enemies, as was noted above, come in many shapes and sizes, the persuasiveness of such claims tends to vary accordingly.

One such enemy is sometimes seen as consisting in those foreign exporters whose domestic customers trade in blissful ignorance of significant adverse domestic effects of their commerce. This argument invokes what we might call 'information deficits'. Here the idea is that foreign trade is a complicated business with many diverse ramifications for domestic wellbeing – ramifications which the state is better placed than domestic private traders to discern. But the trouble with this argument is that the only kind of state-empowerment it sustains is one to disseminate that discerned information, and not one to control what its recipients then do in response to it.

Another enemy, it is often thought, is the foreign exporter of socially undesirable commodities: perhaps certain kinds of pornographic or blasphemous literature, or drugs, etc. These are things which we can well imagine ourselves having moral duties not to consume nor, therefore, to purchase. At the same time, however, the proposal to impede or prevent their importation by legal measures itself presupposes that others among our fellow citizens do not share these moral views and would not authorize that transfer of their property rights that is implied by such measures. And essentially similar things can be said about the converse case where the enemy is the foreign importer who purchases such items as local art treasures and other objects of national cultural significance. In both cases, the argument for state-empowerment rests not on appeals to moral rights, but rather to other values whose demands it proposes to prioritize over those of such rights.

Yet another kind of enemy might be the foreign exporter who sells commodities which are highly socially desirable – so desirable, indeed, that their importation would be sufficiently extensive to drive domestic producers of that type of commodity out of business. This is the classic Corn Laws case. And while it clearly gives those domestic producers some reason to empower the state, it equally clearly furnishes substantial numbers of their fellow citizens with reasons not to do so. Again, this demand for trade restrictions would license the values or interests of some persons to override the rights of others.

But, it has been objected, the absence of such domestic production can, at least in some cases, be quite harmful to the interests of *all* society's members. A future Napoleon might again attempt to blockade British ports and prevent the importation of universally consumed wheat. Viewed in this light, a flourishing domestic wheat industry is an indispensable component of national defence. And national defence, however disputable some of its alleged components may be, is standardly regarded as a 'public good' – with all that is thereby implied about the consensual authorization of state-empowerment to supply it.

This is undoubtedly a strong argument and is widely recognized as such, even by the most committed advocates of trade liberalization. It needs, therefore, to be scrutinized closely. In that regard, it is worth observing that a just world cannot contain a Napoleonic blockade of British ports.[4] That is, certain goods (e.g. national defence) *are* goods only in the face of actual or threatened injustice and not otherwise. Moreover, not all public goods *eo ipso* qualify as components of a just world. For instance, a particularly rapacious Napoleonic conquest of Britain might promise greatly enhanced general prosperity in France. And hence the taxation and conscription measures levied domestically by Napoleon, to secure the military resources needed for that project, would count as public goods.[5] But even though these measures would not violate the just rights of the French, they can hardly be described as elements of a just world. In the *Prisoners' Dilemma* joint non-confession is a publc good, the production of which is precisely a means to securing an injustice.[6] So the fact that some enforced policy supplies a public good – would be authorized by all those subject to it – is not a sufficient condition of its being just, even if it is a necessary condition of it. To be just, it must also not serve as a means for the violation of *anyone's* rights. And not all legal measures needed to secure public goods can satisfy this condition. We can put this another way. Suppose *X* authorizes a policy on the understanding that its results will be used to do an action which violates *Y*'s just rights. Then either (i) that action occurs, in which case *Y*'s rights are violated, or (ii) it does not occur, in which case *X*'s rights are violated.

And this brings us to our final type of enemy. A just world is, trivially, one that contains no unjust regimes. Regimes which practice injustice – say, by instituting systems of apartheid – confer higher levels of wellbeing, more legal property rights, on some subset of their population than it would otherwise possess. Put simply, some portion of those persons' property rights is constituted by the proceeds of theft and exploitation. And hence some trading with that set of persons can amount to the moral equivalent of receiving stolen goods. So I take it that, in such cases, it is at least *permissible* for other states to impose restrictions on that trade and, moreover, to do so regardless of whether these would be authorized by their own citizens, for many or all of whom such trade might be highly beneficial. That is, the fact that some enforced policy supplies a public *bad* – would not be authorized by anyone subject to it – is not a sufficient condition of its being unjust. For no one's just rights can include immunities against being disempowered from acquiring stolen goods.

Whether it would be *mandatory* for states to impose those restrictions raises the thorny issue of whether an individual's moral rights not only correlatively entail others' duties of non-violation, but also imply that those others have (non-contractual) duties to enforce that former set of duties on violators. In a state of nature, I am certainly (and non-contractually) obligated to respect my neighbour's rights and empowered to enforce them against third-party violators. But whether I'm non-contractually obligated to exercise that power is a question to which I currently have no theoretically adequate answer. Does the rule implying my entitlement to equal freedom further imply the permissibility of its reduction to secure that of others? The problem here seems to be that, although decent persons would undoubtedly waive a portion of that entitlement, less decent people also have rights which may include immunities against being conscripted for such purposes.[7,8]

## Notes

1 Cf. Hillel Steiner, *An Essay on Rights*, Oxford, Blackwell, 1994, where arguments for (i) and (ii) are located in ch. 3 and, for (iii) and (iv), in ch. 6.

2 Cf. A.M. Honore, 'Ownership', in A.G. Guest (ed.), *Oxford Essays in Jurisprudence*, First Series, Oxford, Oxford University Press, 1961.

3 'Euro-debate over the citizen's right to property', *Financial Times*, 6.10.80. A similar issue arises in American law in respect of whether state regulation of the use of property counts as a 'taking' under the Constitution's Fifth Amendment which states: 'Nor shall private property be taken for public use, without just compensation'; see Roger Pilon, 'Property and Constitutional Principles', *Wall Street Journal*, 28.2.92, for a discussion of the case *Lucas v. South Carolina*; also Lawrence Becker and Kenneth Kipnis (eds), *Property: Cases, Concepts, Critiques*, Englewood Cliffs, Prentice Hall, 1984, pp. 48–65, on the cases of

*Kaiser Aetna v. United States* and *Robins v. Pruneyard Shopping Center*. More generally, see Richard Epstein, *Takings*, Cambridge, Mass., Harvard University Press, 1985.

4 We will assume here that the blockade is not itself a retaliatory measure against some previous violation of Napoleonic just rights.

5 Public goods, since (for the usual reasons) the prospective net beneficiaries of this conquest would not voluntarily supply the funds and manpower needed to accomplish it.

6 That is, assuming that the prisoners are guilty of violating just rights.

7 For one attempted escape from this conundrum, see Hillel Steiner, 'Putting Rights in Their Place', *Recherches Economiques de Louvain*, 56 (1990), 391–408, pp. 393–7.

8 Work on this paper was supported by an Economic and Social Research Council Senior Research Fellowship.

# 15

# STANDARDS AND TECHNICAL REGULATIONS AS BARRIERS TO TRADE

## Regulating regulations

*Edmond McGovern*

### Introduction

The capacity of national technical regulations and standards to create problems for international trade is well understood. This chapter looks at the opportunities that exist within the WTO system for dealing with these problems, using the extensive experience gained by the EC as an aid to seeing what has been and what might be achieved. Limitations of time and space have restricted this consideration to technical regulations (roughly speaking, those measures that are promulgated with the authority of the state, and are in many cases enforced by sanctions). The focus is on regulations that relate to products.

The EC rules on the subject are to be found in the EC Treaty and in legislation made under the Treaty. Those of the WTO are contained in the GATT, and in the agreements concluded in 1994 on Sanitary and Phytosanitary Measures (SPS), and on Technical Barriers to Trade (TBT). The second of these is a development of the similar agreement – the Standards Code – reached in 1979 as part of the Tokyo Round.

### Regulating regulations

Following the changes made in the Uruguay Round, the strategies available to the WTO and the EC for dealing with trade-restricting national technical regulations are fairly similar. They fall into four broad categories. The first concerns the most obvious problem, and the one most easily dealt with: regulations that discriminate against imports. The second, which concerns limits on all trade-restricting regulations, is essentially an outgrowth of the first, but a rather surprising one because it has no obvious place in a regime ostensibly concerned with international rather than internal trade. The third includes the familiar topic of harmonization, along with the integration of conformity-assurance systems which, although less well known, is perhaps equally significant. Finally there are procedural and institutional measures coming under the general title of transparency.

### *Forbidding discrimination*

The EC rules forbidding discrimination against products of other member states are so well-established that they require little elaboration. Rather than rehearsing the details it may be more fruitful to comment on the general structure of the EC and GATT rules on trade liberalization. In several respects the EC Treaty provisions on trade are developments of those in GATT. Both systems make separate provision for tariff and non-tariff barriers, and as regards financial charges they make a distinction between border measures, i.e. tariffs, and internal measures, i.e. discriminatory taxation. Of course, whereas GATT merely provides for tariff bindings to be achieved in later agreements, the EC Treaty abolishes them entirely. Less importantly from an economic point of view, but perhaps of equal legal significance is the fact that in regard to non-tariff barriers the EC Treaty, unlike GATT, makes no distinction between internal and border measures. In EC law such barriers – including all technical regulations affecting products – are subject to the prohibition on quantitative restrictions and measures having equivalent effect that is principally found Article 30.

According to the GATT categorization, technical regulations are for the most part internal measures of a quantitative character. As such they are subject to rules forbidding discrimination between (Article I) and against (Article III) imports. (If they are imposed at the border the corresponding prohibitions are found in Articles XIII and XI.) The number of panel disputes that have arisen in the area is quite small. In one instance, US state legislation requiring that foreign goods be sold only through wholesalers, or through licensed locally established importers, was found to be inconsistent with Article III:4 (although it was said that where all producers had to sell through licensed wholesalers it would not be discriminatory to require foreign producers who wished to hold a licence to do so through a locally resident employee).[1]

More recently, a panel found that aspects of the US Corporate Average Fuel Economy legislation contravened Article III. Firms were penalized if they did not keep the average fuel consumption of their vehicles below certain levels. However, in calculating these levels foreign- and locally made vehicles were assessed separately, so that US manufacturers of large cars, who could lower their average by buying-in small cars, had an incentive to buy local rather than foreign cars.[2]

The rules are in principle capable of dealing with situations where the discrimination is hidden behind an apparently even-handed measure. Thus, minimum prices on alcoholic drinks that were set to suit domestic producers' costs were found to prejudice the competitive opportunities of imports which could otherwise be supplied below those prices.[3]

The converse situation, rules that on their face are different but are claimed to result in non-discriminatory treatment in practice, were at the heart of the dispute about 'separate but equal' laws in US constitutional law. In the landmark case of *Brown* v. *Board of Education* the Supreme Court ruled that such segregationist laws were inherently discriminatory. GATT panels have not applied this principle to trade disputes, but a country that adopts such measures has the burden of establishing that, despite the differences, the no-less-favourable-treatment standard of Article III is met.[4]

The fact that there have been only a handful of panel decisions involving discriminatory technical regulations is no doubt partly a reflection of the relatively low number of trade disputes that have been resolved by the panel procedure (three or four per year is the recent average). It may also reflect the effectiveness of Article III as a deterrent.

### *Controlling trade-restricting regulations*

Using an anti-discrimination rule to control regulations is a crucial step in the liberalization of trade. It formed a basic element in the establishment of free trade within the EC. However, since the 1980s the European Court of Justice has developed a much more radical strategy for dealing with national regulations, and echoes of this can now be found in the WTO.

#### *EC single market*

The strategy consists in demanding that justification be provided for regulations that restrict trade, irrespective of whether foreign products suffer discrimination. No doubt various considerations led the Court to adopt this bold interpretation of Article 30, but the fact that the EC Treaty does not concern itself with whether quantitative-type measures are imposed at the border or internally (above) may have facilitated the decision. The rule is expressed in the *Dassonville* judgment: 'all trading rules enacted by member states which are capable of hindering, directly or indirectly, actually or potentially, intra-Community trade are to be considered as measures having an effect equivalent to quantitative restrictions'.[5] Thus in its well-known *Cassis de Dijon* judgment[6] the Court held that a German measure that forbade the sale of alcoholic drinks below a certain strength was contrary to Article 30.

For some years it seemed that Article 30 could be invoked in respect of almost any national measure with negative effects on trade. However, since 1993 the Court has found that its scope does not extend to measures affecting the selling of goods, provided that they are applied to all affected traders operating within the national territory and that they affect in the same manner, in law and in fact, the marketing of domestic products and those from other member states. As a result it has been found that limits on sales below cost,[7] on shop closing hours,[8] and on television advertising,[9] are not caught.

*Exceptions*

Of course the prohibitions in Article 30, and GATT Article III, are not absolute. EC Treaty Article 36 lists a number of exceptions that are largely modelled on the general exceptions listed in GATT Article XX. In addition to the list in Article 36 the Court has identified a number of implicit grounds of exception, known as 'imperative requirements'.

Both sets of exceptions are of particular interest in the present context because they cover the very topics, such as the protection of human, animal and plant life and health, which are the typical objectives of technical regulations. The tests that have been evolved in the EC and GATT for applying these exceptions reveal the usual pattern of the two institutions following similar general principles but with the EC having developed them to a greater degree of sophistication. In any event, the exceptions in Article XX are of less significance than those in the EC Treaty for the simple reason that, unlike Article 30, the scope of Article III is confined to measures discriminating against imports (above).

There is not space here in which to elaborate on the ways in which these exception clauses have been applied. However, it should be said that both systems have developed a restriction on the use of exceptions commonly known as the 'least trade restrictive' or 'minimum derogation' principle. As the names imply, this states that, when derogating from the relevant GATT or EC obligation (in this context usually Article III or Article 30) in pursuit of one of the permitted objectives, the country concerned must use the measure which involves the least derogation from that obligation.

At the same time, the Court of Justice has said on several occasions that (in the absence of harmonization, see below) it is for member states to decide what degree of protection of the health and life of humans they intend to assure and in particular how strict the checks to be carried out are to be.[10] In effect, each member state is free to determine the level of risk to which its citizens will be exposed.

One field of application of Articles 30 and 36 that is of particular interest for technical regulations is that of conformity assurance. Where the risks arising from failure to comply with regulations are significant it is common regulatory practice to establish a system for assuring conformity before a product is sold. This can take various forms, such as type approval, examination of systems and procedures, and in the case of particularly high-risk products such as pressure boilers, inspection of individual articles during or after manufacture. Satisfactory products are usually issued with a certificate of conformity.

Faced with the trade barriers created by national procedures of this kind the European Court has attempted to apply the principles already mentioned. It has held that national rules may not require imported products to comply strictly and exactly with the provisions or technical requirements laid down for products manufactured domestically when those under which the imported products were produced afford users the same level of protection.[11] It must follow from this that importers should be allowed reasonable opportunities to establish this equivalence. Probably the onus lies on the importing member state to demand proof, rather than on the importer to establish it before importing the product. In one case the Court held that a member state may require that imports (along with domestic products) be accompanied by test certificates, but may not require technical or chemical analyses or laboratory tests when the same analyses and tests have already been carried out in another member state and their results are available to those authorities or may on request be placed at their disposal.[12] The disappearance of borders checks on goods moving between EC members is an encouragement to manufacturers to import first and answer questions later.

The Community procedure for notification of proposed national regulations (below) gives the Commission the opportunity to recommend the insertion of mutual recognition clauses, a policy which apparently meets with some success.[13]

Establishing equivalence will remain problematic as long member states are entitled to set their own levels of protection. Such differences are removed by harmonization (below), but since Community harmonization measures require acceptance of certificates from other members, the problem is then removed entirely.

### *1994 WTO Agreements*

The experience of the EC is of particular relevance when considering the scope of the two agreements dealing with technical regulations that were negotiated during the Uruguay Round.

Article 2 of the TBT Agreement places two obligations on WTO members as regards the preparation, adoption and application of technical regulations. However, the first of these is merely a repetition of the national and MFN treatment principles found in GATT Articles III and I.

The second obligation is much more significant. Members must ensure that technical regulations are not prepared, adopted or applied with a view to or with the effect of creating unnecessary obstacles to international trade. This part of the obligation was also found in the 1979 Standards Code, but did not attract much attention. The 1994 Agreement states in addition that, for this purpose, technical regulations must not be more trade-restrictive than necessary to fulfil a legitimate objective, taking account of the risks non-fulfilment would create. Such legitimate objectives are, *inter alia:* national security requirements; the prevention of deceptive practices; protection of human health or safety, animal or plant life or health, or the environment. In assessing such risks, relevant elements of consideration are, *inter alia:* available scientific and technical information, related processing technology or intended end-uses of products. Similarly, regulations must not be maintained if the circumstances or objectives giving rise to their adoption no longer exist or if the changed circumstances or objectives can be addressed in a less trade-restrictive manner.[14]

This obligation is capable of being interpreted as merely a detailed expression of the existing GATT rules: i.e. the 'unnecessary obstacle' to trade would be one constituting a breach of the GATT MFN or national treatment obligations, and the legitimate objective would be one of those listed in Article XX.

However, it seems more likely that the intention was to establish a regime similar in principle to that created by the EC Court in decisions such as *Cassis de Dijon*, according to which all trade-restricting regulations must be justified, whether or not they discriminate against or between foreign products. Since a number of cases that rely on such an interpretation are currently being pursued under the WTO disputes mechanism, this uncertainty may shortly be resolved.

The US complaint against the EC ban on hormones in meat invokes this provision of the TBT Agreement along with the corresponding parts of the SPS Agreement, the Agriculture Agreement, and, for good measure, GATT Articles III and XI.

There is also a dispute in which France is accused of restricting the use of the term 'coquille Saint-Jacques' to a particular variety of scallop which, by no coincidence, is the one harvested in French waters, and is not the one exported to France from Canada, Chile and Peru.

The SPS Agreement explicitly adopts the expansive style characterized by the *Cassis de Dijon* judgment. WTO members must ensure that any SPS measure (a) is applied only to the extent necessary to protect human, animal or plant life or health, (b) is based on scientific principles, and (c) is not maintained without sufficient scientific evidence (except in some cases where the scientific evidence is insufficient).[15] The obligation not to discriminate against or between other members is contained in a separate provision.

Of course, this is not the end of the matter. Not only is there the problem of assessing the sufficiency of the scientific evidence, there is also the difficulty (mentioned above in relation to EC law) that states differ in the level of protection that they provide for the various interests, a fact explicitly recognized in the SPS Agreement.

The question of recognizing foreign testing, which in the EC is treated as an aspect of the regime established by Articles 30 and 36, receives specific attention in the 1994 Agreements.

Under the TBT Agreement members must give 'positive consideration' to accepting the equivalence of other members' regulations, even if the regulations differ, provided that they adequately fulfil the same objectives.[16] Such acceptance is most likely to be of significance as an aspect of a more sensitive issue: the recognition of the equivalence of other members' conformity-assessment procedures. However, it is possible that an importing country, having accepted the equivalence of another country's regulation, might be willing to test the conformity of an import against that regulation rather than its own. In addition, members must ensure, whenever possible, the recognition of the results of conformity-assessment procedures in other members as regards central government bodies, even when the procedures differ, provided they are satisfied that they offer an assurance of conformity equivalent to their own procedures.[17]

The SPS Agreement goes a step further. The differing measures of other members must be accepted as equivalent if the exporting member objectively demonstrates that its measures achieve the importing member's appropriate level of protection. For this purpose, reasonable access must be given, upon request, to the importing member for inspection, testing and other relevant procedures.[18]

## *Harmonization and integration*

### *Harmonization*

The constraints on national regulations discussed in the previous sections, whether based on discrimination against imports, or merely on excessive restriction of trade, are of undoubted importance, but it is quite possible for countries to adopt laws that are completely without discrimination and are entirely justified by their objectives, but which cause immense problems for trade. The reason is simply that they differ from, and sometimes contradict the corresponding regulations in other countries, and so require traders to supply products in a variety of forms.

The remedy for this problem is harmonization. This is a subject with a long, and not always happy experience in the EC. In the context of trade liberalization the best known provision is EC Treaty Article 100a, which was introduced explicitly to assist the creation of the Single Market. However, there are a number of other provisions, such as Article 130s regarding environmental measures, and the various powers contained in regimes governing agricultural products.

These powers differ not only as regards their subject matter, but also the applicable voting procedures and the extent to which member states may impose different, usually more demanding, requirements. In the case of measures adopted under Article 100a the opportunities for individual national action are very circumscribed. In particular, member states lose the right to invoke the exceptions listed in Article 36 (above).

In this context mention should also be made of the important drafting technique, adopted as a preferred policy in the New Approach of 1985, of designating particular Euro-standards as satisfying the 'essential requirements' specified in the harmonizing instruments. Curiously the current unpopularity attached to European harmonization has come about at a time when the previously dormant process of international harmonization has been awakened by the WTO Agreements. The TBT Agreement, and more particularly the SPS Agreement have put WTO members under a qualified obligation to use international standards where they exist, and to promote the conclusion of such standards where they do not. The qualification in the TBT Agreement is an exception available when the international standards would be an ineffective or inappropriate means of fulfilling the legitimate objectives being pursued, for instance because of fundamental climatic or geographical factors or fundamental technological problems.[19]

The obligation in the SPS Agreement is to adopt the international standard, or to adopt a level of protection higher than such standard provided that the member has scientific justification demonstrated according to the methodology specified in the Agreement. Although the obligation in the SPS Agreement is therefore more demanding, its effect is limited to three international standards-making bodies: the Codex Alimentarius, the International Office of Epizootics, and the bodies established under the International Plant Protection Convention. Other entities may be added to this list.

The best known international body producing standards is the International Organization for Standardization (ISO). This is concerned with producing harmonized standards rather than technical regulations, but the two cannot always be easily separated.

First, the technique of drafting regulations by reference to standards, which is at the heart of the EC's New Approach to harmonization, means that documents that commence as standards become in effect incorporated into regulations. Furthermore, nowadays many such standards have been explicitly drafted for this purpose.

Second, although substantive product standards often concern matters that are distinct from those covered by technical regulations, there are ISO drafts covering the operations of bodies certifying conformity, and specifying how those bodies should themselves be assessed. In this context there is no reason to distinguish between bodies that examine compliance with standards and those that do the same as regards technical regulations, so the ISO principles are applied to both. (Mention should also be made in this context of the guidelines on good laboratory practice, GLP, that have been developed by OECD and are widely incorporated into national measures.)[20]

In addition to the ISO, the International Electrotechnical Commission (IEC), and the International Telecommunications Union (ITU) are engaged in drafting standards in their respective fields. It is noteworthy that of the three only the ITU is an intergovernmental body, the ISO and IEC being largely comprised of private, national standards bodies (although many of these are state-aided, others are determinedly not so).

If internationally drafted standards are to become parts of national law (often the criminal law) it is reasonable to ask questions about the representative character of bodies producing those standards. Until now, the highly technical nature of the activities of the three entities mentioned in the SPS Agreement has guaranteed them obscurity. It will be interesting to see how their informal structures and procedures, based on a philosophy of cooperation between experts, survive in the more bruising world of the WTO. A foretaste of the future was given in 1995 when the EC was unable to prevent the Codex Alimentarius narrowly voting in favour of a US proposal regarding the acceptable level of hormone residues in meat.

Some progress has been made via bilateral agreements in harmonizing testing methods, for example between the US, Japan and the EC in regard to HFCs. The EC and US are negotiating an agreement involving harmonization of regulations, and possibly mutual recognition of certificates (below), over a wide field of mostly technical goods.

### *Integration*

Harmonization is only a partial answer to the difficulties caused for traders by national technical regulations, particularly as regards conformity assurance requirements. Convenient access to procedures in the importing country (above) is helpful, but ultimately exporters would like recognition by the importing country of the certificates, etc., issued under procedures in their own country. In practice, this goal can be achieved only by some degree of integration of the various national procedures. The EC provides an extreme example, where the regimes established under harmonizing directives normally require the recognition in one member state of certificates issued by the authorities in another. In the international sphere progress depends on the conclusion of mutual recognition agreements. Experience suggests that these are very difficult to achieve.

The TBT Agreement recognizes that consultations leading to understandings may be needed, especially regarding the technical competence of bodies in the exporting member.[21] The SPS Agreement also encourages the negotiation of recognition agreements: members must, upon request, enter into consultations with the aim of achieving bilateral and multilateral agreements on recognition of the equivalence of specified SPS measures.[22] The subject of recognition of foreign certificates is not addressed explicitly in the Agreement, but it can be taken to be included in the term 'measures'. Of the entities mentioned in the Agreement, the Codex Alimentarius seems to have made the furthest progress in this direction: it is trying to develop a system of bilateral agreements for mutual recognition of certificates.

### *Procedural and institutional improvements*

It is not merely the differences between national regulations that cause problems for traders, but also the circumstances surrounding their introduction and modification. What is needed is effective publicity, giving exporters adequate time to react. In addition, exporters like to have the same opportunities to comment on proposed changes as are accorded to local producers. These topics are often grouped together under the heading of 'transparency'.

The EC's rules, contained in Directive 83/189,[23] establish a notification and standstill mechanism. The member states must notify the Commission of proposed technical regulations concerning products, and must delay implementation for three months initially, and then for up to a year if the Commission intends to introduce a harmonizing measure. The Commission vigorously enforces these rules, taking its complaints to the European Court where necessary, and maintains that failure to notify a regulation has the result that it cannot have legal effect against third parties.[24]

The two WTO Agreements contain procedural requirements regarding the introduction of regulations when an international standard does not exist or is not being followed.[25] These oblige members to publicize proposed measures, and to give an opportunity for comments, subject to exceptions for national security, etc.

Unfortunately, the effectiveness of these rules is open to question. The experience of GATT (1947) and the 1979 Codes was that their internal procedures were incapable of deterring widespread disregard of their many notification obligations. The Uruguay Round substantially increased the number of notification requirements, but did little to reform the procedures.

## Conclusion

The four strategies described in this chapter are not precise categories. 'Procedural and institutional improvements' could as easily have been taken as an example of harmonization, and the issue of conformity assurance and mutual recognition might have been assigned a category of its own. Nevertheless, between them they cover most of the ways in which the WTO, and the EC, can attempt to regulate national regulations in the interests of free trade.

The use of the EC's experience is particularly rewarding in a field as wide and varied as this, where abstract hypothesis is likely to identify only a minority of the problems. The approach is also likely to be useful in relation to standards, particularly as regards conformity assurance, where the EC has been active at an institutional level.

In regard to national technical regulations it is evident that the new WTO rules give the WTO the opportunity to adopt several of the strategies developed by the EC, especially the principle that countries should provide justification for any restrictions which they impose on trade. However, it remains an open question whether and to what extent this opportunity will be exploited.

## Notes

1 Report of panel on United States – measures affecting alcoholic and malt beverages, BISD 39S/206 (1993), paras 5.31 et seq.

2 Report of panel on United States – taxes on automobiles, DS31/R, 1994 (unadopted), para. 5.47.

3 Report of panel on Canada – import, distribution and sale of certain alcoholic drinks by provincial marketing agencies, BISD 39S/27 (1993), para. 5.30.
4 Report of panel on United States – section 337 of the Tariff Act of 1930, BISD 36S/402 (1990), para. 5.11; Report of panel on Canada – import, distribution and sale of certain alcoholic drinks by provincial marketing agencies, BISD 39S/27 (1993), para. 5.12.
5 Case 8/74, *Procureur du Roi* v. *Dassonville*, [1974] ECR 837, para. 5.
6 Case 120/78, *Rewe-Zentral* v. *Bundesmonopolverwaltung für Branntwein* [1979] ECR 649.
7 Joined cases C-267/91 and C-268/91, Keck and Mithouard, [1993] ECR I-6097. The same point was made in case C-292/92, Hünermund, [1993] ECR I-6787.
8 Case C-401/92 and C-402/92, *Tankstation 't Heukske* v. *Boermans* [1994] ECR I-2199, Cases C-69/93 and C-258/93, *Punto Casa* v. *Sindaco del Commune di Capena* [1994] ECR I-2355.
9 Case C-412/93, *Leclerc-Siplec* v. *TVI* [1995] ECR I-179.
10 Case 272/80, Frans-Nederlandse Maatschappij voor Biologische Producten [1981] ECR 3277, para. 12; Case 188/84, *Commission* v. *France* [1986] ECR 419, para. 15.
11 Case 188/84, *Commission* v. *France* [1986] ECR 419, para. 16.
12 Case 272/80, Frans-Nederlandse Maatschappij voor Biologische Produkten [1981] ECR 3277, para. 16. See also Case C-373/92, *Commission* v. *Belgium* [1993] ECR 3107.
13 Commission of the EC, *Twelfth annual report on monitoring the application of Community law – 1994*, OJ C 254, 1995, p. 1, at p. 14.
14 Art. 2.2–3.
15 Art. 2.2.
16 Art. 2.7.
17 Art. 6.
18 Art. 4.1.
19 Art. 2.4.
20 E.g., Dir. 87/18, OJ L 15, 1987, p. 29.
21 Art. 6.1.
22 Art. 4.2.
23 OJ L 109, 1983, p. 8; amended by Dir. 88/182, OJ L 81, 1988, p. 75, and Dir. 94/10, OJ L 100, 1994, p. 30.
24 Commission communication, OJ C 245, 1986, p. 4.
25 TBT Agreement, Art. 2; SPS Agreement, Annex B.

# COMMENTARY ON STEINER AND McGOVERN

*Peter Jones*

In recent years there has been a determined international effort to develop freedom of trade although, as Edmond McGovern indicates, the EC has achieved rather more than the WTO. What is the imperative that drives this 'official' commitment to free trade? What sort of evaluation of free trade is implicit in this international endeavour? The answer appears to be essentially utilitarian or welfarist in character. There is a strong presumption that free trade promotes the economic well-being of those engaged in it and it should be promoted and sustained to secure that desirable goal. Thus, the general structure of what I shall call the 'official ideology' is consequentialist: free trade is valued for what it brings about and the goods that it brings about are collective and diffuse in character rather than targeted at the entitlements of specific individuals. (Those who take this view of free trade need not, of course, value everything else in the same way.)

Given its consequentialist structure, this official ideology is well placed to cope with values or with instruments of value that compete with free trade. What we have is a strong presumption of the benign effect of free trade – so strong that it militates against measures which restrict trade indirectly as well as directly, potentially as well as actually (McGovern p. 206). But if free trade does conflict with other significant goods, the official ideology can happily accept that it should be limited for the sake of those goods. Thus, EC and GATT regulations permit a number of legitimate objectives to override the presumption in favour of free trade – objectives such as national security, human safety, protecting the health of animal and plant life, and environmental concerns (McGovern pp. 207, 208). Likewise, if this offical ideology were to confront Steiner's issue of trading with the enemy, it would have no problem in accommodating the claim that states may legitimately prevent their citizens from trading with hostile foreigners or, indeed, from engaging in any kind of trade that might significantly harm their society. Free trade may usually have good consequences but, if it threatens bad consequences, it can be set aside.

The premises from which Hillel Steiner approaches free trade are very different. Readers of his *Essay on Rights* (p. 202, note 1) will know that, for

Steiner, all rights are rights to property and all property is the subject of rights. Property and rights are coextensive. In addition, rights possess a lexical priority over other values (rights always trump other values) and all rights properly so-called are compossible (no right can conflict with another right). Thus any particular property right is absolute: it has absolute weight in the face of all possible considerations to the contrary.

Steiner asks 'do we have moral duties not to trade with the enemy?' If by 'duties' we are to understand *strict* duties, such that we have no right to do what we have a duty not to do, it seems prima facie that his answer must be 'no'. Nothing can trump my right to dispose of my property to whom I choose, including to the enemy. In contrast to the official ideology, Steiner's rights-based liberalism produces a wholly uncompromising and uncompromisable case for free trade.

Moral philosophers sometimes use the term 'duty' more generously as a synonym for what, morally, we 'ought' to do – so that whatever we ought to do, for whatever moral reason, is described as a duty. Thus we might be said to have duties to be kind, generous, forbearing, etc., even though those will normally be duties of less than strict obligation. In this non-strict sense, Steiner might concede that we have 'duties' not to trade with the enemy – duties based in patriotism or a concern for the interests of our fellow-citizens, for example. Yet those patriotic duties cannot displace the *right* to trade with the enemy. People can have a right to do wrong, and trading with the enemy is the sort of wrong that property-owners have a right to do.

So a duty not to trade would preclude a right to trade only if it were a strict duty. How could there be such a duty? Steiner suggests it would arise from a state's having a right to prohibit trade with the enemy. That right would entail a state's having property rights in some of the incidents of things that are otherwise owned by the individuals who are subject to its prohibitions (Steiner p. 200). Since, in Steiner's thinking, all rights are held initially by individuals, a state could have these property rights only if they were transferred by individuals to the state. Why should individuals opt to make that transfer and so entitle the state to limit their freedom to trade?

Steiner is unable to find a good reason. There may be more mileage in collective action problems than he allows. Refraining from trading with an enemy is typically part of a strategy of external defence – a strategy in which all citizens of the relevant state share an interest. Steiner objects (p. 200) that that would not be enough to induce individuals to transfer the relevant powers since they themselves will be aware, or can be made aware, of their shared interest in security and can adjust their behaviour accordingly; in other words, they themselves can choose to refrain from trading with the enemy. But that raises a free rider problem. The danger may not arise if I trade and no-one else does; but, if we all think like that, we shall all trade and our external security will collapse. So we may have reason to transfer powers of control to the state as a solution to that collective action problem.

But perhaps that sort of reasoning is beside the point anyway. Given Steiner's strong theory of individuals' rights, the state's powers cannot be justified merely by there being a *good reason* for individuals to tranfer powers to the state. The state can acquire rights only if individuals *actually transfer* powers to it, for whatever reason, good or bad. That raises the larger question, which I cannot pursue here, of whether Steiner's libertarianism is ever likely to find states (as we know them), even minimal states, legitimate.

That is perhaps why he looks elsewhere for a possible justification for the state's interfering with trade: the prevention of injustice. If you have acquired a good unjustly, you have no right over that good that you can transfer to me. Thus the state, in preventing your trading that good with me, does not violate our rights, since neither of us has a right to the good. But that seems a special case. The central case of trading with the enemy is one in which the trade would be unobjectionable but for its assisting the enemy.

Given the exceptionless way in which he prioritizes rights, Steiner seems bound to have difficulty in circumscribing free trade. Trading with the enemy is a special instance of a more general case. Suppose that A knows that, if he sells something to B, B will use it to violate C's rights or otherwise to harm C. Does A have a (strict) duty not to trade with B out of concern for C? The putative trade might be in cattle infected with BSE or guns or nuclear weapons. At some point most of us, I imagine, would accept that A does incur that duty. But it is hard to see how Steiner can allow that the prospect of B's opting to harm C could justify the curtailing of A's rights.

That is not to say that any sort of rights-based defence of free trade must veto restraints aimed at protecting third parties. But, if a rights-based approach is to accommodate such restraints, it will have to relax the lexical priority of all rights or the compossibility of all rights or some other feature of Steiner's rigorous but unyielding theory of rights.

# INDEX